FINANCIAL MANAGEMENT HANDBOOK

Third edition

Financial Management Handbook

Third Edition

Edited by
Philip A. Vale

A Gower Handbook

Published by
Gower Publishing Company Limited,
Gower House,
Croft Road,
Aldershot,
Hants GU11 3HR,
England

Gower Publishing Company,
Old Post Road,
Brookfield,
Vermont 05036,
U.S.A.

British Library Cataloguing in Publication Data

Financial management handbook. – 3rd ed.
  1. Corporations – Finance
  2. Industrial management
  I. Vale, Philip A.
  658.1'5   HG4026

Library of Congress Cataloging in Publication Data

Financial management handbook.

  Bibliography: p.
  Includes index.
  1. Corporations – Finance – Handbooks, manuals, etc.
2. Business enterprises – Finance – Handbooks, manuals, etc.
I. Vale, Philip A.
HG4027.3.F53   1987   658.1'5   87–40

ISBN 0 566 02623 6

Printed and bound in Great Britain by
Anchor Brendon Ltd, Tiptree, Essex

R

Contents

Contents

PART III   FINANCIAL STRUCTURE

Contents

PART IV   EXTERNAL ENVIRONMENT

Preface

Financial Management Handbook was first published by Gower in 1972 and has proved its value as a practical reference for the financial manager, for the chief executive and for accountable heads of departments. While maintaining the comprehensive and practical character of the earlier editions, the editor of this third edition has updated the Handbook and expanded its scope still further. The objective of the Handbook is to provide an authoratative work on managerial finance with contributions from acknowledged experts in their respective fields. It provides a comprehensive and accurate summary of financial management techniques that can be used as a basis for action by managers in both large and small companies.

The third edition of the Handbook is divided into four sections, each covering a major facet of the subject. These are entitled: Financial Management – an Introduction, Financial Control, Financial Structure and the External Environment. There is an introduction to each of the four parts of the Handbook, termed an overview; this provides a unifying framework for individual chapters provided by the different authors and attempts to outline the broader context of specific contributions.

Part I consists of five chapters and sets the scene for what follows. The fundamentals of financial management are examined opening with a chapter by Peter Ratzer which discusses the role, organization and performance of the finance function. The chapter is a survey of the finance function providing the historical perspective, the objective of financial management, a review of the conceptual framework, the task of financial management, reporting and control and the organization of the finance function. Chapters two and three address the topics of capital investment and working capital management, respectively. Chapter four is new to this edition and introduces the notion of relative price changes in relation to financial measurement; it discusses the effects that an inappropriate treatment can have on an operation's real profitability. Chapter five reviews developments in computer software relevant to many financial decisions and introduces fuzzy models for use in situations that cannot be usefully defined tightly in the traditional mathematical sense.

Part II contains five chapters, which between them provide a full review of the control function. This is perhaps the most important section of the third edition insofar as setting financial objectives is relatively straightforward whereas developing the systems of control that provide relevant, accurate and useful information in a way that does not disrupt or offend an organization is more difficult. The final chapter of the section deals with internal auditing and considers approaches to controlling and monitoring the first level controls.

Part III, Financial Structure, represents a revised presentation of some of the material that first appeared in the second edition. The section is introduced with a new chapter on Capital Structure: this tries to highlight the characteristics of generic funding instruments while providing a background to dispel some common misconceived and emotive reactions to competing capital mixes. Chapter twelve is also new to the third edition; it provides an outline and critique of competing forms of debt. Chapters thirteen and fourteen consider the generation of equity finance from the sale of shares to the public.

Part IV, the final section of the third edition, considers the External Environment and contains chapters on external reporting, acquisitions and mergers, international money management and the taxation of corporations in the UK.

The new material and revised layout of *Financial Management Handbook* are intended to strengthen and build upon the previous two editions so that the Handbook retains its status as a valuable and practical guide to the practising manager.

Philip A. Vale

Illustrations

Figures

Tables

Notes on contributors

Simon Archer *(Costing and internal pricing)* is a senior lecturer in accountancy and finance at Lancaster University. He joined Arthur Andersen from Oxford and became a Chartered Accountant and was formerly a partner in Price Waterhouse Associates, Paris, in charge of Management Advisory Services. Mr Archer is the author of a book and articles on accountancy theory and is a consultant to major companies. He serves on the Editorial Board of the *Accountancy Review.*

Jack E. Broyles *(Managing capital investment)* lectures in Finance at the London Business School. He is the author of two books and numerous articles on financial management, consultant to major companies, banks and H.M. Treasury and former planning manager at Ludlow Corporation. Dr Broyles is a Member of the Board of Editors of the *Journal of Business Finance and Accounting.*

H. W. Calvert *(Costing and internal pricing)* now retired, was Principal Lecturer in Management Accountancy at North East London Polytechnic and formerly Senior Lecturer at South West Essex Technical College. He was a cost accountant with British Celanese Limited and cost accountant and budget accountant with Ilford Limited. H. W. Calvert is an Associate Member of the Chartered Institute of Management Accountants and was a member of the Institute's education committee and of its terminology committee.

Geoffrey P. E. Clarkson *(Managing working capital)* is Professor of Business Administration at Northeastern University in Boston, Massachusetts, where he has been Dean of the College of Business Administration. Previously he was National Westminster Bank Professor of Business Finance at the Manchester Business School and has been Visiting Professor at the Sloan School of Management at the Massachusetts Institute of Technology and at the London School of Economics. He was chairman and Chief Executive of Barker and Dobson Ltd., the UK food conglomerate and is Director of Clarkson & Elliott Ltd., financial consultants. He has written numerous articles and six books on finance and economics. He holds three degrees from the Carnegie-Mellon University, and his PhD thesis won the Ford Foundation Dissertation Prize in 1961.

Ian Cooper *(Relative price changes and financial decisions)* is Lecturer and Baring Brothers Research Fellow in Corporate Finance at the London Business School. He has also taught at the University of Chicago. He is a previous editor of the *Financial Management Handbook* and a consultant to a number of corporations on financial decision procedures.

Elroy Dimson *(The UK new issue market),* is Prudential Research Fellow in Investment and Lecturer in Finance at the London Business School where he is director of the Investment Management Programme. Previously he was visiting Associate Professor of Finance at the University of Chicago and at the University of California at Berkeley. Earlier, he was Operational Research Manager at Unilever and Long Range Planning Officer with Tube Investments. He is Associate Editor of the *Chase Financial Quarterly* (New York) and joint editor of the *Risk Measurement Service* (London Business School). Dr Dimson is the author of many articles concerning corporate finance and portfolio management. He received his BA in Economics from the University of Newcastle Upon Tyne, the MCom. in Business Administration at the University of Birmingham and the PhD from London University.

Myles M. Dryden *(Computers and financial decision making)* was appointed to the first Chair of Management Studies at Glasgow University in 1972 and continued as Head of Department until 1980. He was a member of the Scottish Business School Council from 1975 to 1979. Prior to this he was Reader in Economics at the University of Edinburgh. He spent 1955–63 in the USA. As a National Cash Register Company Scholar he obtained an MBA at Cornell University where he subsequently was awarded a PhD. After a few years as Professor of Industrial Management at the Sloan School (MIT) he returned to Scotland in 1963. His first degree (London School of Economics) was in Economics and Statistics.

He has written numerous articles on capital budgeting, share price behaviour, investment incentives and, more recently, on various aspects of computing.

P. C. Elliott *(Internal auditing)* has been Manager, Corporate Accounts and Central Office Costs, Shell International Petroleum Company Limited, with experience in the Royal Dutch/Shell Group since 1950. He is responsible for the corporate accounts of various subsidiaries of the Group and the administration of budgeting, accounting and cost control for the United Kingdom service companies. Mr Elliott is a Fellow of the Institute of Chartered Accountants in England and Wales, and a past President of the London Chapter of the Institute of Internal Auditors Incorporated.

Julian R. Franks *(Acquisitions and mergers)* is National Westminster Bank Professor of Finance at the London Business School. Other appointments have included Visiting Professor at the University of Cape Town and Visiting Associate Professor at the University of North Carolina at Chapel Hill. Formerly he was Senior Auditor, Esso Europe Inc., and Auditor, Standard Oil of New Jersey. He is currently Honorary Treasurer of the London Council of Social Services and Chairman of its Finance and General Purposes Committee. Professor Franks is the author of numerous articles on corporate finance and co-author of two textbooks, *Modern Managerial Finance* with J.E. Broyles (Wiley, 1979) and *Corporate Financial Management* with Harry Scholefield (Gower, 1977). He is a consultant to major companies and trade unions. Julian Franks obtained his BA(Econ) at Sheffield University, a BA in mathematics at the Open University, the MBA at Columbia University Graduate School of Business Administration and the PhD at London University.

Alan R. Leaper *(Budgets and budgetary control)* was Financial Controller of Hoover Worldwide Eastern Region Headquarters for ten years, in which capacity he was responsible at a regional level for reviewing and controlling the budgets of thirteen overseas subsidiaries. Mr Leaper's experience includes three years in Canada on cost and general accounting assignments and eleven years with the Frigidaire Division of General Motors Limited in various factory accounting positions. Mr Leaper is now managing his own retail and wholesale business and during his career he has obtained considerable practical experience of budgeting and budgetary control in both manufacturing and commercial environments. Mr Leaper is a member of the Advisory Committee to the Management Division of Management Centre Europe where he frequently chairs various seminars and Round Table meetings.

R. L. Mansbridge *(Cash forecasting and control)* is a financial consultant. He was formerly Controller, IMS International Inc. and previously was with Rank Zerox Limited where he spent five years in financial management in the United Kingdom and European operating companies, in various senior headquarters planning and control functions. R. L. Mansbridge is a chartered accountant.

Paul Marsh *(Equity rights issues)* is Bank of England Research Fellow and Lecturer in Finance at the London Business School where he is Director of the London Sloan Fellowship Programme. Previously he was a Systems Analyst with Scicon Limited and with Esso Petroleum Ltd. He is joint editor of the *Risk Measurement Service* (London Business School). Dr March is the author of many articles concerning corporate finance and portfolio investment management. He is a consultant in both the public and private sectors and in the management of financial institutions. He obtained the Bachelor of Science in economics at the London School of Economics and the PhD at the London Business School.

Andreas R. Prindl *(International money management)* has been with Morgan Guaranty Trust Company since 1964 and until recently was on secondment as Chief Executive Officer of Saudi International Bank. Previously, he was General Manager of Morgan Guaranty's Tokyo Office and earlier he managed its International Money Management Group. He is co-author of a book on international money management and has written books on foreign exchange risk and japanese finance published by Wiley. He gained his BA degree at Princeton University and the MA and PhD degrees at the University of Kentucky.

Peter Ratzer *(The role, organization and performance of the finance function)* is currently Controller of the Esso Exploration and Production UK Division of Esso Petroleum Co. Ltd. Formerly he has been Manager of the Planning and Budgets Division of Exxon Corporation in New York and was Assistant Treasurer of Esso Europe Inc and Treasurer of Esso Petroleum Co. Ltd. in London. He was also a Local Councillor for the London Borough of Camden. Peter Ratzer obtained his Bachelors

Degree in Economics and Politics from the University of Glasgow and the MBA from the Harvard Business School on a Teagle Scholarship.

Tessa V. Ryder Runton *(Managing capital investment)* is currently a consultant and part-time lecturer on financial and corporate planning. Formerly, she was Administrative Secretary of the Capital Expenditure Committee at the Rio Tinto Zinc Corporation where she had been a Senior Financial Analyst in Group Planning. Her MA at Cambridge University was in Natural Science and Law, and she studied Economics and Accountancy at the London School of Economics.

Harry H. Scholefield *(Internal auditing)* is currently Audit Supervisor, Esso Europe Inc., based in Hamburg and responsible for internal auditing of operations in Germany, Sweden and Finland. Previously he was General Accounting Group Head, Esso Exploration and Production UK and has held various senior internal auditing positions within the group. He was a Shell Research Fellow in the Department of Economics, University of Strathclyde, is the author of numerous articles and is co-author with J.R. Franks of *Corporate Financial Management* (Gower, 1977). Harry Scholefield received his BA(Econ) at Sheffield University in Accountancy, Business Studies and Economics.

Robert A. Scott *(Taxation of corporations in the United Kingdom)* is a Member of the Institute of Chartered Accountants, Scotland, a Fellow of the Institute of Taxation, runs his own accounting practice and lectures at the University of Glasgow. He is a director of several small companies and his main interest is in small businesses in the UK.

George R. Thomson *(Presentation of external financial reports)* is a financial consultant engaged in advising companies on financial needs, methods of financing, acquisition opportunities and approaches; he is also concerned with grooming private companies for stock market flotation and advising on private portfolio investment. Mr Thomson's experience includes a period as a stockbrokers' investment manager prior to entering financial journalism, when he became City Editor of the *Sunday Express* and City Editor of the *Sunday Dispatch*; he has been a freelance financial journalist since 1961 and is the author of *The ABC of Investment*.

James A. Thomson *(Debt funding)*, was educated at The King's School,

Canterbury and Oriel College, Oxford where he read Philosophy, Politics and Economics. After entering merchant banking with Charterhouse Japhet, has been engaged in lending to both UK and international companies with Hill Samuel – including three years at their German subsidiary – and with Deutsche Bank in London. He joined Hambros Bank in July 1985 as a Director in the Commercial Banking Division with specific responsibility for developing Hambros' lending services to medium sized companies.

Philip A. Vale *(Capital structure)* is Business Fellow at the University of Glasgow, director of the New Enterprise Programme and co-director of the Management Extension Programme. Previously he was engaged at Nottingham University to research the financial constraints restricting expansion and development of manufacturing firms: he is the author of research papers and articles and is retained as financial director and advisor to numerous private companies. Mr. Vale obtained his BSc from Reading University, MSc from the University of Oxford and MPhil from Nottingham University. He is particularly concerned with intra- and entrepreneurial development and represents the Scottish Business School at the Advisory Group on Enterprise Training.

Richard M. S. Wilson *(Reporting and responsibilities)* is the Pannell Kerr Forster Professor of Accounting at Trent Business School in Nottingham. His commercial experience was gained via appointments with a number of organizations covering consumer goods, industrial goods, and services. He is actively involved as a consultant with various organizations, and has also held non-executive directorships. He has published six books and numerous articles generally in the area of financial and marketing management and is editor of *The Journal of Enterprise Management*. He is a Fellow of the Chartered Institute of Management Accountants and of the Association of Certified Accountants and holds degrees in economics/ accounting, management/ marketing and technology/sociology.

Part I

FINANCIAL MANAGEMENT – AN INTRODUCTION

OVERVIEW

Every organization is subject to constraints which restrict its development and efficiency. Some of these constraints have their origins outside the organization; examples might include the legislative requirements applicable at any given time or the appetite of the market for the firm's output. The strategies and tactics developed to minimize adverse consequences arising from such considerations can be more or less successful but the important distinction is that the company is being reactive. More often the effective constraints on performance emanate from within the organization and reflect a poor or incomplete understanding of those factors which determine the profitability or capital growth of a business. The first part of *Financial Management Handbook*, therefore, addresses the key areas of financial management as present in any commercially trading organization. The opening chapter, by Peter Ratzer, details the context in which the financial manager can act pro-actively; it outlines the objectives of financial management and indicates how the sub-functions interrelate.

Chapter 2, by Tessa Ryder Runton, Jack Broyles and Ian Cooper, provides a detailed explanation of the techniques and organization required for effective capital planning. The notion of opportunity cost is developed and the distinction between incremental working capital management and discrete capital investment decisions is highlighted. Testing the viability of capital investments consists of comparing the return from a project with the return required by the company. Various techniques for doing this are described, including the discounted cash flow method. The chapter explains how risk can be incorporated into investment planning using such techniques as sensitivity and probability analysis. The authors proceed to place this technical material in an organizational context, discussing the capital investment decision process and the problem of ex post evaluation of such decisions.

Chapter 3, by Geoffrey Clarkson, considers the area of working capital management. The funds of a business can only be invested in working capital or fixed capital. Working capital, by its very nature, is dynamic, representing net current assets that will have been converted to cash at least once within a 12 month period. Because of the fluidity of working capital this is perhaps where greatest vigilance is required especially in smaller or newer companies. The notions of profitability apply here, but with additional special techniques for managing the various components of working capital efficiently: stocks, cash, debtors and creditors. These techniques are described by Professor Clarkson. In addition, he shows how the cash flows associated with working capital can be analysed to control profitability. He also provides a useful discussion of conventional ratio analysis as applied to working capital, with interpretation featuring rather than just the mechanics of computation.

Chapter 4, by Ian Cooper, focuses on the significance of relative prices. In a dynamic economy, with a private sector characterized by the interaction of supply and demand, money prices can shift significantly. Such price movements can disguise the profitability of a project and can engender erroneous analyses of performance. Real, constant and nominal prices are clearly segregated and the implications for financial decisions discussed. The success of an enterprise is nearly always quantified by numbers that are preceded by '£': the significance of correctly interpreting the meaning of this symbol is paramount.

Chapter 5, the final chapter of Part I, is provided by Professor Myles Dryden: in it he acknowledges the uncertainty surrounding many of the parameters relevant to financial decision making and the fact that decision criteria themselves are not necessarily inflexible. The reader is introduced to the notion of fuzzy logic and the application of software that can assist in the analysis of less structured aspects of finance.

4

1

The role, organization and performance of the finance function

Peter Ratzer

'In the broadest sense the function of the financial viewpoint is to serve as the point of contact between the uses of funds within an enterprise and its sources of funds'. This was Ezra Solomon's view of the finance function in his classic work *The Theory of Financial Management.*[1] It still stands as a practical definition today.

In this introductory chapter the definition is elaborated upon and related to four specific concerns of the financial manager: employing funds, controlling funds, structuring funds and the external environment.

HISTORICAL PERSPECTIVE

Until the 1950s and early 1960s the primary focus of the finance function was on raising funds. Even today many people still think of the Finance Director or Treasurer as responsible solely for finding money that others in the company need to implement their business plans.

The shift to a concern with the whole financial structure of the company, with both sides of the balance sheet, owes much to Joel Dean's pioneering work in the USA on capital budgeting.[2] In the UK the work of Merrett and Sykes[3] provided a similar stimulus to broadening the finance function's responsibility. The 1960s saw many firms in the UK change their methods of appraising capital expenditures and shift to approaches such as Discounted Cash Flow (DCF) or Net Present Value

(NPV), that recognized the time value of money and emphasized the expected pattern of cash flows, rather than the book profit of a project. Allied to this development was the work being done on the cost of capital and on the criteria that should be used to judge the acceptability of capital investments.

This work provided the crucial link between the two sides of the balance sheet; between the mix of assets and the mix of finance. It led to the formulation of the key objective of the finance function as maximizing the value of the firm. The challenging and complex fields of risk analysis and modern portfolio theory followed.

Out of this and related work came three ideas — market efficiency, capital market opportunity cost and the required reward for risk — that provide the conceptual framework for financial management today. We are likely to see the wider implications of these three concepts having a growing influence on the practice of financial management.

These key concepts are described in more detail shortly, but it is necessary to stress that, although the theoretical underpinnings of finance are important, the main conclusion to be drawn from this brief historical sketch is that the finance function needs to be interpreted broadly if it is to make its full contribution to a company and to meet corporate goals. As Hunt, Williams and Donaldson[4] put it, the successful financial manager must not only be a 'money man', he must also be a businessman. He is part of the operating team.[5]

OBJECTIVES OF FINANCIAL MANAGEMENT

Profit maximization has long been recognized as one of the main goals of a company. To some it is the only goal. The problem is to define profit maximization in a way that makes business sense and that can be used to guide practical decision making in a company.

How is profit to be defined? Are we talking of maximizing operating earnings or net profit attributable to the shareholders? Does it mean an immediate, short term profit? How can a company balance longer term profit potential against shorter term costs? What about risk? These are just some of the questions that come to mind when trying to define profit maximization.

The solution which has been adopted is to focus on maximizing the value of the firm. Valuation is at the heart of the finance function's activity and a key technique is that of discounting. In essence, discounting provides a link between the present and future by the use of a discount or interest rate. It enables all the cash flows of a business at various dates to be valued on a consistent basis at one common time. This is normally the present, hence the term present value, but it can equally well be some time in the future.

Discounting solves the problem of short versus long term profit maximization. It enables different cash flow profiles to be compared in terms of their present values and it provides a simple tool for determining which profile has the highest present value.

Usually the focus is not on operating earnings or net profit, but on cash flows before any financing charges or depreciation. Financing charges, primarily interest, are omitted since they are a function of a company's financing structure; they determine how the total value of a company is split between shareholders and lenders. Depreciation is omitted since it is a non-cash charge and is only an estimated allocation of earnings to cover the use or decline in value of fixed assets such as plant and machinery. The forecast cash flows are the key to profitability of a company or project. They represent funds that will be available in the future to service debt, pay dividends or make new investment. The forecast cash flow profile is therefore used to determine the viability of companies and of projects.

Although the net profit of a company over its life is ultimately the difference between the company's total cash inflows and outflows, after allowing for the return of capital to its providers, it is the timing and the pattern of these flows that determine the value of a company and the return that it earns. Two companies could be expected to generate the same net profit over a period but the cash flows, and hence the value of each company, could be very different.

Another factor that affects the value of companies is risk. Two companies could have similar cash flow outlooks, but their values could differ widely if the cash flows of one are subject to considerable risk whereas the cash flows of the other are dependable. This brings us to the question of the appropriate discount rate to use for valuing future cash flows given their risk.

Assuming the company has investments that yield more than the rate of interest on additional borrowing, the apparent return to the shareholders could be raised by borrowing more and by increasing its gearing or leverage, or the debt/equity ratio. In the long run this will only increase the riskiness of the shareholders' cash flow since a higher proportion of the total cash flow is allocated to lenders. The shareholders are left to bear potentially greater swings in their cash flow. As the risk increases, so the rate at which these cash flows will be discounted or capitalized by the shareholders will increase. Thus the apparent advantage of additional debt is offset by the greater risk and higher discount rate for the shareholders' equity. Hence the total value of the firm may be unaffected by the way in which claims on assets and cash flow are divided between equity holders and debt holders. The well known Modigliani — Miller theory[6] states that the value of a company is unaffected by how it is financed. An increase in debt will result in a matching decline in the shareholders' interest. Put as baldly as this it might suggest that the financing structure of a company is irrelevant.

In summary, the key objective of financial management is to maximize the value of a company. The value is a function of the expected cash flows and their riskiness.

CONCEPTUAL FRAMEWORK

Three pillars of modern financial management are the efficient market hypothesis, capital market opportunity costs and the required reward for risk. They relate to the valuation of a company and this explains their central role in financial management.

An efficient market is one in which prices reflect all information available to participants in the market. The stock and bond markets are considered efficient and therefore, for example, share prices reflect all the available information about a company. This implies that, in the absence of 'inside' information, there is no way of consistently predicting share price movement. The next price movement bears no relationship to the last movement — hence the term 'random walk'.

Capital market efficiency also implies that the value of a quoted company is the market value of its securities on the stock exchange. This allows the financial manager to draw conclusions about the expectations of shareholders and their attitudes to risk and returns by observing the behaviour of security prices. This information can be fed back into the financial planning of a company.

There is growing evidence that financial markets are efficient. Undoubtedly more research will be done for the benefit of financial management in the coming years on the way the markets work and on the ramifications of this behaviour.

The concept of market efficiency can also be applied to other financial markets such as foreign exchange. This has considerable implications for the way a company manages its foreign exchange activities if it trades or invests abroad. If the market is efficient the expected gain from taking views on future foreign exchange rates is zero. Speculative activity will not pay in the long run.

Financial management has now moved almost full circle from the detailed descriptive work on capital markets and securities that characterized the teaching of finance before the 1950s to a fundamental understanding of how the financial markets work. One of the tasks of the financial manager is to ensure that management takes advantage of the implications of the new insights when running the business.

The concept of capital market opportunity costs is the second pillar of modern finance. It takes as its starting point the valuation of a risk-free cash flow; that is, from a short-term government bond. The discount rate used to value the cash flow from such an asset is the government borrowing rate. This is the minimum required return for a risk-free investment.

Capital market opportunity costs imply that a higher return is required for higher risk assets. This accords with common sense since there is no reason why any person or company should accept some risk unless they are offered a return above that available from government bonds. Some inducement is needed to give up a secure, guaranteed income.

The discount rate for valuing the expected cash flow of a company, normally called the cost of capital, will therefore be equal to the risk-free return plus a premium for risk. The amount of the premium can be estimated with reasonable accuracy from long-run market data. It is at this point that efficient markets and capital market opportunity costs come together. The required reward for risk, the third pillar of modern finance, therefore provides a link between efficient markets and capital market opportunity costs.

One of the more controversial conclusions of modern financial theory is that, from a strictly financial point of view, a company will not benefit by attempting to spread its risk by diversification. The reason given is that investors can equally well diversify their own portfolios. Although such a conclusion omits consideration of the benefits of lower risk to managers and employees, which can also benefit shareholders indirectly through lower wage costs, shareholders do diversify. Thus, the risk for which investors ultimately need compensation is the risk of movement in the general economic situation. That is a risk which investors cannot escape by further diversification of their portfolios.

Again, it is the task of the financial manager to help management understand how the market value of the company is determined and to help management draw the right conclusions on, for example, return criteria for different risk classes of investment, on diversification and on mergers and acquisitions. In this introduction only the foundations of modern financial management will be sketched. The topics are discussed in more detail in later chapters.

FINANCIAL MANAGEMENT

The main elements of the conceptual framework — that markets reflect all available information, that a premium is required for risk and that investors diversify their portfolios — may seem self-evident, but it is hoped that it has been indicated that even self-evident assumptions about the way markets and investors behave can have controversial implications when it comes to practical financial management. This is one of the factors that makes financial management such a challenging and stimulating activity. It also gives the job a significant educational component.

In this section some of the key issues on the agenda of the financial manager are summarized. The basic objective of maximizing the value of the company as given will be taken. The key long term financing decisions are the target debt/equity ratio, the debt structure and dividend policy.

The author explained earlier how increased gearing has a cost in the form of extra risk for the shareholders, which offsets the fact that the interest rate on debt is below the overall cost of funds to the company. This does not mean that the value of a company is unaffected by its financing structure. Since interest is tax deductible, shareholders can benefit from the introduction of some debt into a company and the total market value of shares plus debt securities will be increased by the present value of the tax saving on interest.[7] The cost of capital will decline.

At higher levels of debt a company is likely to run up against increasing reluctance on the part of lenders. This can push up the cost of new debt by more than the tax benefit of additional gearing to shareholders. Lenders and shareholders may see increasing risks of bankruptcy and this can lead to a decline in the total market value of a company and to an increase in the cost of capital. The financial manager's job is therefore to recommend a target debt/equity ratio appropriate for the business in question. This is the point at which uses and sources of funds come together since the target debt/equity will be a function of the type of investments and their riskiness, with an added element of market convention reflecting rates applicable to similar companies in the same business.

The USA has rating agencies that grade the quality of corporate debt issues. In such circumstances a company may set a policy of maintaining its rating at a particular level and then design a debt/equity ratio (plus other ratios such as the coverage of all fixed charges) that it is believed will maintain the required rating. 'Believed' is stressed, since the agencies do not work to mechanical ratio limits. They are also influenced by the quality of company management.

The debt structure or mix of a company is the balance between long, medium and short term debt and, if appropriate, between the currencies of debt. Again, this will be a function of the business, its assets and cash flows, and of the availability of finance. The financial manager needs to be aware of the various sources of finance and their costs and of any opportunities provided by less conventional sources such as leasing companies. He needs to understand the cash flows of the business well since they will determine the basic needs for short term financing to keep interest costs at a minimum and avoid accumulating surplus, idle funds.

Dividend policy is a controversial subject and the literature on this topic alone is immense. One of the most stimulating contributions was made by Miller and Modigliani[8] who argued that dividend policy was irrelevant to the valuation of a company, that shareholders should value dividends and retained earnings equally. As with their argument on the debt/equity ratio this is a simplified proposition that ignores various factors such as taxes and the information value of dividends. Taxes are relevant if the average shareholder pays a different effective marginal rate of tax than the company on income from investments. The information value of dividends can be important since changes in dividend levels may reflect more accurately than reported earnings how the directors of a company see the future. It is up to the financial manager to frame recommendations on long run dividend policy that take into account the future needs for retained earnings to support capital investment and, as necessary, additional debt. At this point dividend policy becomes an integral part of the financial planning and business strategy of a company.

The three key financial decisions just discussed — the debt/equity ratio, the debt structure and dividend policy — form the basis of any long term financial plan. They are all related and together make up a company's capital structure plan. The capital structure plan should be one of the financial manager's main planning tools.

REPORTING AND CONTROL

So far the focus has been primarily on the basic principles and objectives of financial management, on the conceptual framework and on the major policy elements that make up the capital structure plan of a company.

As the range of chapters in this handbook indicates, the role of the finance function includes many other responsibilities; the main one can be summarized under the heading 'Reporting and Control'.

Reporting can be divided into external and internal areas. External reporting covers the reports to shareholders and other interested parties, such as lenders. There has been considerable debate within the accounting profession on the role of published accounts and a useful review of the key issues can be found in 'The Corporate Report', a discussion paper published in 1975 by the Accounting Standards Steering Committee. [9]

External financial communications will absorb a greater share of the finance function's time during the 1980s than during the 1960s and 1970s. Part of this emphasis will reflect the growing reporting burden imposed by new accounting standards, but the rest will be dictated by the need to explain in greater detail the contribution a company has made to society.

Internal reporting is an essential part of management control. It is the finance function's responsibility to develop and run the systems for monitoring and reporting all the operations and profitability of a company. Such systems, which are outlined in more detail in later chapters, are an essential control tool. Management needs both current and forecast data to control and steer the business. Internal reporting is another area where the finance function can excercise its own judgement in drawing management's attention to issues or trends that may be a cause of concern. Closely related to reporting is control. Control covers the proper and accurate recording of all financial business transactions, the development of appropriate and secure systems for handling all receipts and payments, and internal audit activities. These are all major responsibilities of the finance function and their scope is more likely to increase than to decrease.

ORGANIZATION

Obviously the organization of the finance function in any company will depend upon its size, the nature of its business and its history.

The range of titles that people in the finance function carry is very wide and indicated below is the general pattern among UK companies. To a great extent this pattern follows USA precedents.

The Finance Director has responsibility as a board member for the whole of the finance function. As a board member he participates in all corporate decisions and can bring the financial viewpoint to bear on the company's business decisions. In view of his wide board responsibilities he has to delegate many of his responsibilities to the Controller and Treasurer. In larger companies the Finance Director may also have a Tax Manager reporting to him and also other departments such as Purchasing.

The focus here is on the activities of the Controller and Treasurer since the division of responsibilities between them mirrors the distinction between reporting and control and financial management discussed earlier.

The Controller is the company's accounting and financial control manager. He is responsible for external and internal reporting, for the accounting and information systems, for controlling all receipts and payments and for internal audit and control. The size of a company and its activities will determine how these responsibilities are split into manageable divisions or groups, for example capital budgets, reporting and forecasting, payroll, costs, sales accounting, information systems and so on. It should be added that in some companies the computer operations and systems do not form part of the Controller's responsibility, because he is just one of many users. The Controller has the vital task of liaising with the company's statutory auditors. This is a key relationship which is critical in external reporting and in maintaining the financial soundness of a company, since a qualification to the accounts by the auditors can be very damaging.

The Treasurer is the company's finance manager. He is responsible for developing the capital structure plan and basic financial policies outlined earlier. He must ensure that finance is available to meet the needs of the company, both new investments and working capital, and that the flows of cash in and out of the company are managed efficiently. He is the company's main contact with the financial community. He advises on appropriate return criteria for investment decisions. Normally the Treasurer is also responsible for risk management and insurance and for advising on pension fund management. He is also likely to be the point of contact with the company's actuary and must advise on the appropriate valuation assumptions to be used in computing pension liabilities and determining the company's contribution to its pension fund.

If the company is involved in overseas investment or in importing and exporting, then it will be vulnerable to movements in exchange rates. The Treasury, whose department is responsible for all purchases and sales of foreign exchange, must develop appropriate policies for managing foreign exchange exposure. This is another topic that has absorbed an increasing amount of management time and effort in many companies. It was mentioned earlier that taking views on exchange rates is an unprofitable activity over the long run. Although some would not accept this statement, it can be argued that it is a useful working assumption for managing exposure. It ensures that more effort goes into control and management of foreign exchange risk than into trying to forecast exchange rates.

Although both the Controller and Treasurer are part of the same function, they have a check and balance relationship. While the Treasurer manages the company's cash, the Controller provides the necessary control to ensure that the cash is used as authorized in accordance with company policies.

In summary, every company needs key personnel to shoulder the various responsibilities of the finance function. How these responsibilities are allocated will differ from company to company, but it is clear that an increasing number of companies in the UK have set up separate Treasurer's Departments reporting directly to the Finance

Director. In the 1960s this was still a novelty. By 1980 a new professional body, the Association of Corporate Treasurers, had been founded in recognition of this trend.

CONCLUSION

Ezra Solomon posed three interrelated questions for financial management:

1 What specific assets should an enterprise acquire?
2 What total volume of funds should an enterprise commit?
3 How should the funds required be financed?

Although financial theory has developed significantly since he wrote *The Theory of Financial Management*, the questions are still pertinent. An outline has been provided of some of the basic considerations that a financial manager should take into account when making recommendations on these topics to management. The following chapters provide more detailed descriptions of the concepts.

REFERENCES

1 Solomon, E., *The Theory of Financial Management*, Columbia University Press, New York, 1963
2 Dean, J., *Capital Budgeting*, Columbia University Press, New York, 1951
3 Merrett, A. J. and Sykes, A., *The Finance and Analysis of Capital Projects*, Longman, London, 1963, 2nd Edn 1973
4 Hunt, P., Williams, C. M. and Donaldson, G., *Basic Business Finance*, Richard D. Irwin, Homewood, Illinois, 3rd Edn 1966
5 Gerstner Jr., L. V. and Anderson, M. H., 'The Chief Financial Officer as Activist', *Harvard Business Review*, September-October 1976
6 Modigliani, F. and Miller, M. H., 'The Cost of Capital, Corporation Finance, and The Theory of Investment', *American Economic Review*, June 1958
7 Modigliani, F. and Miller, M. H., 'Corporate Income Taxes and the Cost of Capital: A Correction'. *American Economic Review*, June 1963

8 Miller, M. H. and Modigliani, F., 'Dividend Policy, Growth and the Valuation of Shares', *Journal of Business*, October 1961

9 Accounting Standards Steering Committee, 'The Corporate Report', 1975

2

Managing capital investment

Tessa Ryder Runton, Jack Broyles and Ian Cooper

Capital project planning and investment is the process by which companies allocate funds to various projects designed to ensure profitability and growth. Evaluation of such projects involves estimating their future benefits to the company and comparing these with their costs. Such analysis is appropriate not only to the purchase of long lived physical assets, but to any decision which has impacts extending into the future. Thus capital project planning can encompass, for example, long term contracts for goods and services, marketing expenditures, disinvestment by sale, mergers and plant closures.

The key requirements for capital project evaluation are:

1 Access to the appropriate information.
2 Knowledge of the company's required financial return.
3 Realistic evaluation of the prospective cash flow and profit impacts of projects.
4 Analysis of the costs and benefits of projects with attention to the timing of their occurrence.
5 Evaluation by senior management of the strategic implications of large projects.
6 A well-defined approval process.
7 Consistency with strategic planning and budgeting procedures.
8 A review procedure.

GOALS OF PROJECT PLANNING

Businesses have responsibilities to various interested groups including employees, customers, suppliers, bankers and shareholders. The commercial goal is met by maximizing the total market value of a company's shares. The capital market values shares at the present value of current and future cash flows attributable to shareholders. If the company maximizes the net present value of all the operations that make up its business, the sum will be the maximization of the value of the company. This value net of debt belongs to shareholders. Companies pursuing other objectives, whether social or technological, must primarily be profitable. Should shareholders, corporate members or financiers become dissatisfied with the company's operations, they may withdraw their support, causing such awkward problems as loss of morale and personnel, shortage of funds, a fall in the company's share price if it is publicly quoted, or stormy annual general meetings. Any of these can lead to undesirable vulnerability and result in a takeover, closedown, or governmental interference.

REQUIRED RATE OF RETURN STANDARDS AND COST OF CAPITAL

Cost of capital is a standard of comparison used in financial analysis and is a vital company statistic needing careful calculation. The return on capital resources must equal or exceed the cost of that capital. Although zero or negative returns are acceptable in special cases, the necessary subsidies may lead to costs in another form.

The realities of commercial life have caused the cost of capital to be a very complex subject. Any comparisons must be made between like numbers. A percentage profit before tax made on a hotel in Bermuda bears no relationship to the same figure made after tax on a farm in Scotland. A profit expressed as a percentage of capital employed should not be compared with a discounted cash flow internal rate of return. Many measures of company performance can be devised but these are valuable only to those who are completely familiar with the definitions involved. The appraisal of projected cash flow discounted at a rate equal to a carefully estimated required rate of return leads to fewer pitfalls. In particular, the time-value of money is taken into account, all the financial effects are assessed and tax and inflation are taken into account in the calculation of the cash flow and the estimation of the cost of capital.

Capital investment analysis aims to discover the financial truth about the plan under investigation. If it does not meet the survival standard of the organization, that fact should be stated clearly before the discussion as to its desirability begins. In practice, many apparently unprofitable processes go on in any business because they enhance the profitable activities which, of course, should outnumber them. Obvious examples are the provision of catering and other services for the work force, advertising, research and so on. It used to be thought that discounted cash flow analysis led to categorical 'yes' or 'no' judgements on any plan; in fact, all it does is marshal the financial facts for the guidance of the decision takers. In addition, it can point to the least unprofitable way of tackling a loss-making but necessary job.

Cost of capital to the firm

Most companies raise funds from many sources – retained earnings, new equity, grants and many forms of loans. The overall cost of capital to the firm is the return it must earn on its assets to meet the requirements of all those providing it with financing. Lenders require interest payments and shareholders expect to receive dividends and see capital growth.

In the past, UK shareholders have expected to earn a real net return of about 8 per cent after tax on average risk shares. To obtain this required net return in money terms, the expected inflation rate must be added. If this expected inflation rate is 10 per cent, the required return on the company's present equity and retained earning is 18 per cent. The cost of new equity raised by means of 'rights' is a little more than this to allow for the cost of the issue. Other forms of new equity issues incur further costs of about 2 per cent.

Although the average real expected return on shares is about 8 per cent, companies in risky industries or with high gearing (borrowing relative to equity funds) will have more vulnerable shares than average. The real return required by their shareholders will be commensurately higher. This means that borrowing is not necessarily a cheap way of raising funds. Although the interest rate on borrowing may be lower than the return expected by shareholders, increased gearing will raise the risk of shares and not change the overall cost of funds to the company. This is discussed later in this chapter (for a more detailed analysis see Franks and Broyles, 1979).

If a company maintains a proportion of debt capital agreed with its lenders, it can compute a weighted average cost of capital. For example, if the interest rate on debt is 10 per cent, and the company has 25 per cent debt and 75 per cent equity, the weighted average cost of capital in money terms including 10 per cent average inflation is (0.25 × 10 per cent) + (0.75 × 18 per cent) = 16 per cent. This cost does not allow for the tax savings from interest payments. This benefit is added separately.

In deciding the appropriate standards for an organization, the marginal cost of capital is a vital guide. In a growing company, new capital will be needed and, therefore, the return on a project of normal risk should be judged against a standard of the weighted average cost of new capital. Companies making investment decisions continuously should use this marginal cost of capital as the standard for all projects with risks normal to the company's business. If a project cannot pass this test, it will diminish the company's value.

Required rate of return on projects

Obviously projects involve differing risks. Some, such as cost saving investments and lease or buy decisions, are of low risk; others, such as research projects, involve greater than average levels of risk. A company should classify its risk categories for projects and set required returns for each. A large project with risk significantly different from normal can alter the overall character of a company, its cost of capital, its accepted gearing and the returns expected by financiers.

The required rate of return for a project can be significantly different from weighted average cost of capital for the company. High risk projects are characterized by high fixed operating expenditure and high revenue variability. These should be expected to earn high rates of return. The exact return required will depend upon a judgement about the level of risk in the project compared with the average risk of the company. In the case above, where the weighted average cost of capital in real terms is 6 per cent, the real required return on a project twice as risky as the market should be 12 per cent. With 10 per cent expected inflation the money required return should be 22 per cent.

The use of a separate required rate of return for each individual project is most important when the projects are large relative to the company and/or when the projects being considered have long lives. A typical classification scheme, in increasing order of risk is: cost reduction, replacement, scale expansion, new products. The risks of these different types of investment differ, and so should their required returns.

By evaluating different projects at different required rates of return, the company seeks to protect its shareholders. Shareholders require higher rates of return for higher levels of risk, and receive compensation for high risk in the capital markets. Companies undertaking high risk asset investment decisions must seek to achieve higher returns than their shareholders can earn for that level of risk in the capital markets.

Effect of debt on required returns

Unless there are non-financial incentives, a project is acceptable only if it stands on its own feet; that is, its cash flow should at least meet the company's return criterion for the risks involved. With the possibility of debt financing is the position changed? A typical case arises when new assets simply increase the total assets on a proportion of which debt is available. Some people argue that, even apart from tax advantages, debt is cheap since the interest rate is lower than the cost of equity funds. This argument ignores the hidden cost of debt: the increased vulnerability of the equity as more borrowing is undertaken. The total operating risk of the company remains constant as more debt financing is used, so it is unrealistic to believe that the overall cost of funds can be reduced thus.

One advantage that borrowing does confer is the reduction in taxes caused by the deductibility of interest payments. The impact on cash flows of this tax saving is simply the future stream of tax payments that are saved by the interest payments on the debt. The value of these tax savings can be added to the value of the operating cash flows from the project to get an overall value including the benefits of debt financing. This is preferable to using a weighted average cost of capital including the cost of debt at an after-tax rate. Use of the latter assumes that the debt available for a project will be very long term and will be the same proportion of the project financing as it is for the company. Both these assumptions can be erroneous when projects have short maturity debt or very high or low gearing.

Care needs to be taken when a project merits special loans. Usually these are projects of significant size for which government incentives are available, or for which special working capital loans can be raised, or involving mortgageable property. If the result is a new company finance structure, then cost of capital and risk classifications must be reassessed. Some large capital investments, such as in mining, involve parent companies in special financial guarantees and these need special attention. Other capital investments such as in research, do not result in increased total assets which can be partly debt financed.

TRADITIONAL TECHNIQUES FOR TESTING VIABILITY

The natural question: 'When do I get my money back?' has often been answered by the traditional technique of adding up the forecast net cash inflow (sometimes the sum of the profit before depreciation from the forecast profit and loss account) year by year until the amount of the original capital investment is reached, thereby giving the years to payback. Such a calculation is inconclusive because standards vary, definitions of the original capital vary, tax is not always deducted and most of the benefits of tax allowances are obscured. The method ignores the time-value of money, cannot cope with inflation and takes no account of the later profits, if any. Whether, in fact, any profit is made on the investment is not measured at all. Payback calculations give some guidance in matters of liquidity in which case the cash inflow should be carefully defined and be free of any 'accounting numbers' such as 'tax provision' instead of 'tax payable'. A better payback calculation is the discounted payback, which is computed using the present values of the future cash inflows.

Another traditional technique involves the use of accounting ratios for current and proposed operations. These include the ratios of profit to capital employed, of profit to sales, and many others concerning stock, current assets and liabilities, and working capital. These ratios are useful for regulating smooth operations but are unhelpful for judging profitability, owing to definition problems and the choice of standards, but mostly because the time-value of money is not included.

One ratio used is the return on capital, known as 'the accountant's return' or the 'book rate of return'. An average profit, before or after tax, is calculated for a number of years of the proposed project and this is expressed as a percentage of the capital employed. The latter is often defined as the initial investment or the average capital employed of the years, thereby allowing for further investment and depreciation. This procedure suffers from the same snags as the techniques mentioned above and, in addition, smooths out the effect of irregular annual profits. Clearly, quick profits are preferable to a slow build up, but advantages or disadvantages are obscured.

MODERN TECHNIQUES FOR TESTING VIABILITY

The traditional techniques take no account of the time-value of money.

But money received today is much more valuable than the same money received later. Inflationary conditions magnify the difference. This is the principal fact which modern analysis techniques have incorporated to improve on past procedures. Analysis concentrates on the incremental cash flow of a project. The cash flow is discounted at the project's discount rate to the present time, giving a present value. The work involved has increased, but once an analysis discipline has been set up, decision takers can expect that the realities of the given data for some plan will be clearly identified. They can then concentrate on the non-financial problems involved, judge whether the data is sufficient with which to work and act accordingly.

The concept of moving money in time using the relevant discount rate is not new. Today's quoted price for benefits to be received in the future can be judged by netting the price, or capital cost, from the present value of the future cash flow. A positive resultant Net Present Value (NPV), if properly calculated shows that the transaction is financially worthwhile. The value of the transaction can also be assessed by judging its Internal Rate of Return (IRR).

CASH FLOW DISCIPLINE IN PROJECT ANALYSIS

The discounted cash flow techniques use as their raw material the incremental cash flow resulting from some plan. Profit flow study is necessary for proper annual accounting as required by shareholders, but it is the cash flow that should be studied to identify the return forecast and the finance that is required. Provisions for depreciation are excluded, but expenditures on working capital and capital expenditures are included. The cash flow of a project is a forecast of the total monetary effects computed periodically (usually annually or monthly) over the whole life of the project, including scrap values. Such items as tax savings achieved on other profits of the organization because of allowances due to the new project or any other cash effects would not occur without the new project; for example, the cost of head office extensions or replacing an executive who would be transferred, should be included. Interest payments are often wrongly deducted from the cash flow, but they are not operating flows, being part of the cost of funds included in the cost capital. A project can be defined as any procedure which alters the organization's cash flow. Projects, therefore, include opportunities for cost savings and productivity improvements, where capital cost is not necessarily involved. What, therefore, is analysed is the total cash flow effect of an opportunity, that is, the net incremental cash flow, which is the difference between the cash flow in the company if the project is undertaken and the cash flow if it is not.

This analysis must be in real terms or in money terms with respect to inflation and, if necessary, alterations must be made so that real terms cash flows are judged by a real terms required return standard, and so that money cash flows are judged by a money terms required return standard. Tax allowances and loan servicing schedules are always in money terms but sales and cost figures are usually forecast in real terms. It is usual for the marketing and production departments to project schedules showing changes in sales percentages or production costs without allowing for external price changes. However, the estimation of taxable profits and taxes requires that these data be converted to money terms. In cases of high inflation forecasts, or different effects on prices and costs, and for lengthy projects, some estimate must be made of the inflation pattern over the life of the project. This estimate could differ for use on prices, on costs and on the overall situation including the cost of capital. All figures must then be converted to money terms so that expected tax payments can be estimated.

It should go without saying that cash flows are forecast after the effects of company taxes when paid. Because tax allowances are normally in money terms, consistent cash flows almost certainly have to be forecast in money terms, unless real terms tax allowances can be calculated. Sometimes it is necessary to consider any likely future changes in tax structure. In this, as in treating inflation and in all problems of data uncertainties, it is important not to be over meticulous, particularly at the outset. Analysis of the most roughly prepared cash flow will show whether it is worth spending any further time attending to the details. The first question to answer is: 'What is the profitability of the given set of data, warts included?' If the answer looks promising it is then sensible to take the time to examine the given data, prepare a detailed net incremental cash flow in money terms and look at possible outcomes of the project as opposed to one set of the data. The analysis should then examine sensitivities, risks and probabilities and the effect of the project on the organization as a whole. Decision takers prefer consistent analysis disciplines so that they can use consistent standards of judgement and comparison.

NPV and IRR in more detail

The use of the concept of present value (NPV)

The net present value, NPV, of a project is the net present value of the net incremental cash flow discounted at the project's required rate of return. A zero NPV shows that the project repays the capital invested plus the minimum acceptable return on the invested capital throughout the project's life. The minimum acceptable return is equal to the opportunity cost of that capital including a return required for the risk taken by investing in that operation for that period. NPVs show that the minimum return is achieved plus extra value. Given a discount rate of 11 per cent for a project, the NPV is found as shown in Table 2.1.

Other things being equal, this project looks financially acceptable. One could pay up to £199 more for the opportunity and still not lose. NPV represents the analyst's estimate of the net increase in the value of the company which would accrue from the project. If the discount rate used is the capital market's capitalization rate for the risk of the project, the NPV represents an estimate of the incremental market value of the firm due to the project. The NPV technique thus gives a simple assessment tool, but is inaccurate if there is doubt or dispute as to the correct discount rate.

Table 2.1
Calculating the net present value (NPV)

Time in years from today	Cash flow (£)	11% Discount factor	Present value (£)
0	(1500)	1.000	(1500)
1	100	0.901	90
2	1000	0.812	812
3	1000	0.731	731
4	100	0.659	66

The NPV, the sum of the present values of the cash flow = + £199

Use of the concept of internal rate of return (IRR)

The internal rates of return, IRR, is also known as the discounted cash flow yield, the DCF return or the actuarial return. IRR is defined as the break-even financing rate for the project. This is not to say that the capital released by the project earns such a return. Reinvestments, whether wise or not, should be kept separate from the analysis of a project on its own merits. The IRR of a project is judged against the cost of capital standard or the minimum required return.

The mathematical definition of the IRR is that it is the discount rate which, when used to discount the net incremental cash flow, gives a zero net present value for the project. The NPV (which is calculated at the

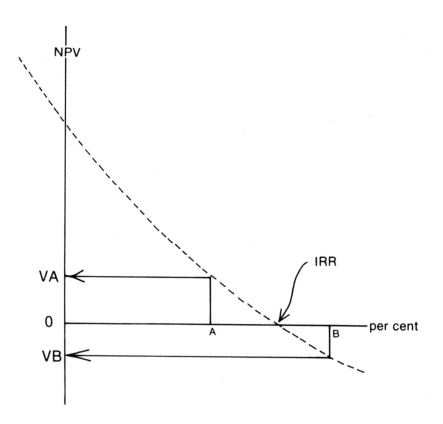

Figure 2.1   The use of trial rates to calculate the internal rate of return

project's required rate of return discount rate) should not be confused with the many net present values which can be calculated using other rates.

The calculation of the NPV consists in setting out the cash flow, discounting it to the present time and adding up the net total. IRR calculations necessitate trial and error. If, however, the graph shown in Figure 2.1 is borne in mind, the process need not be lengthy.

Most practitioners find it convenient to calculate the NPV first. If this shows, for example by being positive, that it is worth doing more sums, a guess must be made of the next trial rate. A positive NPV indicates that the IRR will be greater than the cost of capital rate; how much greater can sometimes be guessed by the size of the NPV. Trial rate A per cent is used and will give a net present value VA. Consideration of this result might lead to trial rate B per cent and VB. Having thus both over and underestimated the answer, we can find the true IRR by mathematical interpolation, or by drawing a similar graph (always provided that the trial rates are not more than one or two percentage points apart – if they are, the curve that represents the relation will give too inaccurate a result, which should be checked by another trial and interpolation or extrapolation).

Table 2.2 shows how this procedure applies. Suppose the cost of capital is 11 per cent and an investment is being considered which costs £1500, lasts four years and has no terminal value.

Table 2.2
Finding the true internal rate of return (IRR)

		Cash flow discounted at:							
		11 per cent		20 per cent		17 per cent		16 per cent	
Time in years	Cash								
from today	flow £	Discount factor	value	factor	value	factor	value	factor	value
0	(1500)	1.000	(1500)	1.000	(1500)	1.000	(1500)	1.000	(1500)
1	100	0.901	90	0.833	83	0.855	86	0.862	86
2	1000	0.812	812	0.694	694	0.731	731	0.743	743
3	1000	0.731	731	0.579	579	0.624	624	0.641	641
4	100	0.659	66	0.482	48	0.534	53	0.522	55
Net present values			199 this is the NPV		(96)		(6)		25

By interpolation between the net present value calculated at 16 per cent and 17 per cent the IRR is calculated to be

$$16 + \frac{25}{31} = 16.8 \text{ per cent}$$

The same result is obtained extrapolating from the 17 per cent and 20 per cent figures

$$\text{IRR} = 17 - \frac{3 \times 6}{90} = 16.8 \text{ per cent}$$

Interpolation between the 11 per cent and 20 per cent figures, however, gives the answer

$$11 + \frac{9 \times 199}{295} = 17.1 \text{ per cent}$$

which may be too inaccurate, although in this case the return would probably be quoted at 17 per cent. These figures could also be found graphically.

Use of present value: mid-year discounting

Discount tables are available for all periods — weeks, quarters, years — and to various numbers of places of decimals. It is not helpful normally to calculate the cash flow in too small periods or to discount it using more than four-figure tables. It is more important to notice that the tables usually refer to points of time and the cash flows represent a total for a period. A fitting assumption is needed. It is easy if the majority of receipts and payments occur at the begining or at the end of the periods. For flows which are continuous and irregular over the periods, the total cash flow is often assumed to arise mid-year. The calculation should therefore be refined. If only annual discount tables are available, the half-year discount factor at r per cent can be calculated from the equation:

$$\text{Discount factor} = \frac{1}{\text{Square root of } (1 + r \text{ expressed as a decimal})}$$

Examples

(A) In the example suppose the investment is bought today and the operation is immediate and continuous. The NPV calculation becomes as shown in Table 2.3.

Table 2.3
The net present value (NPV) calculation

Time from today	Cash flow £	Present value at 11 per cent Discount factor	Present value
0	(1500)	1.000	(1500)
½	100	0.949	95
1½	1000	0.901 × 0.949	855
2½	1000	0.812 × 0.949	770
3½	100	0.731 × 0.949	69
		NPV = 289	

The IRR now needs to be recalculated to take account of the refined timing. The IRR is now 21½ per cent because of the earlier cash flow.

(B) Suppose again that the operation were to be built up and paid for over one construction year. In this case the £1500 cash flow is similarly assumed to be mid-year and the other cash flows occur six months later than before. The NPV can then be obtained from the first calculation, which has so far given a present value six months from today, by discounting the result by six months. NPV today is equal to

$$199 \times 0.949 = £189$$

The IRR is 17 per cent in this case, as at first, because it is mathematically true that the same yield is given wherever period zero is assumed to occur if the succeeding time periods bear the same relationship to period zero.

In some cases, such as natural resource projects, which involve large negative cash flows at the end of the project, a special problem arises in using IRR. Projects of this sort can have more than one IRR, some of which may be above the required return and some below. Complex techniques have been developed to salvage the IRR method in these circumstances. These adjustments usually involve procedures similar to the present value approach, and fewer problems will be encountered by the use of the NPV rule in these circumstances.

Use of present value: optimization of mutually exclusive alternatives

Financial analysts are constantly being asked to advise as to which of two viable alternatives is financially preferable. Such choices include large long life machinery versus cheaper short life machinery, labour versus automation, the choice of site, speed of construction, shaft versus open pit mining, air transport versus sea transport, and so on; in each case choice of one excludes the possibility of choosing the other alternative. Use of the net present value calculation is the easiest approach. Suppose that in a company with a cost of capital of 11 per cent the choice is between: method A (which is capital intensive) showing a NPV of + £1500 and method B (with a lower capital cost) showing a NPV of + £1500.

If the analyst calculates the NPVs using the minimum acceptable return discount rate for the risk of the project, different discount rates might be appropriate to A and B. For example, one method might involve installing a possibly risky unproven technological improvement, whereas the other method would re-equip as before.

The actual question to be answered, since both methods are financially desirable, is whether the expenditure of the extra capital involved on Method A is worth while. The incremental investment which is represented by the difference between the cash flows of the two alternatives (cash flow A and cash flow B, for each period), shows NPV of + £200 (NPV A − NPV B). It is therefore worth spending the extra money. Where the patterns of the alternative cash flows are very different, the incremental approach avoids problems in comparing projects with different levels of capital expenditure. Indeed, different cash flows can arise from the same total capital invested but the incremental cash flow analysis still gives the financially preferable operational plan.

Use of the DCF/IRR approach is also straightforward but contains a snare for the unwary. The question of whether the incremental investment would be desirable is answered by finding the DCF/IRR on the incremental cash flow (cash flow A minus cash flow B, for each period). If the incremental IRR is greater than the company's minimum acceptable return, then alternative A is financially preferable. When setting out the results, however, an apparent problem frequently arises (see Table 2.4).

Table 2.4
A problem with the internal rate of return (IRR)

Method		11 per cent NPV	IRR
A	Expensive	+ £1 500	14 per cent
B	Cheaper	+ £1 300	16 per cent
A—B	Incremental investment	+ £200	13 per cent

It looks as though one should choose method B because the IRR is better than in A. This is an illusion because the capital on which the yield is earned is different in each case. The analysis of the incremental investment points to the same answer whichever method is used. It is often argued that, perhaps, the incremental capital should be spent on some other investment which might show a better return than the 13 per cent here. This could be the case in conditions of severe capital rationing when investments yielding 13 per cent cannot be financed. In other conditions there is no conflict and both investments are desirable. Of course, more than two projects might be available, in which case, several incremental investment choices would be necessary. It is easier simply to compare the NPVs; the most preferable choice has the highest NPV.

Some practitioners approve the calculation of the NPV but find the answer, which is of necessity expressed in currency, difficult to use. The profitability index is therefore sometimes used, particularly when projects need to be ranked because budgets are limited. The index is calculated by dividing the present value of the net cash returns by the present value of the net cash investments. In the example given earlier the profitability index is 1699/1500 = 1.13 which means that every unit of investment earns 1.13 units of present value in the project. Care must be taken not to confuse this with the IRR, which is 17 per cent. In practice analysts report the profitability of a project both in terms of NPV in currency and of IRR as a percentage, to assist understanding.

When mutually exclusive opportunities are being analysed, equal project lives should be compared. This is often difficult, but a three-year life machine can be compared with a five-year machine by assuming that the longer life machine will be sold at the end of the third year.

Alternatively a fifteen-year period can be taken with five three-year machines compared with three five-year machines. The most sensible assumption will be obvious.

Present value and expected value: decision trees

Much of capital investment planning involves arranging a continuous series of actions which may be altered in the light of future events or future actual patterns of marketing. It is possible to set out likely outcomes in a map known as a decision tree — it grows as it is extended further into the future. NPVs of each likely chain of events can be prepared and this could help the decision that must be taken later. Very often decision tree calculations are of the expected value of the outcome. To calculate expected values, the probabilities of likely intermediate events of outcomes are incorporated. Decision trees have been described extensively. A decision tree is shown in Figure 2.2.

Figure 2.2 Example of a decision tree

Faced with the need to decide whether to install a computer, the possibilities or likely events might appear as shown. The decision taken would depend, financially, on the relative NPVs or expected values of the three good possibilities. Expected values are weighted by the relevant probability; for example, if there is a 60 per cent chance of an NPV of £1000 and a 40 per cent chance of an NPV of zero, the expected value is £600.

COMPUTATIONAL RESOURCES

Although computers, large and small, are invaluable as calculating aids for complex problems they should not be used indiscriminately because the cost and the time taken to eliminate errors can become disproportionate to the problem being analysed. Time sharing on computer terminals using borrowed working programs can be invaluable. Modern analytical methods can generally be employed for simple problems, using everyday hand calculators.

Calculation shortcuts and standard procedures for all problems are often sought in the field. If, however, they are used without understanding or without necessary adaption to the different circumstances of each case, much more time can easily be wasted than if the problem were initially approached from first principles.

DATA

The collection and sifting of project data normally leads to far more problems than the analysis. This is no reason for allowing less than rigorous analytical techniques. If a quick look at the first set of data indicates a promising idea, it is sensible to re-examine the data before extending the analysis. Data is given, begged, borrowed or stolen, but in spite of, or because of, the uncertainties involved, the best way to obtain good understanding leading to better decisions is to establish good communications with the project initiators as a top priority.

Discussions should be held 'on site' as early as possible so that there is no suggestion of 'ivory tower' thinking. Diplomatic approaches to hard-worked estimators who have to grapple with difficult forecasting problems can lead to a good understanding, not only of the best realistic guess at some figure, but also of the possible range in which it may lie and of the probabilities involved. Conversation with outsiders often helps clarification. The best hunches are those agreed by two or more experts. Special and outside experts can be called in to advise on variables found by sensitivity analysis to be critical enough to merit the cost of the advice.

A special problem to be tackled is that of inflation, particularly when costs are subject to special pressures leading to price rises greater than the general rate. The analyst will have to take a view as to when it is safe to assume that, on balance, costs and revenue will be similarly inflated (See also Chapter 5).

Missing data — reverse economics

Very often, data is simply not available for such vital factors as the achievable price for a new product, the size of the reserves in a new oil field, the time required to obtain safety clearance or planning permission or the market or technological life period. Reverse economics is the formal technique whereby it is possible to define the achievable or viable range for the missing data. If a graph is drawn of the profitability (NPV or IRR/DCF) of the project against invented values of the missing data, it is possible to find the value that gives the minimum acceptable result. If that value is very unrealistic, it may be possibe to conclude that the new product will not be profitable, or that the oil field cannot be exploited economically under present circumstances. A decision might then be taken to stop any further expenditure on the promotion of the idea. If a project must be killed off or frozen it is far better halted early, before reputations become involved.

This technique is also useful when considering the merger, takeover or sale of a company, or its flotation on the public market. An attempt is made to forecast the foreseeable cash flow of the company, possibly including benefits caused by savings in the new managerial context. The difference between the present value of the forecast cash flow and the debt divided by the number of issued shares will give a measure of the acceptability of a quoted or offered price, or will indicate what price to set at the beginning of negotiations. In a takeover situation the buyer should use the incremental required return for the project, that is, the required rate of return for the risk of the company being taken over. If the company is quoted, the value of its equity share capital is given in the market place, unless there are undisclosed facts such as merger. The premium paid should be less than the NPV of the merger benefits (see also Chapter 16).

Uncertain and erroneous data

A good approach to uncertain data is to attempt to identify the range in which the answer may lie. This is sometimes done by adding to the best guess two more guesses, one of which is the most pessimistic and the other the most optimistic. In this way it may be possible to exclude too much subjectivity on the part of the estimator, who might previously have thought that his future depended on the success of his estimates and who therefore, understandably, introduced too much conservatism. In large organizations a chain of conservatism may be introduced. In such cases the analyst must try to assess the realities and it is helpful if the motivations of the personnel are adjusted so as not to interfere. Overestimating can be as wrong as underestimating and can easily lead to raising too much finance, or to premature expansion.

Often data is manipulated, either innocently or deliberately, to achieve the desired result — perhaps acceptance of a scheme by head office or of a contract in a tendering competition. The results can lead to public embarrassment, if not disaster. A good review discipline can help to avoid or to sort out such problems.

Once the range in which critical data lies is found, sensitivity analysis can be carried out. Alernatively, a calculation of the likely profit or loss, should everything turn out for the worst, can help in discussion. If the organization simply cannot survive such a loss and the chances of it are significant, then the project may well have to be forgone.

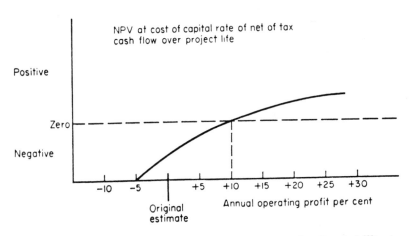

Figure 2.3   Graph of the sensitivity of the project's viability to profit variation

SENSITIVITY ANALYSIS

This technique can highlight the facts and problems caused by the risks and uncertainties of the plan under discussion. It has limitations but can be carried out with a minimum of calculating aids if necesary. The aim of this analysis is to discover the value of an uncertain variable at which the project is just profitable. Two or three calculations will give the necessary sensitivity curve.

Table 2.5
Variables in profit estimates

	Original estimate	Acceptable estimates					
Price per unit £	20	21	20	20	20	20	20.3
Volume/Number sold	10	10	10.5	10	10	10	10.15
Labour cost £	40	40	40	30	40	40	38
Materials cost £	50	50	50	50	40	50	47.5
Overhead cost £	10	10	10	10	10	0	9.5
Operating profit	100	110	110	110	110	110	111.045

Example

A project is showing a negative net present value at the company's cost of capital rate. What would need to be done to make it profitable? The sensitivity graph is drawn (Figure 2.3) and shows that the operating profit would need to be raised by 10 per cent to give a zero NPV of the net incremental cash flow for the project. All other things are assumed at first to remain constant (capital cost, speed of coming into operation, life of the project, tax, inflation, etc.). Table 2.5 shows data which give the desired result.

It is thus possible to say that the project would be acceptable if either the price could be raised by 5 per cent, or the volume sold is increased by 5 per cent, or if the labour cost could be lowered by 25 per cent, or the material cost by 20 per cent or the overhead cost by 100 per cent. Another possibility to explore would be if (as shown in the final column) both the price volume sold could be raised by 1½ per cent at the same time as all costs are reduced by 5 per cent. However, one should try to ensure that joint changes in variables are not contradictory and fit a plausible and consistent scenario.

The graph could have been plotted using IRR and the company's required rate of return as the cut-off line but this involves more sums.

One more uncertainty can be explored to extend the analysis. Suppose, for example, that the market for the product is thought to last ten years but could be hit by competition in eight to twelve years' time; further calculations give the graph shown in Figure 2.4. Annual operating profit is thought likely to lie between 95 and 120. Assuming the variable examined to be the most critical, the profitability 'envelope' is shown by the two outer curves and the dotted connecting lines. This envelope is divided into two parts by the cut-off line of zero net present value. By inspection of the two areas it is possible to conclude that the project has roughly only a 40 per cent chance of being viable. The worst likely outcome is also shown. The decision may then be taken more easily.

Figure 2.4   Two-variable sensitivity analysis graph

Should the whole envelope be above the cut-off line it would be possible to conclude that the project is profitable in spite of the uncertainty in the variables considered, which are then defined as uncritical. Further effort could then be concentrated on other variables. This technique is limited to two dimensions. It is, however, of great value, even without calculating aids, because of its simplicity in demonstrating the effect of apparently daunting uncertainties.

PROBABILITY ANALYSIS

This is the ideal towards which sensitivity analysis is the first step, but the calculation usually requires the help of a computer. Great efforts are being made by large organizations and consultants to prepare flexible computer programs to conduct probability analysis on a wide variety of projects.

Sensitivity analysis tells one the impact of each variable on the profitability of the project. If probabilities can be assigned to each variable in different parts of its range, the probability of various outcomes for the profitability of the project can be examined. Subjectivity is not avoided by this, but the further discussion can sometimes help clarify the situation. The results could be shown for each variable in a histogram, which is a practical approach to the underlying mathematical curve. An example is shown in Figure 2.5.

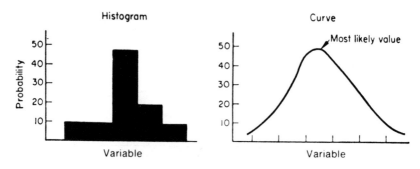

Figure 2.5   Examples of probability distributions

Mathematical sampling using such data for each significant variable results in the type of profitability/probability graph shown in Figure 2.6.

Figure 2.6 Example of a profitability/probability graph

The peak of the curve shows the most likely outcome, but there is a significant chance that the yield might be negative or that the original investment would not be recovered. The area under the curve being taken as unity, the area to the left of the cost of capital or required rate of return cut-off line, if measured, gives the probability of unprofitability. The use of sensitivity and probability analyses does not remove uncertainty and subjectivity of data; it helps decision takers to judge the likelihood of profit or loss in projects.

RISK

Uncertainty of data is not the only unknown bedevilling projects. Many possible events could have a highly significant effect. Such events include acts of God (earthquake, flood), of governments (tariffs, nationaliza-tion), of competitors, of technological improvement. Some risks can be insured against. In every case it is helpful to define the risk and assess its possible effect (what happens if . . .?), and in particular when such an effect might occur. If the likely loss caused by the risky circumstances were to be disastrous to the company, then perhaps the venture is too risky. There are several ways in which organizations of different kinds can proceed to minimize the effect of risk. Obvious examples are diversification, both geographically and in the nature of the business, the tying of customers or suppliers to long term contracts, and the cautious introduction of new or different scale business. Other risks can be eliminated through markets in which risk is traded. A surprising variety of risks can be insured against and others, such as commodity price variation and exchange rate variations, can be hedged in future markets.

DISCUSSION FORUM FOR CAPITAL INVESTMENT PROBLEMS

Good decision taking depends more than anything else on good communication. The decision takers (at the level appropriate to the size of the proposal) do well to arrange a free debate between the project sponsors, the experts, the analysts and themselves. Documentation of the proposal, the analysis, the decision and any argument or discussion are of great value to all concerned in future planning, as well as the relevance to interrelated projects in the context of the organization's future as a whole. The techniques described in this chapter contribute only by assembling such facts as can be established and highlighting the likely probabilities. This, however, is of great value in releasing management effort for the interpretation of the problems.

Most private organizations are to some extent limited as to the amount of capital available, particularly for unspectacular investments. It would be convenient if all projects turned up simultaneously and could be ranked in order of profitability and then accepted in turn until available funds were used up. (Such a procedure is to a certain extent available to the public sector at budget time.) In most companies, however, capital investment or operational optimization opportunities turn up irregularly. It is therefore highly desirable to establish and monitor a clearly understood set of criteria and discount rates, reflecting the company's required rates of return for different risks, against which each scheme can be measured as it arises and progresses. With the aid of the right criteria there is some chance that a good source of investments will have been chosen so that, at the minimum, returns can exceed costs and the company's value can be increased, leading to a healthy financial context for future development.

Tactics

When analysis precedes or accompanies negotiations with governments, financiers, associates or opponents, it is usually helpful to make calculations in order that one can understand the opposite point of view, which might be based on different methods or criteria.

Few organizations can avoid differences of opinion which lead to apparent or very real conflicts. The experienced decision taker and his advisers can normally recognize the behavioural signs. Discussion is not always avoided for good reasons, such as a real emergency. Emergencies can be contrived by skilful delays and, perhaps, decisions can be precipitated by prompted outside pressures. Decisions taken in real emergencies should be appraised and documented as soon as possible. If a decision taker is known to be susceptible to private discussions, then project sponsors will be quick to arrange suitable lobbying. Such a situation has obvious dangers.

A very real problem can arise in planning investments which can or should be phased. The purchase of options or expenditure on pilot plants, which lead either to subsequent large investment or to embarrassment if the second stage is deemed unacceptable, should not be appraised in isolation. Appraisal of the first stage should be accompanied by a best guess of the likely subsequent history, and the project should be discussed at the level relevant to the whole operation, in which case the decision will be taken after consideration of the future commitments. The decision tree technique examined earlier can help.

When a superficially attractive proposal is financially marginal, special care must be taken. At this time criticism may be made of the company's criteria which were otherwise accepted when the proposals were better than marginal. Such criticism at this time may not always be valid. In this situation excessive subjectivity may be introduced into uncertain data; in fact, some estimators claim to be able to produce estimates which pass company tests. Wide discussions of parameters, perhaps calling in outside advice, as well as the discipline contained in carrying out sensitivity and probability analysis, go some way to reduce the risk. Afterwards, a well-established routine or project monitoring reappraisal, review or ex-post evaluation, or whatever the subsequent comparison of forecast with actual results is called, may be especially appropriate.

REAPPRAISAL: EX-POST EVALUATION AND CAPITAL EXPENDITURE REVIEWS

It has been said that, without subsequent re-examination, formal planning appraisal techniques are largely counter-productive. Ex ante evaluation – the prior preparation of forecast results – is very necessary when raising finance for a project, either internally or externally, and obtaining the desired go-ahead. There is, however, no certainty that the combined estimates and skills which resulted in the forecasts have been optimized unless a subsequent view is taken.

There are well-established commercial routines whereby periodic (weekly, monthly, quarterly, annual) accounts are compiled of both financial and physical resources used and benefits achieved, and reports are made to relevant technical and financial monitors. Usually the results are compared with annual and three or five-year plans for the project or the organization as a whole. Variations are studied and adjustments are made.

Projects which were initially appraised using cash flow disciplines should be reviewed using the same discipines. If the conclusions drawn differ, speedy action may be desirable or, if it is not, it would be nice to know that it is not.

Unfortunately, it is necessary to take a cynical look at projects built for less than the forecast cost, sales that noticeably exceed budget, and other successes. If the planners' faults were not in their stars but in themselves they should remain underlings. People have gone as far as saying that it is useless to plan at all unless one also reviews the results. But, as always, too much is as bad as too little.

It is not always clear who should conduct reappraisal reviews. Conflicts may be avoided if the project operators undertake the review in to normal course of their duties. It is highly desirable also to include some sort of outside view to ensure a balanced opinion as to why the resulting return differs from the first forecast. The review should, of course, cover all the unquantifiable as well as the measurable aspects. If the organization sets up a separate reviewing team, its members may need great powers of diplomacy as well as of detection and endurance.

Reviews are discussed preferably at the same forum as are capital expenditure proposals, or, at least, the decision takers should check that re-evaluation has taken place. Very often the lessons do not need to be driven home but have been learnt in the course of the operation.

The introduction of this routine is often problematical. As usual, opposition may be a cover. Other avoidance tactics can include radical changes of the scope of a project leading, among other things, to a delay in the review date. Significant changes of scope should be appraised as rigorously as new projects.

FURTHER READING

Brealey, R. A. and Myers, S. C., *Principles of Corporate Finance*, McGraw-Hill, New York, 1984

Franks, R. J. and Broyles, J. E., *Modern Managerial Finance*, John Wiley & Sons, Chichester, 1979

Merrett, A. J. and Sykes, Allen, *The Finance and Analysis of Capital Projects*, 2nd Edn, Longman, London, 1973

Merrett, A. J. and Sykes, Allen, *Capital Budgeting & Company Finance*, 2nd Edn, Longman, London, 1973

Thomas, H., *Decision Theory and the Manager*, Pitman, London, 1972

3

Managing working capital

Geoffrey P. E. Clarkson

Working capital is that proportion of a company's capital which is employed in short-term operations. It is customary to divide working capital into two categories: gross and net. Gross working capital is the sum total of all current assets, whereas net working capital is the amount by which the value of current assets exceeds the value of current liabilities. The former presents the financial manager with the problem of how to manage the individual components which compromise the list of current assets. The latter has financial significance for two reasons. The amount of net working capital represents the net volume of current assets which are being financed by long-term sources. Though current assets and liabilities customarily are turned over within relatively short periods of time, the net balance of current assets is that proportion which requires permanent financing by the company. The second point is that creditors have a particular interest in the net working capital position and regard these assets as the ultimate source of funds for the repayment of their loans.

Current assets consist of all stocks (inventories), including finished goods, work in process and raw materials; debtors; short-term investments (near cash) and cash.

Current liabilities are the sum total of a company's debts which must be settled within the following twelve months. They include creditors, overdrafts (short-term bank loans), current portions of long-term debt due, as well as the remaining credit obligations of the firm. They may require early settlement, or involve an interest charge which can vary from zero in the case of net monthly accounts due, to bank charge rates on overdrafts. Current liabilities represent the total amount of short-term debt. They are the cheaper forms of debt but involve the highest insolvency risks. Current liabilities have relatively short-term due dates for payment and cash or further credits must be found to settle these accounts.

It is the function of financial management to fund the company debt at the lowest cost consistent with acceptable risk. This is readily evident when the net working capital position is examined. Since net working capital is the net value of current assets this balance must be totally financed from long term sources. Since long-term funds are usually more costly than short-term funds, the management of current assets and current liabilities is an important part of financial management.

WORKING CAPITAL RATIOS

The liquidity and solvency of a firm are closely related to its working capital position. Solvency represents the time state of liquidity. To be solvent entails an ability to meet debt payments on due dates by having money available in the form of cash, near cash or unused credit. To be and remain solvent, it is not necessary to be liquid. It is only necessary to be able to become sufficiently liquid should the need arise.

The ability to become liquid is a function of time and the state of assets in relation to cash. If too high a proportion of assets exist in a state far removed from cash, a problem of solvency can arise. To be unable to generate cash or credit when required creates the risk of insolvency. This condition is known as overtrading. Firms which overtrade cause concern in the minds of their creditors. This can lead creditors to shorten credit lines, and in some cases, to demand immediate settlement of their debts. If sufficient cash cannot be obtained, the company may be declared technically insolvent.

Technical insolvency, as distinct from legal insolvency, occurs when a firm has sufficient assets to meet all financial obligations but not enough time to convert those assets into cash. Legal insolvency is a condition of permanent cash shortage no matter how much time is provided.

A customary way to measure a company's liquidity is to divide its current assets, the gross working capital, by its current liabilities to get what is called the current ratio.

$$\text{Current ratio} \quad = \quad \frac{\text{Current assets}}{\text{Current liabilities}}$$

This ratio, sometimes called the working capital ratio, provides a rough measure of the safety afforded the firm's short-term creditors. For, in the event of a technical liquidation, current assets are more likely to yield a high percentage of their book value than are many of the fixed assets. Moreover, short-term lenders look to the current assets as the prime source for the repayment of their loans. Clearly, the higher the value of the current ratio, the greater is their feeling of security.

Despite the feelings of security it may generate, the working capital ratio is frequently misleading. Often it has little value as a tool for financial management. To calculate the ratio, figures are taken from a balance sheet. These numbers reflect the past activities of the firm. Though it may comfort a manager to know that his current ratio was in a satisfactory state last month, this data point may not relate to present activities. Not only do balance sheets usually represent the past, but they are also summary statements of the accounts. They do not provide information on timing, particularly with reference to the periods within which the current liabilities are falling due. A company could have a current ratio of four to one at the time of its audit, but if its current assets were primarily made up of work in process and most of its current liabilities were due at the end of the month it might face a severe shortage of cash. On the other hand a company which acted as an agent buying and selling finished goods for clients could have a low current ratio and a sound liquidity position.

One way of coping with the inadequacies of the current ratio is to recognize the inherent illiquidity of most companies' stocks (inventories), particularly if the majority of their value is tied up in work in process. A first solution to this problem is to exclude all stocks from consideration and focus attention instead on the current assets that stand nearer to cash. Under this approach, a quick ratio is created which takes as the numerator the value of cash, near cash and debtors (accounts receivable), and as the denominator the value of the current liabilities.

$$\text{Quick ratio} \quad = \quad \frac{\text{Cash} + \text{near cash} + \text{debtors}}{\text{Current liabilities}}$$

The quick ratio unquestionably provides a stricter test of a firm's liquidity. But it still does not represent or measure the underlying short-term credit strength of a company. Nor does it reflect or measure the timing of the flow of funds.

One way to overcome the inadequacies of the current and quick ratios is to calculate the borrowing power of a company's current assets. This borrowing power or potential is then compared to the actual borrowings of current liabilities to determine the proportion of its short term borrowing power the company has already consumed. Since existing borrowings, namely the current liabilities, are known with accuracy, the only difficulty in calculating this ratio lies in assessing the borrowing power of a company's current assets.

Borrowing power depends upon holdings of cash, near cash, debtors and stocks. In order to calculate the total borrowing power, it is necessary to look at each item separately since each has a different liquidity value and hence a different borrowing power.

Cash and near cash have the highest liquidity. Although near cash may well represent 90- or 120-day deposits or securities, their borrowing power is quite high. Clearly, instead of borrowing against such assets they could be sold for cash. Frequently, however, there are severe interest penalties for early encashment. Hence, genuine savings can be affected by borrowing against the market value of such time deposits and securities. Although conditions can vary, particularly in periods of rapid inflation, it is realistic to assume the borrowing power of cash and near cash combined to be 95 per cent of face value.

Debtors can readily be used as security for short-term loans. The borrowing power of a company's debtors is calculated as a percentage of their book or face value. This percentage is directly related to their quality which in turn reflects the credit worthiness of the customers as well as their payment record. Banks and finance houses that specialize in granting loans on debtors make it their business to assess accurately the quality of such assets. Though percentages will vary between companies, it is realistic to assume that the borrowing power of their debtors is 80 per cent of face value.

Stocks are by far the hardest to assess. In order to calculate their borrowing power, it is necessary to break stocks down into the three main categories of raw materials, work in process, and finished goods. Companies that use raw materials listed on commodity exchanges can borrow a high proportion of their market value. Such items as steel, copper, silver, crude or refined petroleum products, hides for leather, chemicals, grains, and so on, may vary in price from day to day, but their liquidity remains high. When used as security for a loan, the bank or lender will lend a proportion of their market value, usually specifying a minimum level which must be maintained. Percentages vary with the liquidity of the item, but in general, it is realistic to assume that the borrowing power of these raw materials is 80 per cent of their market value.

Some companies use as the raw materials for their manufacturing process sub-components or assemblies built by other firms. Though listed on their books as raw materials, the borrowing power of such items is in the same category as that of work in process. Work in process can have a high scrap value, particularly if the scrapping process is neither lengthy nor complicated. But scrap value is not a good indicator of borrowing power as bankers and other financial institutions are not in business to behave as scrap merchants. Hence, unless a company's products have some unusual or special features, the borrowing power of work in process is effectively zero.

Finished goods can have a high level of borrowing power. Once again, the exact percentage will depend on the time and effort it customarily takes to sell these items. For example, a specially designed machine tool will have less value as security for a loan than a like value of standard sized ball and roller bearings. On average, however, a company should be able to borrow up to 70 per cent of the book value of its finished goods stock.

The liquid asset ratio is thus given by dividing the value of liquid assets by the value of the current liabilities.

$$\text{Liquid asset ratio} \quad = \quad \frac{\text{Liquid assets}}{\text{Current liabilities}}$$

The liquid asset ratio has several important features. The first is that it provides the financial manager with an accurate assessment of the company's short term liquidity and solvency. If the ratio has a value greater than one, the firm still has additional credit available to it should the need arise. A ratio of less than one says the borrowing power of the current assets is no longer sufficient to cover the current liabilities already on the books. From a financial point of view, the most efficient use of short-term borrowing power is being made when the liquid asset ratio is approximately equal to one. At that point, the minimum amount of current assets is being kept in a needlessly liquid condition.

Despite the refinements provided by the liquid asset ratio, none of the above ratios deal with the flow of cash through the company's accounts. This flow is of prime importance to the company's operating liquidity and solvency.

DECISION MAKING

The management of working capital is concerned with two distinct but interwoven sets of activities: short-term and long-term financial operations. The former poses the problem of managing the individual current asset balances which make up the gross working capital position. Long-term working capital management is concerned with providing and funding the volume of net working capital required by the company's current and future activities.

An obvious problem concerning the management of a company's net working capital is the impact of inflation on the value of these assets. In times of high rates of inflation the money values of stocks and debtors can rise very rapidly. The value of trade creditors will also rise, but if the company is engaged in manufacturing, the impact of inflation is greater on the asset side of the balance sheet. As a result, incremental long-term funds have to be found to finance this inflationary addition to the value of net working capital. To the extent that the company's long-term funds are partly represented by long-term debt, the exposure of these net assets to erosion by inflation is lessened. Incremental debt brings incremental financial risk. To achieve an acceptable balance this risk has to be weighed against the certain erosion of value caused by inflation.

It would be very convenient it if were possible to prescribe the precise amount of gross and net working capital each company needs. Unfortunately, such is not the case. Manufacturing and merchandising enterprises, to mention but two examples, will invest different proportions of their total available monetary resources in working capital. Furthermore, some businesses will buy their fixed assets such as land, buildings and machinery, whereas others will lease these items. Each situation creates its own working capital problems that must be decided within the constraints and plans of the individual company. The object of this chapter, therefore, is not to tell managers what working capital they require. Rather it is to present a number of analytic techniques which will identify the decisions to be made when applied to the data of any company. It is management's job to make and take decisions. All that technical analysis can do is to identify the decisions that have to be made and the paths to their resolution.

The fundamental problem posed in the management of net and gross working capital can best be illustrated by examining the effects on a company of an increase in sales. To fill new orders extra units must be produced. Extra production requires additional raw materials, labour and overhead expenses. Even after the sale is effected an interval of time will elapse before payment is received. Throughout the manufacturing, selling and delivery period the company's activities have to be financed. Though the effects of this financing will eventually be reflected in the current and quick ratios, it is the pattern and timing of the expenditures and receipts that generate the company's current liquidity and solvency.

Table 3.1

Balance sheets   **(all figures £'000s)**

Liquidity Company

	£			£
Net worth	4 000	Fixed assets		2 500
		current assets		
Current liabilities	500	Stock	500	
		Debtors	1 000	
		Cash & deposits	500	2 000
	4 500			4 500

Efficiency Company

	£			£
Net worth	3 000	Fixed assets		1 700
		current assets		
Current liabilities	1 500	Stock	1 000	
		Debtors	1 300	
		Cash & deposits	500	2 800
	4 500			4 500

EXAMPLE OF WORKING CAPITAL FLOWS

Consider the consequences of the following sequence of events on the much simplified balance sheets of two companies. Liquidity Company Limited and Efficiency Company Limited, whose starting balances are given in Table 3.1. Both companies now receive an order for £500 000 of their products. The order itself has no effect on their working capital, it merely becomes an entry in the order book. Suppose each firm has sufficient productive capacity available to handle the order. To manufacture the products each company has to buy £100 000 of raw materials. These materials are purchased on terms of net cash monthly. Gross working capital grows immediately by £100 000. So do current liabilities, since the increase in gross working capital is being financed by the supplier who is not paid until the end of the month.

Table 3.2
Working capital effect of accepting an order

Liquidity Company		
	Before	**After**
Cash & deposits	500	500
Debtors	1000	1000
Stock	500	800
Liquid assets* (95:80:50)	1525	1675
Current assets	2000	2300
Current liabilities	500	800
Net working capital	1500	1500
Current ratio	4 to 1	2.88 to 1
Quick ratio	3 to 1	2.25 to 1
Liquid asset ratio	3.05 to 1	2.09 to 1

Efficiency Company		
	Before	*After*
Cash & deposits	500	500
Debtors	1300	1300
Stock	1000	1300
Liquid assets* (95:80:50)	1540	1690
Current assets	2800	3100
Current liabilities	1500	1800
Net working capital	1300	1300
Current ratio	1.87 to 1	1.72 to 1
Quick ratio	1.20 to 1	1 to 1
Liquid asset ratio	1.03 to 1	0.94 to 1

*Borrowing power is taken as cash 95%; debtors 80%; stock 50%

The raw material begins its passage through the manufacturing process and a direct wages bill of £100 000 is incurred. By the time the products are manufactured, labour, overhead and other costs have risen to a total of £200 000. Thus, to produce these orders the companies have had to find £300 000 and current liabilities register a similar increase. As can be seen in Table 3.2, both companies are now noticeably less liquid, although the Efficiency Company has incurred a proportionately greater reduction in its current liquidity.

Consider now the effects of completing the sale transaction. The orders are delivered and invoices are sent out for £500 000 with terms of net cash monthly. By sending out the goods, as well as the invoice, the stock of finished goods is turned into a debtor valued at the selling price, presuming no loss due to bad debts. The value of liquid assets for both firms rises immediately, as do their quick and liquid assets ratios. Current liquidity has improved when judged by these ratio tests, but a cash shortage will remain until the buyer pays for the goods he has purchased.

TIMING OF FLOWS

The pattern of payments and receipts which are a part of all business operations, depicts the occasions when financing is required. The purchase of materials generates trade creditors, and the manufacturing process creates labour and overhead expenses, all of which have to be paid for. Stocks of work in process and finished goods have to be handled, stored, and shipped. Each operation incurs additional expense that has to be paid for as it comes due. Finished goods which have been sold are then delivered, usually on credit terms. Credit sales generate trade debtors: it is at this point that cash shortages reach their peak. Companies face a variety of cash demands, including tax payments, all with individual timing. As a rule, there is only one main source of cash revenue: credit sales which have yet another timing.

The management of the cash flows is crucial to the financial life of an enterprise. It may be necessary, as well as desirable, to finance cash shortages with short-term borrowing. Such borrowing must be planned. It is as foolish to borrow money and not use it as it is to discover need for cash that can only be satisfied by an immediate increase in short-term loans. Banks, like other lenders, dislike lending at short notice. They also have their cash flow problems. Further, when a company needs cash urgently the risk of insolvency is at its highest, and willing lenders become scarce as the risk increases. Many profitable firms have gone bankrupt because they ran out of cash. Solvency can always be maintained by holding large amounts of cash or deposits, but excessive cash implies a high level of net

Table 3.3
Comparison of quarterly balance sheets

	Fourth quarter	First quarter	Increase (decrease)	Second quarter	Increase (decrease)	Third quarter	Increase (decrease)
Net worth	£	£	£	£	£	£	£
Ordinary shares	220 000	220 000		220 000		250 000	30 000
Retained earnings	275 000	293 000	18 000	316 000	23 000	341 000	25 000
Total	495 000	513 000		536 000		591 000	
Long term liabilities							
Mortgages	180 000	180 000		180 000		200 000	20 000
Machinery loans	90 000	100 000	10 000	103 000	3 000	121 000	18 000
Total	270 000	280 000		283 000		321 000	
Fixed assets							
Building & property	230 000	227 000	(3 000)	224 000	(3 000	250 000	26 000
Machinery	320 000	340 000	20 000	345 000	5 000	360 000	25 000
Total	550 000	567 000		569 000		610 000	
Net increase (decrease) in long term funds			11 000		24 000		52 000
Current liabilities							
Bank overdraft	33 000	85 000	52 000	29 000	(56 000)	41 000	12 000
Creditors	95 000	145 000	50 000	112 000	(33 000)	153 000	41 000
Other payables	17 000	8 000	(9 000)	15 000	7 000	10 000	(3 000)
Total	145 000	238 000		156 000		204 000	
Current assets							
Stock	230 000	268 000	38 000	245 000	(23 000)	298 000	53 000
Debtors	105 000	150 000	45 000	130 000	(20 000)	165 000	35 000
Cash and deposits	25 000	46 000	21 000	31 000	(15 000)	46 000	15 000
Total	360 000	464 000		406 000		508 000	
Net increase (decrease) in short term funds			(11 000)		(24 000)		(52 000)

working capital. Net working capital is financed from long term sources. An efficient financial manager will determine the minimum cash required, will study the pattern of receipts and payments, and will plan both his short-term borrowings and investments so that the company is neither wasting its funds nor running unnecessary risks. He will manage the company's cash so that it is neither idle nor overtraded.

FLOW OF FUNDS

The pattern of payments and receipts described above gives a simple example of the flow of funds through a company's activities. These flows are usually audited on specific dates such as the end of each month, quarter or year. Over such intervals of time, the total net flows represent a balance of all cash transactions. Receipts from sales, for example, are balanced against the funds used in the generation of those sales. Similarly, cash borrowed during the period is offset by payments made on the debt.

Total net cash flows are calculated by comparing balance sheet entries for consecutive time periods. Table 3.3 represents a simplified statement of a company's balances at the end of each of three consecutive quarters. In addition, two columns note the increases or decreases in assets and liabilities that took place during each period. The changes in assets and liabilities are important, for they identify the fund transfers that have been made. A decrease in an asset's value implies that a corresponding increase in cash has been generated from this asset. Alternatively, an increase in an asset's value means that additional funds have been invested, which implies a decrease in cash. A decrease in cash can also be achieved by reducing liabilities, whereas any increases in liabilities or net worth, or shareholders' equity, mean an increase in funds. These sources and uses of funds can be summarized as follows:

Sources of funds	*Uses of funds*
Decrease in assets	Increase in assets
Increase in liabilities	Decrease in liabilities
Increase in net worth	Decrease in net worth

In order to illustrate how to identify these flows of funds in detail, the flows of three quarters' worth of balance sheets are set out in Table 3.4. As can now be readily seen, during the first quarter cash was generated by negotiating an increase in bank borrowings, by taking an increase in trade credit, by financing new machinery purchases partly with term loans, and by earning enough profit to increase retained earnings after taking care of taxes and dividends. Most of these funds were used to build up current assets in the form of stocks and debtors. During the second quarter, this pattern of sources and uses is reversed. Funds are

Table 3.4
Sources and uses of cash for first three quarters

	First quarter	Second quarter	Third quarter
	£	£	£
Sources: long term			
Ordinary shares			30 000
Retained earnings	18 000	23 000	25 000
Mortgages			20 000
Machinery loans	10 000	3 000	18 000
Buildings & property	3 000	3 000	
Total	31 000	29 000	93 000
Uses: long term			
Buildings & property			26 000
Machinery	20 000	5 000	15 000
Total	20 000	5 000	41 000
Net sources (uses): long term	11 000	24 000	52 000
Sources: short term			
Bank overdraft	52 000		12 000
Creditors	50 000		41 000
Other payables		7 000	
Stock		23 000	
Debtors		20 000	
Cash & deposits		15 000	
Total	102 000	65 000	53 000
Uses: short term			
Bank overdraft		56 000	
Creditors		33 000	
Other payables	9 000		3 000
Stock	38 000		53 000
Debtors	45 000		35 000
Cash & deposits	21 000		14 000
Total	113 000	89 000	105 000
Net sources (uses): short term	(11 000)	(24 000)	(52 000)

still raised from the re-investment of retained earnings and by raising more machinery loans, but the largest sums are generated by reducing the value of current assets. These funds are applied to the reduction of current liabilities. The funds flow in the third quarter is very similar to that of the first, the one main exception being the sale of additional equity.

From the flow of cash depicted in Table 3.4, it is possible to make a number of inferences about the company's financial behaviour throughout the three quarters. The company began the year by increasing both stocks and sales. Either sales are subject to seasonal swings or the firm has launched a new sales campaign. The effect of increasing sales on current assets and cash flows has already been partially described in the analysis of the activities of the Liquidity and Efficiency Companies (see Table 3.2). There it was noted that a growth in sales needs to be supported by a corresponding growth in raw materials, work in process and finished goods and debtors. All these activities require cash, and it can be seen from Table 3.4 that this company chose to finance its first quarter growth by borrowing short term from its bankers and suppliers, and long term by financing new machinery purchases, and by making an adequate and retainable profit.

By the end of the second quarter either the sales drive has come to an end or the company does produce seasonal items. In either event, the growth rate of sales fell during this quarter. Typically a lower rate of sales generates cash if there is a corresponding reduction in creditors and stock. During the second quarter most of the cash generated by the reduction in current assets was used to reduce current liabilities. One could therefore infer that the company was working itself back to a level of sales and production based on its experience of demand in the previous fourth quarter.

The third quarter, however, was another period of rapid growth in sales. Once again the surge in current assets was financed by borrowing short term from bankers and suppliers. This time, management must have judged the rate of growth in sales to be reasonably secure because additions were made to buildings as well as machinery. These additions were financed by increasing both the amount of the mortgage and the machinery loan. Another indicator of management's belief that the sales had indeed grown at least to a new plateau is the fact that they chose to raise further funds by selling additional equity during this quarter.

Another interesting feature of these cash flows is that in each quarter the company was taking cash raised from long-term sources and investing these funds in short-term assets. As can be seen in Table 3.4, the amount of cash invested in short-term assets increased each quarter. As a result, one can conclude that over these three quarters the company was becoming progressively more liquid. In effect, the company has been a net borrower of long-term funds which it has chosen to invest in current assets.

PRODUCT CASH CYCLE

An equally important aspect of working capital behaviour is the way cash flows are related to the life cycle of individual products. The life cycle begins when a company decides to develop a new product. Development costs may be large or small but inevitably they require cash payments. In addition to design and development costs, the firm may have to incur the costs of extensive market testing. Also, some reorganization of the manufacturing process may be required if the tests indicate that the new product should go into production. In addition, various engineering and other costs will be incurred if a new production line has to be set up. Raw materials must then be purchased and labour and overhead expenses be applied in order to create the required stock of partially and completely finished products. During this last stage, some form of sales campaign must be launched. Finally, if orders are generated, deliveries can begin.

The design, development, marketing and production stages may represent years of time and effort. However long the time period, the cash flows during this part of a product's life cycle are wholly negative. It is not until some weeks after the first delivery has been made that the first sales revenue is received. For many products, particularly those requiring advanced technology, the research and development phase alone occupies a number of years. Testing and refining prototypes can add many more months, as faults are discovered and improvements are made. Manufacturing and marketing also take time. Throughout this period the firm has to finance the new product's development from revenue and money sources to which the new product is not yet contributing. In order to manage and control these expenses, companies frequently set up a research and development department with its own budget. This department or division then becomes responsible for initiating studies and helping to make marketing and production decisions which identify and create profitable additions to the product line. Research and development is expensive. It is successful only when a new product sells sufficiently well to earn a suitable share of the company's profit. No product, however, earns cash returns while it is being developed. All such development must be financed, perhaps by an advanced sale of a franchise or royalty rights, perhaps by government grants or from internal funds. Whatever the cost, the required volume of funds as well as the timing of the outlays must be estimated, and the necessary funds obtained, or the new product cannot be developed, let alone brought to the market to earn profits.

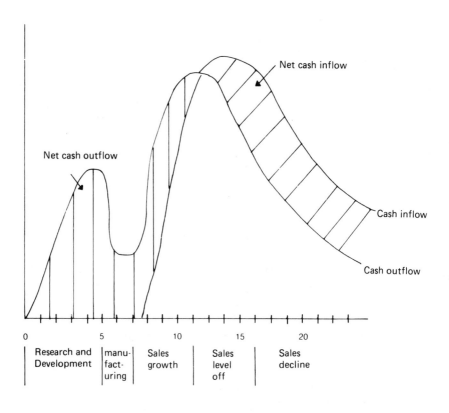

Figure 3.1 Product cash cycle

Example of the cash flows of a new product

Figure 3.1 provides a graphic illustration of the behaviour of the cash flows for a product that is launched successfully. At first, the cash revenue is small. As sales and deliveries build up, cash receipts rise. It is frequently the case, however, that the cash costs of generating sales and effecting the deliveries rise faster than the cash inflows from those sales. The net result is an extended period of cash shortages, shortages that are not relieved until the rate of growth tapers off. A rapid growth in the sales of a product can eventually be very profitable, but it always causes a heavy drain on cash.

Taking a closer look at Figure 3.1, one can see that if the intervals on the horizontal axis represent quarters, the first net cash receipts are not received until two and a half years after the first expenses are incurred.

This schedule of cash flows is typical of many products. There are some products, notably fashion items, which can be created, developed and brought to the market in a matter of months. Equally, there are high technology products for which the intervals of time in the cash cycle are measured in years. Whatever the duration of the cash outflows, it is important to notice that large net cash receipts only begin when the rate of growth in sales slows down. The greatest net inflow of cash occurs when manufacturing expenses decline and the product can be sold without extensive advertising and marketing costs. This is a period where the growth in sales is declining. It may well signify that the useful life of the product is coming to an end.

The net cash inflows that are generated during the later, or mature, stages of a product's life can be, and frequently are, used to finance the development of other new products. When companies state that 80 per cent of their current sales comes from products that didn't exist five years ago and that this pattern is expected to continue, it is clear that these firms have learned to balance and manage the many streams of cash flows.

MANAGING DEBTORS

Trade debtors are a product of credit sales. If a company were to make all sales for cash it would have no debtors and no need to finance its sales by the use of current debt. Most companies, particularly in manufacturing, sell on credit and it is these companies with debtor balances that this section concerns.

Net cash value

The average collection period (or age) is an important indicator of the liquidity of receivables. The longer an invoice goes unpaid the less likely it is ever to be paid. Doubtful accounts turn into bad debts when they are left uncollected. Hence, to assess the liquidity of a given balance of receivables it is necessary to investigate the relation between the age of an account and the likelihood of its being collected. An inspection of past accounts will reveal the proportions to use. For illustrative purposes suppose the collectable percentages are as follows.

Age of accounts (days)	Collectable percentages
1 – 30	99
31 – 60	98
61 – 90	95
91 – 120	70
121 +	50

Applying these percentages to the receivables balance recorded at a particular time period will produce the net cash value of those receivables. Thus a £100 000 credit sale in the age category 1 – 30 would have a net cash value of £99 000. The same sized sale in the 121 days plus category would have a net cash value of only £50 000. It follows that an increase in the average age of receivables means a deterioration both in liquidity and real value.

Suppose that management has decided to do something about its deteriorating receivables position. What are the possible actions it can take and what credit policy should be adopted? Solutions vary from leaving things as they are to the opposite extreme of withdrawing credit facilities and insisting that all future sales be contracted for cash. Every solution will generate its own pattern of cash receipts and, depending upon its stringency, will entail certain costs. Thus, an increase in cash flow can be measured against the cost of generation. The net value to the company, given by a variety of alternatives, will help management to decide which credit policy to adopt.

It is most unlikely that a new, more stringent credit policy can be effected without cost. Management will wish to determine the probable cost of persuading customers to pay their bills within a new time limit. Obviously, such cost must not exceed the benefits to be derived from the new policy. The limit to the cost is determined by calculating the discount which the company could afford to offer as an incentive leaving itself no worse off than under the old credit policy. In other words, the interest rate or discount that will equalize the present value of these two streams of income must be calculated.

Financing debtors

Encashing receivables, like obtaining an overdraft or trade credit, is an important part of short-term working capital management. The basic objective in financing accounts receivable is to generate the maximum cash inflow at the lowest possible cost. One possible strategy was noted above: to offer a discount for prompt payment and a maximum credit period of 30 days. Although there is a large range of alternative financing policies, three important types of approach exist. The first is to sell, each month, all receivables to a commercial factor for cash. The second is to borrow against the receivables balance. The third is to develop a credit and collection department of such capability that other companies' receivables can be purchased and processed with the company's own assets to yield additional earnings.

Factoring debtors

The factoring of debtors is accomplished by offering the entire collection of receivables to a commercial factor. If a satisfactory price is negotiated and the sale is made, the factor takes on the responsibility for collecting all accounts due. As a consequence he also accepts the risk that some accounts will prove to be uncollectable. The purchase price is determined on the basis of the net cash value of the receivables balance. Though practices can differ, the purchase price is usually stated in terms of an advance payment of, say, 90 per cent of the net cash value. The balance, less service and financing charges, which may amount to 4 or 5 per cent, is paid to the company on the average due date for the accounts.

For example, suppose a company has a debtor balance with a net cash value of £100 000. The average age of these receivables is 30 days. The factor offers £90 000 cash now, and the balance less service and finance charges in thirty days. The amount of this balance depends upon the quality of the receivables. If the credit worthiness of these accounts is high, the factor's charge is low. It increases in line with the risk of bad debts.

The total cost of factoring can be quite heavy, particularly in times of high interest rates. However, if a company uses a factor for all its credit sales then the company has no direct collection charges of its own. The criterion is the company's cost of its own credit and collection department for the year. Moreover, cash today is worth more than cash at some future period. In any assessment of the cost of factoring the fact that the company's own credit department will not produce 90 per cent of the cash value of all receivables on the first day of every month must be costed and allowed. Hence the factoring cost may well look quite attractive compared to the alternative costs.

Borrowing on debtors

An alternative method of raising money on debtors is to pledge them as collateral for a loan. Many companies do not like the thought of having a factor collect from their customers. None the less, they cannot afford to tie up cash in receivables. A loan based on these receivables can be readily negotiated with commercial or merchant banks and may well provide a more acceptable financing vehicle.

With a loan of this type, the company retains the obligation to collect the debtors as well as the risk of doubtful accounts becoming bad debts. The usual practice is for the finance house to lend the company a proportion, say 70 or 80 per cent, of the net value of the receivables. Interest can be charged either on a daily basis or on the actual cash advanced. A service charge may also be included. Usually, the company will pay off the loan as debtors are collected and, as a result, the net cost to the company will be less than that charged by the factor on an outright sale. It must be noted, however, that the factor carries out credit accounting, ledger keeping and collecting as part of his services. The company is responsible for all these activities if it merely borrows money on its receivables.

BUYING DEBTORS

Many companies are in a position where they manage and finance their own credit sales. Such companies have credit departments and managers whose task is to service their customers' accounts and collect the receipts when due. One alternative to selling or borrowing on debtors is to go into the business of collecting receivables in a serious way. If the company already has a credit department, why not put it to work in a more efficient and effective manner? A satisfactory credit department will find little difficulty in providing a collection service for receivables from other companies with similar customers. The question to answer has two parts and can be stated as follows: is it cheaper to sell receivables outright to a factor or to process them? Whatever set of reasons persuades a company not to sell its receivables, economies of scale suggest it will be cheaper, per account collected, to behave as a factor and buy other companies' receivables. For debtors can be purchased just as they can be sold.

MANAGING STOCKS

Stocks of raw materials, goods in progress and finished goods pose a number of management problems. On the one hand there are the questions of warehousing and storage. Decisions on what levels of stock to keep are determined by economic order and production batch size considerations. These, in turn, help to specify the minimum and maximum stock levels required. On the other hand there is the question of how to finance these stocks and how to control the investment of funds in this type of asset.

The average age of stocks on hand can be computed. The stock balances at the begining of the period are divided by the purchases expected during the period and multiplied by the number of days in the accounting period. This calculation can be made for each category of stock as well as for the total balance. For example, within the raw material stocks used in a particular company's manufacturing process there is a variety of items such as sheet steel, copper bars and metal rods, which are purchased in substantial quantities. Raw materials, as far as this company is concerned, also include items which are the finished products of other companies, such as die castings, gear assemblies and many types of fittings. The manufacturing process takes some time to complete and in so doing produces a number of stages of goods in progress. Raw materials have been partially assembled into finished goods and stocks of goods in progress are normally held at a fairly high level, representing a substantial amount of invested funds. Finished goods stocks are not large and every effort is made to keep them within reasonable bounds.

Suppose the age classification of the die casting stocks are as given in Table 3.5. It can be readily seen that over 60 per cent of these die castings have been on hand for more than 45 days. Suppose a check on the composition of these aged stocks shows that some castings are used early in the productive process whereas others are not employed until much later. Moreover, some of the castings are speciality items which may remain in stock for many months at a time. In short, the company really uses two classes of die castings: those which are processed within 30 days and those which may take many months to clear.

Table 3.5
Age classification of die castings

Classification (Days)	Amount £	Percentage each is of total
0–15	17 000	16.0
16–30	13 000	12.2
31–45	9 000	8.5
46–60	29 000	27.4
61 +	38 000	35.9
	106 000	100.0

Efficient management of raw materials requires that these stocks are turned over rapidly. The longer a given item remains in stock the more difficult it becomes to collect the full cost through the sale price. In many instances, however, there are some items, such as special die castings, sub-assemblies, and so on, which cannot be moved through the productive process with the desired speed. The financing of stocks can be readily geared to the ageing process, and it is this criterion which is featured in Table 3.5 and discussed in the next section.

Types of stock finance

Stocks can be used to raise funds in a number of ways. The simplest procedure is to use these assets as collateral for a secured loan from a commercial or merchant bank. To do so the value of each item or class of items must be noted and approved. As in the case of debtors, the loan will be based upon an agreed percentage of the net cash value of the stocks. As stocks are consumed in the productive process, the net cash value declines and unless the balance is maintained by new purchases the size of the loan has to be reduced by a proportionate amount. As a result, taking a secured loan on rapidly moving raw materials is a complicated process and may not be worth the effort. An analysis of the age classification reveals those stocks which remain unused for the greatest periods of time. These are the items to use as collateral if loan financing is desired. If the average age of certain materials, say die castings or other speciality items, is 80 days, this length of time is sufficient to make a collateral loan worthy of investigation.

Raw materials which are purchased in bulk and which take some time to be delivered to the company can be financed en route by means of a trade bill and/or warehouse receipt. In either case, the financing instrument is, in effect, a secured loan on the value of the itemized goods. Warehouse receipts are issued by the warehousing company and can be used by the company to reclaim the goods when required; to borrow funds by pledging the receipt as collateral; or to sell the goods in question by presenting the receipt for sale on the commodity market. The trade bill is based upon the bills of lading, which represent the goods in transit from the supplier. These bills become negotiable if endorsed by a commercial or merchant bank and can be sold outright or used as collateral for a loan. In both of these cases the company is delaying the investment of its own funds until such time as the goods are actually delivered to its factory for processing.

MANAGING CREDITORS

The management of trade creditors is essentially a simple operation. As indicated earlier, it is both informative and useful to maintain control over the average age of the outstanding trade credit. The decision whether to settle these accounts at once or later depends upon the discounts, if any, that are offered for prompt and early cash payment. If discounts are available from suppliers, then advantage should be taken of the offer. Such reductions in cost can always be compared to the value of keeping the same amount of credit unpaid. In most cases it is a sound financial rule to accept cash discounts whenever possible.

Some suppliers do not offer cash discounts. In this event, they should be approached with a view to striking a bargain. The promise of prompt settlement will often produce an agreed discount even if this is not part of the company's normal sales policies. If all efforts to achieve discounts for immediate cash payment fail, there is no incentive to settle the account and every reason to delay payment until the last possible moment.

The management of trade creditors can be broken down into two parts.

1 For all accounts on which attractive cash discounts are available, ensure that settlements occur before the cash due date.
2 For all accounts with no discount, ensure that payment is not made until the maximum due date, but no later.

Financial management is responsible for maintaining the credit standing of the company as well as generating the necessary credit financing. To be known as a late payer does not enhance the company's reputation. To be known as a company that is aware of the value of money and insists on bargaining for its most effective use engenders respect and, in all likelihood, will lead to even higher credit rating.

The remaining current liabilities offer little scope for active financial management. PAYE withholdings are taken out of wages and salaries every time employers are paid. These withholdings do not have to be paid to the appropriate authority until certain calendar dates have been reached. Companies have free use of these funds for an average 30 to 40 days. If total wage and salary payments are rising, so will be the amount of credit that this free source of funds represents. Since the size of the withholdings is outside the company's control, management only has responsibility to use these funds while it can and to make sure they are paid to the tax authorities when due.

Similar comments pertain to payment of the company's tax obligations. Though tax assessments must be paid, there is no justification for paying them in advance. Tax reserve certificates are offered for sale to tempt companies, by a small discount, to settle their obligations in advance. But a tax reserve certificate can only be used in dealings with the Inland Revenue. All other short-term or long-term investments have a degree of liquidity and many exist which also provide higher rates of return. Thus, before purchasing tax reserve certificates their rate of return should be compared with other available short-term investments. The money market can always supply an investment with a high degree of liquidity and a due date coincident with tax outlays.

4

Relative price changes and financial decisions

Ian Cooper

Relative price changes are the essence of financial profitability. Suppose that you buy a property for £100 000. You hold it for a year and sell it. Was it a good decision? This depends on what has happened to the price of the property relative to the interest rate on the debt used to finance the purchase. This comparison involves comparing the price change of the property with another price: the interest rate is the price of the time-value of money.

Before the property is purchased one is faced with a slightly different problem. The price change in the property must be forecast relative to the interest rate. Note that the interest rate is known at the time of the decision to purchase the property, whereas the price change of the asset to be bought is uncertain. It is easy to see, in this case, that the profitability of the financial decision depends almost entirely on a relative price change. Since the return to a speculative asset purchase of this sort is the price change of the property, the link between the relative price change and profitability is obvious. It is slightly less obvious that decisions to invest in continuing operations are just as dependent for their success upon relative price changes.

Suppose that a decision is made to develop a new product. The product requires investment in capital assets and overheads and will generate a contribution stream. The contribution is equal to the volume of product sold multiplied by the gross margin per unit. The profitability of the project depends, therefore, on the gross margin. But the gross margin is determined by the difference between the sales price and the direct cost per unit: the relative prices of output and input.

The purpose of this chapter is to demonstrate in detail how relative price changes should be incorporated into good financial decisions. In the next section two important notions are introduced: the real interest rate and real price changes. Next is illustrated, with a detailed example, the incorporation of relative price changes into cash flow analysis of decisions. The section which follows on page 72 explains a common misconception: that constant prices are the same as a constant price level. The magnitude of relative price changes is then illustrated, and forecasting price changes is then discussed. Finally, two common errors made by those analysing financial decisions are illustrated, and the chapter concludes with a short summary of the major points.

REAL INTEREST RATES AND REAL PRICE CHANGES

Let us return to the example of buying property. Suppose that the property made a return of 20 per cent over the year, including price appreciation. The general inflation rate was 8 per cent. We can state this information in two different ways. The return was 20 per cent stated in nominal, or 'money-of-the-day', terms. This return was 12 per cent in excess of the rate of inflation. The latter is called 'real' terms. This restatement in real terms is just a convention and should not be thought of as having any significance beyond that.

Is this return good or bad? Suppose that we compare it with the return we would normally require for an investment of this type and risk level. This 'required return' might be 16 per cent in nominal terms. We can also state the required return in 'real' terms by subtracting the inflation rate. In this case the real required return is 8 per cent (16 per cent minus the 8 per cent inflation rate).

This procedure is summarized in Table 4.1. Note that the comparison between what was earned and what was required gives the same result whether we make the comparison in nominal or real units. The investment earned 4 per cent more than the required return. The procedure of adjusting for inflation has not changed the basic message as to whether this was, or was not, a good investment. Indeed, the adjustment is merely a mechanical calculation, it cannot change what has happened. It would be odd, therefore, if it resulted in a different impression of the profitability of the investment.

Table 4.1
Nominal and real returns

	Return earned (%)	Return required (%)	Excess return (%)
Nominal return	20	16	4
Less inflation	−8	−8	
Real return	12	8	4

We can go a bit further with the breakdown between real and nominal rates. The required return is normally viewed as consisting of the interest rate plus a premium for risk. In this case the 16 per cent nominal required return consists of a 10 per cent nominal interest rate plus a risk premium of 6 per cent. We can equally think of the real required return as consisting of a 2 per cent real interest rate plus the same 6 per cent risk premium. This is illustrated in the lower half of Table 4.2.

Table 4.2
Nominal and real required returns

	Interest rate(%)	+	Risk premium(%)	=	Required return(%)
Nominal	10	+	6	=	16
Real	2	+	6	=	8

Everything so far is purely mechanical. It affects the way that information is presented, but it does not affect the content of the information, or its implication for financial decisions. Yet the inability to keep clear this 'nominal' versus 'real' distinction leads to some very odd statements and decisions in practice. It is probably the largest single source of confusion in the way that people think about financial decisions.

NOMINAL PRICE CHANGES

Although general inflation in the last example was 8 per cent, the price of the property changed by a different amount. Table 4.3 shows that the property grew in value by 15 per cent and gave a rental yield of 5 per cent. This resulted in an overall return to the property of 20 per cent. The 15 per cent price appreciation can be thought of as 8 per cent general inflation plus a positive relative price appreciation of 7 per cent. This relative price movement was the key to the profitability of the investment.

Table 4.3
Cash flow analysis including relative price change
and general inflation (nominal terms)

Time	0	1
Property purchase and sale	− 100	+ 115
Property rent		+ 5
Total	− 100	+ 120
PV at 16 per cent	− 100	+ 103.4

Suppose we switch perspective and are now trying to make the decision as to whether or not to purchase the property. Suppose that the rental yield is known, and the 15 per cent price appreciation now represents our expectation of what will happen to the value of the property. The cash flows are as before, but they are now forecasts. The standard way to analyse the decision is to take the present value of the future cash flows, using the required rate of return of 16 per cent to perform the discounting calculation. This results in a net present value (NPV) of 3.4. This is equal to the present value of the forecast future cash flow of 103.4 less the investment of 100.

Would this be different if we exclude the impact of general inflation? The answer is no. Table 4.4 shows why: in this table, the cash flows are shown in 'real' terms, with the impact of the 8 per cent general inflation rate excluded. The value of the property now inflates at 6.5 per cent, which is the relative price move of the property compared with the general inflation rate. The 6.5 per cent is not quite the same as the 7 per cent obtained by simply subtracting 8 per cent inflation from the 15 per cent property price appreciation. The latter is an approximation. The correct procedure is shown at the foot of Table 4.4.

Table 4.4
Cash flow analysis showing general inflation, including relative price changes (real terms)

Time	0	1
Property purchase and sale	− 100	+ 106.5*
Rental		+ 4.6†
Total	− 100	+ 111.1
PV at 7.4%‡	− 100	+ 103.4

*106.5 = 115/1.08.   †4.6 = 5/1.08.   ‡1.074 = 1.16/1.08.

Although Table 4.4 presents the information about the investment in a different way to Table 4.3, the net result of the analysis is the same. Since the cash flows are in real terms, they should be discounted at a real discount rate. The appropriate real discount rate is the 16 per cent nominal required return adjusted for the 8 per cent inflation rate. This gives 7.4 per cent. Discounted at this rate, the present values of the cash flows are exactly the same as before.

Given that there is no difference, other than presentation, between the two types of financial analysis, what reason is there to prefer one form to the other? On the whole, those who use the 'real' style of analysis tend to do so either because they think it is easy (which is a mistake) or because they believe that it facilitates aggregation across different currencies (which is also a mistake). Many companies have a strong preference for including in their financial decision-making procedures the impact of all future price changes, including general inflation. This requires that the financial analysis be in nominal terms. This approach almost always leads to fewer errors of the type discussed in the section 'Common Errors' on page 76. Forecasts of cash flows should be made in 'nominal' units including all forecasts of inflation and relative price changes. These should be discounted at a rate which reflects the nominal interest rate plus an appropriate risk premium. The nominal interest rate is the actual rate charged by lenders, since part of this is an allowance for general inflation.

If, for reasons of exposition, it is desired to restate the analysis in real terms, then the cash flows and the discount rate should both be adjusted for the general inflation forecast. This adjustment is illustrated by the steps taken to convert Table 4.3 to Table 4.4.

CONSTANT PRICES AND CONSTANT PRICE LEVELS

Some people confuse the 'real terms' financial analysis outlined in the previous section with something very different: assuming that prices remain unchanged. The difference is that real analysis assumes that the general level of prices remains unchanged, which is very different to assuming that all prices stay the same. Table 4.5 illustrates this with an example of an operating project. This project is very simple and is a stylized version of real projects.

Table 4.5
Analysis of operating project: nominal terms

Time (yrs)	0	1	2	3	4
Capital investment	− 200				+ 40
Sales revenue*		+ 300	+ 315	+ 331	+ 348
Operating costs†		− 200	− 240	− 288	− 346
Working capital‡	− 50	− 10	− 12	− 15	+ 87
Net cash flow	− 250	+ 78	+ 63	+ 28	+ 129
Present value at 15%	− 250	+ 78	+ 48	+ 18	+ 74

*Constant volume of 100. Initial price 3. Price increase of 5% pa.
†Constant volume of 100. Initial cost 2. Cost increases of 20% pa.
‡Working capital required is 25% of operating costs.

The cash flows in Table 4.5 include forecasts of particular rates of sales price and unit cost increases. These are 5 per cent and 20 per cent, respectively. The net present value of the cash flows is −32 using a discount rate of 15 per cent.

Table 4.6 restates the same cash flows in 'real terms' after allowing for a general inflation rate of 10 per cent. The discount rate is also adjusted by this amount of forecast inflation, to give a real discount rate of 4.5 per cent. A comparison of Tables 4.5 and 4.6 shows that the overall result of the appraisal is unchanged. The net present value of the project and the present value of each future cash flow are the same. The difference here lies entirely in presentation rather than substance.

Table 4.6
Analysis of operating project: real terms (10% inflation)

Time (yrs)	0	1	2	3	4
Capital investment	− 200				+ 27
Sales revenue		+ 273	+ 260	+ 249	+ 238
Operating costs		− 182	− 198	− 216	− 236
Working capital	− 50	− 9	− 10	− 11	+ 59
Net cash flow	− 250	+ 82	+ 52	+ 21	+ 88
Present value at 4.5%*	− 250	+ 78	+ 48	+ 18	+ 74

$*1.045 = 1.15/1.10$

Table 4.7, however, presents a completely different picture. In Table 4.7 the same volume forecasts have been used, but the price and unit costs figures used throughout the four years are those pertaining to the first year. The net present value is now + 152. This huge swing in apparent profitability is caused by a simple, but common, error. The error is confusing real terms, which means at a constant general price level, with constant prices, which means all prices and costs staying the same. The latter omits the relative price moves which are the main cause of profitability, or the lack of it.

It is quite easy to see this by looking again at Table 4.6, the analysis of the project in real terms. In this case, although the impact of general inflation has been excluded from the cash flows, there are still two large relative price changes included. The first is the 5 per cent real price decline of the output. The second is the 10 per cent real rise of the operating costs. The analysis in Table 4.7 has omitted the impact of these relative price changes. It is based upon the false assumption that prices in the future, when adjusted for the general rate of inflation, will be the same as they are today.

Table 4.7
Analysis of operating project: constant prices

Time (yrs)	0	1	2	3	4
Capital investment	− 200				+ 27
Sales revenue*		+ 300	+ 300	+ 300	+ 300
Operating costs†		− 200	− 200	− 200	− 200
Working capital‡	− 50	0	0	0	+ 50
Net cash flow	− 250	+ 100	+ 100	+ 100	+ 177
Present value at 4.5%	− 250	+ 96	+ 92	+ 88	+ 148

*Volume of 100 multiplied by price of 3.
†Volume of 100 multiplied by unit cost of 2.
‡25% of operating costs

RELATIVE PRICE CHANGES

Table 4.8 shows the changes in four price indices measured relative to the retail price index (RPI) for the period 1980−85. These real price changes show some common features. Year-to-year relative price changes are large in some years for all the series. These short-term swings are caused by temporary supply and demand shifts which can change the real price by significant amounts over a single year. Over the medium term, represented by the entire six year period, the effects of these short-term imbalances even out. Average real price moves over the six years are not large, when stated as a percentage per annum, but do have a large cumulative effect. These medium-term real price moves are caused by medium-term changes in supply and demand resulting from changing wealth levels, consumption patterns, productivity, substitution and technology.

The price moves illustrated in Table 4.8 are for inputs and outputs aggregated across fairly broad groups. If the table included, for instance, the inputs purchased by an individual company for an individual project we would see even larger year-to-year swings. We are, therefore, left with the conclusion that relative price changes can be large in the short term and cumulatively large in the medium to long term. Since these relative price changes are one key to profitable financial decisions, we are confronted with a crucial question: can we forecast relative price changes?

Table 4.8
Real price changes: price change relative to RPI, %

Year	Oil	Manufacturing wages	Instrument Input	Engineering Output	Food Input	Food Output
1980	+ 37	+ 4	− 5	− 5	− 12	− 7
1981	+ 16	− 3	− 8	− 2	− 3	− 3
1982	− 5	− 4	− 3	0	− 2	− 2
1983	− 8	− 4	0	− 1	0	− 1
1984	+ 1	− 1	+ 2	0	+ 2	+ 1
1985	− 6*	0	− 1	− 2	− 7	− 3
Average	+ 4	− 1	− 2	− 2	− 4	− 2

*First three quarters

FORECASTING RELATIVE PRICE CHANGES

The last section illustrated relative price changes in both the short term and the medium term. Short-term changes are caused by temporary shifts in supply and demand. The real oil price rise in 1980 was induced by the OPEC cartel, the real price fall of food inputs in 1985 was caused by agricultural surpluses. The long-run changes, though small as annual averages, have a large cumulative impact. They are caused by innovation, changes in wealth and demand patterns, competition and substitution. The real decline in input prices for instrument engineering has been caused by innovation in the industries that supply instrument components. The real decline in the output price for this industry has been caused by competition within the industry by those who use the cheapest available inputs.

Can one forecast these changes? Short-term forecasting requires detailed knowledge of the demand and supply conditions in a particular market. Knowledge of the possible success of OPEC in reforming the oil cartel would clearly help in forecasting the short-term move in the real oil price. Knowledge of the EEC policy on food surpluses would help in forecasting the short-term price change of outputs from the food industry. Thus detailed analysis of individual markets is vital to short-term forecasting of relative price changes. It is a mistake, however, to make medium-term and long-term forecasts based on extrapolation of these short-term forecasts. There are powerful economic forces that mean that short-term supply and demand imbalances cannot persist indefinitely.

For medium-term and long-term changes in relative prices this powerful set of economic forces comes into play. Those forecasters who predicted that the oil price could continuously rise at a rate far in excess of general inflation ignored three powerful economic phenomena: substitution, competition, and innovation. Substitution by users of energy reduced their dependence on oil. Competition destroyed the OPEC cartel in its original form. Innovation in response to the jump in the real price of oil facilitated both of these effects.

Thus those who forecast medium- and long-term real price changes for a particular product, commodity, or input face the burden of proving that such real price changes will be sustainable in the face of substitution, competition and innovation. It is clear that such long-term changes do occur, but the long-term behaviour of a price is quite different to its short-term behaviour. Demand and supply changes induce responses from current and potential competitors and from consumers of the product. One must be very careful if one bases financial decisions on medium-term price forecasts that do not incorporate the effects of this competition and substitution.

COMMON ERRORS

In making financial decisions using forecasts of cash flows, the best technique is to make all forecasts in nominal or 'money-of-the-day' units which include all forecast price changes including the general inflation forecast. These cash flows should then be discounted at a nominal discount rate which is equal to the nominal interest rate plus a risk premium. Those who approach the problem differently expose themselves to a host of potential errors. Two common ones involve the treatment of tax and working capital. The problem with tax arises because many tax cash flows are paid some time after they are incurred.

Suppose, for instance, that a nominal tax liability of £100 is incurred now and paid one year later. This gives rise to a nominal payment of £100 in year 1. If inflation is expected to be 10 per cent the inflation adjusted real equivalent of this is only £91, since the amount of the tax payment is not indexed for the inflation between incurring and paying the tax. A common error is to allow for the postponement of the tax payment but not to recognize that its real value falls. This is illustrated in the third row of Table 4.9. Here the tax cash flow has been lagged by one year to allow for the delay in payment, but not adjusted to keep it in 'real' terms.

Table 4.9
Treatment of tax cash flows

Tax of 100 incurred in year zero, paid in year one. Inflation rate 10%

Time	0 (tax incurred)	1 (tax paid)
Nominal cash flow		− 100
Real cash flow		− 91*
Incorrect real		− 100

*91 = 100/1.1

Table 4.10
Treatment of working capital

Constant working capital stock of 100 real, inflation 10%

Time	0	1
Nominal stock	100	110
Nominal cash flow		− 10
Real stock	100	100
Real cash flow		− 9.1*
Real stock	100	100
Incorrect real cash flow		0

*9.1 = 10/1.1

A similar misconception can arise with working capital flows. Table 4.10 illustrates a situation where, because of the impact of inflation, cash is being invested in working capital to maintain its real level. This cash flow is correctly stated in nominal terms and real terms in the first two blocks of Table 4.10. Note that the correct real cash flow is obtained by first analysing the situation in nominal terms and then converting the cash flow to real terms. A common mistake is to perform the forecast in the way shown in the third block. Because the real level of working capital is constant, it is tempting to believe that no cash flow is required to maintain the working capital balance. This is incorrect, and the correct treatment is given in the second block. Although the real level of working capital is constant, there is still a cash flow required to sustain this level of working capital.

CONCLUSIONS

The impact of relative price changes on the profitability of financial decisions is enormous. There are no short-cut techniques for dealing with this problem. Those who believe that making decisions in 'real' units, that omit the impact of inflation, helps address the problem are usually making one of a number of large errors. The most common of these is to confuse the analysis of financial decisions in real terms (which is merely a presentational device) with the forecast that all relative prices will remain the same (which is almost always wrong).

Good financial analysis confronts directly the issue of which prices will move relative to each other and the general inflation rate and by how much. Short-term forecasts of these price moves should be based upon detailed knowledge of current demand and supply conditions and imminent changes in these. Long-term forecasts should not be extrapolations of these short-term effects. They should explicitly recognize the powerful medium-term impacts of substitution, competition and innovation. These economic forces limit the size of plausible forecasts of medium-term real price changes.

FURTHER READING

Brealey, R. A. and Myers, S. C. *Principles of Corporate Finance*, Chapter 6, McGraw-Hill, New York, 1985

Carsberg, B. and Hope, A., *Business Investment Decisions under Inflation*, Institute of Chartered Accountants, 1976

Franks, R. J., Broyles, J. E., and Carleton, W. T., *Corporate Finance: Concepts and Applications*, Chapter 7, John Wiley & Sons, Chichester, 1985

5

Computers and financial decision making

Myles M. Dryden

This chapter differs from most others in this book in that it is concerned less with the nature of financial analysis *per se*, focusing instead on the *way* in which many decisions of a financial nature can now be considered given the increasing availability of relatively new analytical techniques. These techniques are in the form of computer software. Rather than concentrate on particular items of software which will only run on specific pieces of hardware − which may indeed become obsolete before these words appear in print − the discussion will be kept at a general level; but almost all of the general points concerning software noted in this chapter are associated with software which runs on one or other of the better known 16-bit micro-computers; for example the IBM PC or one of its various lookalikes.

Although there is clearly some resistance to the computerization of managerial decision making − supported by a number of well-publicised disasters − it is unlikely that the upward trend will not persist, resulting in both a deepening and widening of the financial decisions which are amenable to analysis of a kind possible only by using high speed digital computers. Here we are more concerned with the deepening aspect, that is, the use of software to assist in the analysis of the less structured aspects of financial decision making and we ignore the issues raised by the computerization of the relatively routine aspects of financial management, for example those associated with the classification and recording of transactions. In this respect it is probably worth noting that financial management, probably more than any other business function, lends itself to these new developments, although clearly other managerial functions such as personnel management also offer some scope for their application. This trend will be strengthened too by economic factors. The real cost of micro-computers is falling, particularly in key components such as memory. White collar costs meanwhile continue to rise creating further pressure for substitution.

INTELLIGENT TASKS

The origins of interest in developing computers and associated software which would tackle intelligent tasks has a long and chequered history but for many years this interest was limited primarily to researchers working in the field of artificial intelligence. In that much of this effort was of an esoteric nature and associated with large mainframe computers, relatively little of this work manifested itself in commercial applications and of these hardly any were business applications. All this has suddenly changed, partly as a result of the economics of computing noted above but, perhaps more significantly in this context, as a result of the Japanese decision to mount a very large program in this area resulting in renewed, if not almost frenzied, interest in this type of computer application in the USA, the UK (the Alvey Program) and in Europe (EEC's Esprit Program). Although the longer-term objectives of these programs are extremely ambitious some of the short-term developments are already begining to have an impact in the general area of business decision making.

SPREADSHEETS AND LOGIC MODELLERS

Before proceeding to the new developments in computer-assisted decision making it is worth noting briefly the kind of software currently used by financial managers and its limitations. To some extent the effectiveness of the newer methods will be judged by their ability to transcend these limitations. Much of current financial modelling work is undertaken by software which falls under the general description 'spreadsheet'. The creation of packages which replaced the traditional spreadsheet of businessmen with an electronic spreadsheet really did not offer much new – which perhaps explains the extremely rapid penetration of such products into the business community! No new concepts had to be learned. What these products offered was speed in calculation and the capability of exploring many different scenarios — 'what if?'. Over the years many, many variants of these products have appeared. The earlier ones were primarily arithmetical in their orientation and simply replicated the typical traditional hand calculations. VISICALC is probably the most widely known example. Such spreadsheets, however, usually failed to offer suitable consolidation facilities — for example allowing the aggregation of the budgets of several different departments to produce an overall budget — or significant report generating or graphics facilities. The second category is perhaps better described as 'logic modellers'. These provided a wider range of facilities including many which were probably not in the traditional hand-calculator's kitbag. MICROMODELLER is probably one of the better known products in this second category. Apart from the commonly used arithmetical processes of addition, subtraction, multiplication and division, these logic modellers included a number of logical functions and built-in financial functions, such as compound interest, present value and so on. In addition, the file-handling capabilities of these packages were much superior to those of the primitive spreadsheets, allowing the user to separate the basic raw data from the model (logic files). Furthermore, where functions were not available within the package, facilities were provided to allow the user to access a program language from the package and create the appropriate function. Spreadsheets and logic modellers were broadly differentiated on the basis of the particular sub-set of facilities offered.

Even the most sophisticated of these packages, however, rarely provided suitable methods of modelling uncertainty. Bearing in mind that uncertainty is almost always intrinsic in any type of financial decision, this is a serious limitation. Nor were such packages useful in coping with problems where outcomes are dependent on several variables. Indeed, it is questionable to what extent these packages really provided 'models' of financial relationships. Relationships of the form

Closing inventory = Opening inventory + Production − Sales

are easily handled using spreadsheets. Indeed, most of the examples in the software manuals and textbooks are of this kind, but these are simply accounting identities, statements true by definition. On the other hand, the level of a company's sales will depend on the product's price and probably on the price of its main competitor. In contrast to the identities described above the relationships of this latter type are of an empirical nature which in many cases are simply assumed away in spreadsheet analysis. Without wishing to minimize the usefulness of spreadsheets – which can be used in a very versatile and creative manner – there are clearly limitations to their playing a central role in those financial management decisions which are of a less routine nature, where variables are subject to uncertainty, where choices are subject to complicated constraints and are made on the basis of expertise which is not readily programmable, or indeed readily imparted to others.

EXPERT SYSTEMS

Software, partly stemming from the renewed interest in artificial intelligence, is now beginning to provide some support in dealing with these limitations of spreadsheet software. The software described below is concerned primarily with the problems of uncertainty and building in expertise, although it contains many other features. Additionally, however, there are some packages which are explicitly designed for simulating expertise – 'expert systems' – whereas still others occupy an intermediate position between sophisticated spreadsheets and expert systems, and are broadly described as 'decision support systems'. The package described as REVEAL contains elements of each, can be run on a microcomputer and incorporates a number of new concepts which are likely to become increasingly available in new software products. It provides, therefore, a suitable vehicle for illustrating the nature of the generation of software products which has followed the spreadsheets and for highlighting the likely course of future developments in financial-modelling software.

FUZZY SETS

An important new concept appearing in some of the recent decision support and expert systems is that of fuzziness. Earlier models – such as linear programming – which were popularized in the 1950s and 1960s and which are still used, depend on precise specification. For example that the capital expenditure budget should not exceed £x of which not more than £y is spent next year, £z the following year, and so on and where x, y and z are stated numbers. The mathematics used to solve such problems is based on set theory where, for example, all numbers less than or equal to x are potential solutions to the problem and any number greater than x is not; and similarly for y and z. A number is either a member of a set (true $= 1$) or not (false $= 0$). Apart from such methods leading to unsatisfactory solutions, the formulation of the problem is, as any financial manager is aware, unrealistic. Goals and constraints are frequently stated in fuzzy form — for example, to secure 'about' a 30 per cent share of the market, to have the product's price 'low' in relation to that of competitors and so on. Such formulations of the problem have now become possible with the development of fuzzy set theory. Instead of a number being simply a member of a set or not there are shades or degrees of membership. Thus, whereas the set of numbers greater than 100 constitutes a conventionally defined set, the set of numbers which are much greater than 100 is a fuzzy set. The price paid for this flexibility is that it is necessary to define the shades of membership. This definition constitutes the membership function. In this example the membership function $f(x)$ could be defined as equal to zero for values of x less than or equal to 100 and equal to $(x - 100)/x$ for values of x greater than 100. It is a matter of convention how the membership values are scaled. Usually the values of the membership function are set at 0 for no membership and 1 (or sometimes 100) for complete membership. Degrees of membership are therefore numbers between 0 and 1 (or 100).

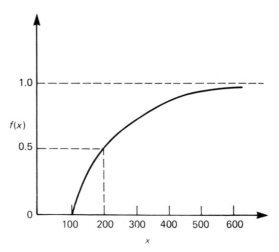

Figure 5.1   Membership function for fuzzy variable

The membership function defined above is illustrated in Figure 5.1. For a number a little greater than 100, say 105, the membership function is f(105) = 0.05. For a much larger value of x, say $x = 400$, the membership function is $f(400) = 0.75$, reflecting as would be expected, a much higher degree of membership. For variables which are to be regarded as fuzzy, packages such as REVEAL offer a choice of membership functions. In many cases one of these may well suit the user. In the other cases it is necessary either to specify one's own function say $g(x)$, or alternatively input separate membership values corresponding to each value of x. Whatever the method adopted it is important that this function reflects the decision maker's own perception of the situation. The danger is to opt for a built-in 'black box' function which does not match the user's specification.

The distinction between the conventional deterministic models and the use of fuzzy models may be seen in the following simple hypothetical example. Assume that an electronics company is in search of potential acquisitions and that these must be drawn from the company's own industry. Furthermore, assume that interesting companies must have sales in excess of 500 and return on assets of at least 10 per cent.

Table 5.1
Deterministic and fuzzy models

	Sales (1)	Return (2)	Conventional (3)	Fuzzy (4)
A	400	10	0	0
B	440	15	0	0
C	490	13	0	0.4
D	510	10	1	0.37
E	810	9	0	0.25

Details of a few of the companies in the industry are listed in Table 5.1 in columns (1) and (2) which show the sales and return data for each of five companies. Column (3) shows the selection of companies which meet the non-fuzzy criteria, sales greater than 500 and a return of at least 10 per cent. D is the only company to be designated as meeting these criteria. Any sensible financial manager would, however, wish to keep company C under consideration although strictly it does not satisfy the criteria specified. But what would happen if the hypothetical data in Table 5.1 were expanded to include all of the companies in the industry and that their performance with respect to say half a dozen separate criteria are to be considered, and not simply their sales and return performance? The matrix of data would be far too large for the financial manager to process visually, identifying interesting marginal cases in the manner described above with a very small data set. This is where the use of fuzzy variables and fuzzy logic can assist us. Suppose that the problem is re-stated to allow consideration of companies for acquisition whose 'sales are high' and 'return is acceptable'. Further we define the set 'high sales' to be that with membership of 0 for sales less than 450 and membership of unity for sales greater than 550. The fuzzy set of acceptable returns is defined by membership equal to 0 for returns less than 8 per cent and equal to unity for returns greater than 12 per cent. Column (4) gives the corresponding membership values for each of the five companies (assuming that membership functions have been fully defined). Unsurprisingly company D is still signalled as being of potential interest. Company C is also signalled as being interesting and indeed more interesting than D! Using this approach the financial manager is now in a position to devote his energies to considering the subject of companies which broadly meet the criteria knowing that no company has been excluded from consideration simply on account of its failure to meet narrowly defined criteria.

An extension of this approach is demonstrated in the following example. Here the fuzzy reasoning − or approximate reasoning − of REVEAL is combined with the use of linguistic variables, qualifiers and

Table 5.2
Fuzzy reasoning and profit projections

Month	1	2	3	4	5	6
Price	15.90	16.05	16.25	18.10	17.00	17.15
Unit variable cost	11.15	11.37	11.60	11.83	12.07	12.31
Volume	100	100	100	100	100	100
Fixed costs	200	200	200	200	200	200
Competitor's price	16	18	18	22	25	25
Net profit	275	268	265	427	293	284

hedges. In addition, typical spreadsheet facilities are included. The problem is to consider the effect on monthly profit projections of various assumptions concerning the competitor's price. Table 5.2 shows the consequences of a simplified set of relations for a single product company.

REVEAL can be given the usual accounting definitions – as in spreadsheet analysis – namely:

Margin	=	Price – Unit Variable Cost
Revenue	=	Price * Volume
Profit	=	Margin * Volume
Net profit	=	Profit – Fixed costs

But in addition to these identities the competitor's price is to be used as a guide to setting the company's own price, but not in a mechanical manner. The model is, therefore, further defined by the following (fuzzy) goals and constraints:

If the competitor's price is not very high then our price should be
    near the competitor
Our price should be low
Our price should be about 1.5* unit variable cost

Finally, unit costs are defined to increase systematically from month to month (reflecting cost inflation), again using a built in function as in a typical spreadsheet analysis. The input to REVEAL is virtually in the form specified above. 'Linguistic variables' such as unit costs can be used together with qualifiers such as 'low' or hedges such as 'about'. All other terms – except the logical ones such as 'if' and 'then' – are ignored by the package and are treated as noise although clearly they have meaning to the user and are important to other users who wish to examine the model. As with the previous example the fuzzy variables, qualifiers and hedges must be suitably specified by their corresponding membership functions, either built in ones or those supplied by the user. Assuming this has been done, that is, the terms such as 'high' and 'low' have been defined, the package then converts the above policy into actual projections, an example of which is shown in Table 5.2.

Initially the competitor's price is deemed sufficiently low to be the basis for the company's price which, however, edges upwards as unit costs rise. Thereafter the policy of keeping the price low and approximating 50 per cent greater than the unit cost influences the company's price, lowering it in month 5 against large increases in the competitor's price. The precise outcomes in Table 5.2 will of course depend on the detailed specification of all of the membership functions, the definition of what constitutes 'high', 'low', etc.

There is nothing intrinsic in packages like *Reveal* to limit the applications to the kind described above. Manpower planning, determining the credit rating of customers, choosing capital projects and deciding on their financing as between external versus internal funds, are just a few of the topics which the modelling facilities allow. The applications too can vary from those drawing primarily on spreadsheet facilities to those requiring the modelling of probabilistic relationships and managerial expertise expressed in the form of approximate rules. The effective use of such packages will probably depend less on increased financial knowledge on the part of financial managers and more on their ability to understand the new concepts embodied in these packages.

FURTHER READING

Alves, J.R. and Selva, M., *Multiplan Business Users Guide: Controlling Financial Planning with Multiplan*, Business Books, (London, 1984). Step by step guide to the use of MULTIPLAN, a typical spreadsheet package. Takes over where manual leaves off. Supported by software.

Byte, (May 1984) Vol. 9, No. 5 features a wide range of articles on the use of computers to assist decision makers.

Drew, R., *Microcomputers for Financial Planning*, Gower, (Aldershot, 2nd Edn, 1987). Introduction to Financial Planning and how computer systems can assist. The elements of computer systems are described. Some useful appendices (evaluation check lists etc.)

Expert Systems, published by Learned Information and *Expert Systems User*, published by Expert Systems User Ltd., are two of the many new journals in this field. Both provide useful surveys, information on new products, etc..

Forsyth, R. (Ed), *Expert Systems: Principles and Case Studies*, Chapman & Hall, (London, 1984). Useful all round practical approach with chapters on principles (e.g. Fuzzy Reasoning, Chap. 5) and applications (e.g. REVEAL, Chap. 9).

Goodall, A., *The Guide to Expert Systems*, Learned Information, (Oxford, 1985). Designed to introduce the key concepts of expert systems: although not specifically oriented to managers this contains relevant material on how to build such systems.

Horner, H., *Computing in a Small Business*, Hutchinson, (London, 1984). Very basic introduction to selection of software and hardware for the small business.

Webster, R., 'Revealing Business Solutions', *PC*, April 1985, Vol. 4, No. 8, pp 125–130. Describes REVEAL. This issue of *PC* also features a number of articles on other expert systems for personal computers.

Part II
FINANCIAL CONTROL

OVERVIEW

Financial measurement is an essential ingredient in all commercial activities in a market economy. Thus the challenge of financial management lies in the interdependence of finance and all other activities in the firm. Financial management encompasses not only the treasury function, that is, raising capital and the management of working capital and of capital investment, but also the controllership function involving the operation of a financial control system which aims to depict the financial aspect of all the firm's planned and actual activities. This means that as well as being a financial specialist, a financial manager may need to be a management systems generalist. Financial information systems must be articulated with operational information systems in sales and marketing, production, physical distribution, personnel and so on. Hence, when discussing control, one should consider companies and their various parts as systems and sub-systems (systems within systems).

Part II of this handbook deals with these control aspects of financial management. Broadly speaking, control requires that objectives be established, that actual outcomes be measured and compared to objectives, and that actions be taken to avoid any major divergences between expected outcomes and objectives. For the financial manager, the relevant aspects of objectives and outcomes are the financial ones, that is, in the last analysis, cash flows. Certain financial objectives and outcomes can be, and often are, also expressed in terms of profits, which are perhaps best considered as cash flows which have been smoothed by removing two kinds of fluctuations:

1 Fluctuations due to the operation of the working capital cycle;

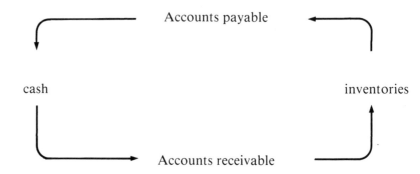

Accounts payable

cash

inventories

Accounts receivable

2 Fluctuations due to the lumpy nature of expenditure on fixed assets.

How far this kind of smoothing contributes to the usefulness of the information will depend on the circumstances in which it is being used. It should be recognized that because the financial control system works by abstracting the financial aspects of the firm's activities, a degree of abstraction is essential to the system. An excessive degree of abstraction is, however, a common failing in accounting systems.

To achieve control, a management system has two interrelated kinds of systemic requirements: an information system or systems, and a system of responsibilities or management organization. These requirements are the subject of Richard Wilson's chapter, 'Reporting and responsibilities' (Chapter 6). Within this system, the budget control subsystem is concerned particularly with the expression of operational objectives in financial terms, and the comparison of financial outcomes (profits and cash flows) with these objectives. This forms the subject of Alan Leaper's chapter, 'Budgets and budgetary control' (Chapter 7).

Both the establishment of objectives and the measurement of financial outcomes require information subsystems which provide knowledge of the costs of the organization's final outputs (products) and of intermediate outputs (goods and services produced and used within the organization in the production of those final outputs). These subsystems for costing and internal (or transfer) pricing are the subject of Chapter 8 by H.W. Calvert and Simon Archer.

'Cash forecasting and control' (Chapter 9), by R. L. Mansbridge, sets out possible procedures to maintain appropriate liquidity consistent with the overall financial plan. This represents the most crucial primary-level control subsystem.

Finally, the internal audit subsystem is intended to provide a check on the operation of the management system as a whole. As described in the chapter, 'Internal auditing', by Harry Scholefield and P.C. Elliot, it constitutes an off-line or second-level appraisal activity designed to evaluate the adequacy, efficiency and effectiveness of the company's on-line or first-level control subsystems. 'Internal auditing' (Chapter 10) is not part of financial control as exercised by the Financial Manager; rather, it is complementary to it.

Thus the five chapters deal with the principles which govern the design and operation of financial control systems in business organizations. Certain important system requirements tend, however, to be specific to particular kinds of business (retailing, for example, as compared with manufacturing or transport); others may be specific to certain areas of the business (marketing, production, etc.).

Such situation-specific requirements are potentially vast in number. Part II does not aim to cover the control requirements of particular types of business or, in detail, of particular areas in a business; rather, the aim is to deal with those principles and approaches which apply to a wide range of business situations. As with most areas of financial management, the final prescription reflects the judgement of the financial manager.

6

Reporting and responsibilities

Richard M. S. Wilson

The aim of this chapter is to indicate how the accountant might design and develop reporting procedures under the total systems concept by adopting a control perspective.

SYSTEMS DESIGN IN MANAGERIAL ACCOUNTING

The objects of managerial accounting systems design are: to assist managers to take planning and control decisions in the light of their financial impact on the whole organization; to motivate employees towards a high level of performance; and to evaluate actual performance. Internal financial reporting is the 'output' subsystem of managerial accounting designed to supply managers with relevant and usable information. Other subsystems of managerial accounting are concerned with collecting and processing raw data to provide these outputs.

Planning and control systems: the cycle of control

The necessary company-wide perspective for establishing reporting systems is given by the cycle of control. Diagramatically, this can be shown as in Figure 6.1. Reporting systems should be designed to include

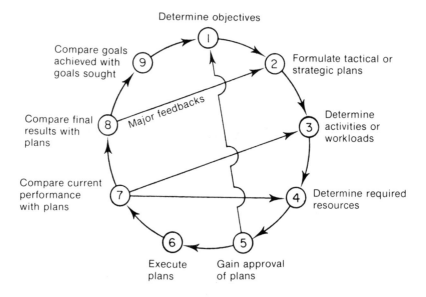

Figure 6.1   The cycle of control

procedures for carrying out each of the steps within the cycle. This requires

1   Means of determining and communicating the objectives that the system is to serve (step 1).
2   Means of adding the additional detail to complete and gain approval of the planning phases (steps 2, 3, 4 and 5).
3   Means of communicating with the performance groups (step 7).
4   Methods of comparing performance with the plan and identifying significant variations (steps 7 and 8).
5   Methods of reporting accomplishments (step 8).
6   Identification of the various corrective actions which may be taken and the means of taking them (steps 8 and 9).

In these terms, the managerial accounting system forms a significant part of a web of management information systems designed to facilitate the articulation and achievement of the company's objectives. These information systems, in turn, form part of the overall set of operational activities making up the business enterprise as a total system.

Operating principles of systems design

Decision needs and associated information flows are the primary centre of attention for accounting systems designers, and the actual design of accounting systems must concentrate on the desired arrangement of resources and activities within the organization and on the desired outputs from those resources and activities.

Initially, then, the systems designer must know

1   What the organization and its sub-units are required to achieve.
2   To what standards they are required to do this.
3   How their performance is to be evaluated against these standards.

The requirements of the system can then be expressed in terms of information outputs that its reporting subsystem must produce; data that its data input subsystem must accept; processing operations that its data processing subsystem must perform; and resources that it is constrained to use.

Its performance may then be measured in terms of whichever criteria are appropriate. For example, relevant criteria of system operating performance will usually include some of the following

1   Cost
2   Timeliness
3   Accuracy
4   Reliability
5   Security
6   Quality
7   Flexibility
8   Capacity
9   Efficiency
10 Acceptability

The successful operation of a managerial accounting system depends upon both the accounting techniques employed and the behavioural response of the result. Given this, the basic steps in designing a new system are to

1   Study the enterprise and the information needs of its decision makers.
2   Develop a basic system design: overall system and major subsystems.

3 Identify the activities to be performed within each subsystem and the interfaces between the various subsystems.
4 Specify the resources needed to perform these activities and assure the interfaces.
5 Prepare a preliminary plan for system implementation.
6 Determine the impact of the design on profitability (or other objectives or constraints).
7 Document the new system design.

These steps are often best accomplished by a project team comprising representatives from the main decision making units and account and data processing specialists, directed by a project leader. The responsible individual must ensure that he has the authority of management to implement the system once it has been designed.

The installation of a new accounting system involves recruiting new staff, re-training existing staff, re-allocating duties, etc. As a result, job classifications, job specifications and the proper division of labour must be considered carefully. If the system is large, phased implementation is preferable to a single complete change, due to the latter's sheer complexity.

Every system should possess sufficient flexibility to allow for a constantly changing environment. (For example, sufficient free classifications should be built into an account coding system to allow subsequent expansion to be accommodated.) Furthermore, a system producing too much information can obscure that which is relevant, whereas a system producing too little information does not favour good decision making. Balance and flexibility are prerequisites for success.

If an existing system is to be improved, four basic steps should be followed; it is necessary to

1 Identify the critical aspects that need to be planned and controlled (i.e. ascertain the types of decisions to be made).
2 Determine what specific information is required, and amend the system by adding omitted data flows and deleting unnecessary data flows.
3 Motivate and train line-management to use the revised system, involving it in its design to an appropriate extent.
4 Determine the best method of improving the required information within prescribed time limits.

This highlights the need for a systematic, rather than an *ad hoc*, approach.

Control as the perspective for accounting systems

If progress towards goals is to be supervised, it must be observed and measured; there must be some assessment of where the organization is, compared to where it ought to be. This is achieved through control. Control involves the use of a reliable, readily understood and sensitive system of information and standards as a basis for the management decisions that have to be taken.

All control is not necessarily financial or accounting-based. The company consists of the subsystems of production, marketing, R and D, personnel, administration, etc., all of which have their specific control aspects. However, the accountant or financial manager, by the very nature of his duties, is in a better position than most to see the total spectrum of corporate activities in an integrated manner, even though this overall view is biased in favour of emphasizing the aspects most readily expressed in terms of money at the expense of those not so readily expressed. Yet, money is certainly the most convenient, if not the only, common yardstick for planning and gauging performance; and this is the accountant's or financial manager's domain. The accountant can discharge the responsibility adequately, however, only if the type of decisions made and the nature of the activities to be controlled are appreciated. Indeed, there are good reasons to believe that improvements can be made on the stereotyped accountant's approach to reporting.

Additionally, the accountant is in a good position to consider the economics of control. The aim should be to provide an information system that facilitates control in such a way that the value is maximized for a given cost, (or alternatively, cost is minimized for a given level of control information).

In the capacity of controller, the accountant will be responsible for

1 Selecting the key factors and control points.
2 Segregating the non-controllable factors so that the picture of the controllable aspects is not confused.
3 Relating the plans and controls to individual accountability at the various organizational levels.
4 Ensuring that the setting of standards meets the needs of the control system and can be built into departmental plans.
5 Co-ordinating the building up of the overall plan from subsidiary plans.
6 Designing the reporting system for effective display of required feedback data.

Distinctions in accounting systems for planning and control

In the context of designing financial reporting systems for control purposes, it is helpful to distinguish the various types of accounting, namely: financial (or external) accounting and management accounting in its cost, decision and control aspects.

Financial accounting systems report to the outside world on management, rather than to management. (See Chapter 15.) The traditionally aggregated figures must meet the criterion of objectivity, but this often conflicts with the more important control criterion of usefulness. Although financial accounts focus on the whole business, they must be compiled in accordance with statutory requirements and are historical in perspective. It will be evident, therefore, that financial accounting is of little value to management in exercising control.

In contrast, the term management accounting is used to designate a subject of information systems which fall into three main categories: cost accounting, decision accounting and control accounting. Such systems are intended as tools for management, and their outputs are not subject to the objectivity criteria and formal requirements characteristic of financial accounting.

Cost accounting is concerned with specific segments of the company, relating costs and revenues (and, hence, profits) to products, processes and divisions. Operational control is made effective through the analysis of variances from standard, but, essentially, cost accounting is concerned with planning and controlling costs in great detail, often at the unit cost level.

Decision accounting is perhaps more aptly referred to as economic decision analysis. It aims to provide information that is useful to management for specific decisions or planning purposes. Thus, its activities consist of a series of one-off studies of particular problems which routine cost or control accounting activities are designed to illuminate only partly, such as whether to produce internally or to subcontract certain manufactured items or service activities.

The purpose of control accounting is to indicate how successful the company is in achieving its goals. It permits the inclusion of goals other than profit (or cost reduction), and pays special attention (through the planning phase) to securing consistency among the objectives of the company as a whole and the objectives of its constituent parts.

Inevitably, these four broad types of accounting overlap considerably, but the demands of a variety of primary and secondary goals within the control process require that the control aspect of management accounting, supplemented by the other forms as appropriate, be the focus of attention for designers of reporting systems.

Accounting control systems considered

Given the purpose of accounting for control, several accounting subsystems can successfully supplement the budgetary control system (which is discussed in the next chapter).

Internal control is the process and means of safeguarding assets, checking the reliability of accounting data, monitoring operational efficiency and encouraging adherence to managerial policies with which the accountant is normally associated. However, in its broadest sense, internal control embraces every type of accounting technique and even extends beyond internal audit to the rigorous management audit. Since any system of control requires human application, internal control exists, essentially, to ensure that the human factor acts in accordance with instructions, plans and policies.

Conventional product cost accounting can be usefully supplemented by distribution cost analysis, thereby bringing marketing and distribution activities under the same microcontrol as production activities.

It is worth bearing in mind that cost itself is not a homogeneous concept, although the notion of sacrifice is common to all cost concepts. The costs of tangible phenomena can be defined and measured in many ways depending on how money values are assigned to the resources involved and precisely which resources are considered as being involved. Opportunity cost, direct cost, indirect cost, overhead cost, fixed cost, variable cost, marginal cost, incremental (or differential) cost, semi-fixed cost, semi-variable cost, average cost, full (or absorbed) cost, joint cost, separable cost, sunk cost, avoidable cost, imputed cost, controllable cost, uncontrollable cost, replacement cost, standard cost – this list indicates the multiplicity of cost concepts which a systems designer may have to consider.

Clearly, the accountant must consider carefully (in conjunction with those who will use his reports) the types of cost to include in any financial reporting system. His role will be both provider of information and educator on how to use it.

It must be borne in mind, then, that any accounting technique has limitations. For example, allocations of indirect costs between products and of fixed costs to units of product, are arbitrary; ratios may hide compensating factors or trends and cost-volume-profit (or break-even) analysis is essentially a static technique, being largely based on static assumptions of linear, that is, straight-line, relationships between volumes, on the one hand, and revenues and costs on the other.

Nevertheless, the distinction between fixed and variable costs and the related flexible budgeting approach help to depict the financial implications of alternative scenarios and in the analysis of past performance. Ratio analysis can also be used to assist in the same process.

KEYS TO CONTROL

The first and perhaps the most obvious requirement is that measurement must be relevant to management's needs, and measures themselves must be designed to aid interpretation.

What to measure

Many companies tend to measure only material factors that are readily expressed in production or financial terms, such as time, quantity and quality. However, it is important that certain non-material factors should be measured, especially those indicating the performance of responsible individuals throughout the company.

Interpretation

Interpretation is the essential link between measurement (information) and decision making (action). The demands on top management are such that it is important that reports emphasize departures from plan or standard (exception reporting) and interpret the exceptions, in order both to conserve the manager's time and aid him in decision making. A policy decision must be made therefore in designing control systems to determine the extent to which the interpretation of exceptions and the resultant decisions can be delegated as routine procedures to subordinate staff.

Where practicable, trends should be displayed graphically as, for instance, the behaviour of overhead costs in relation to the level of productive activity.

Selectivity

When considering the scope of exception reporting, one must bear in mind that control can break down because management attempts to control too much, and really important issues become submerged in a mass of irrelevancies. In any control series, a small proportion of elements will tend always to account for a large proportion of effects. Examples of the frequently-met 80/20 rule illustrate this when 80 per cent of a company's sales are accounted for by 20 per cent of its customers, or 20 per cent of items in stock account for 80 per cent of the value of inventory. Accordingly, the key factors for control must be selected carefully and reporting systems should be designed to highlight significant items.

In practice, most managements attempt to control many factors which, in a control sense, are unimportant because their behaviour pattern will follow that of other more essential factors such as the level of sales.

Accountability and controllability

It is essential to the success of any financial control system that an individual (the budgetee) is only held responsible for results when the following conditions prevail

1   That he knows what he is expected to achieve.
2   That he knows what he is actually achieving.
3   That it is substantially within his power to regulate what is happening.

When all these conditions do not exist simultaneously, it may be unjust and ineffective to hold the budgetee responsible, and the desired control will become impossible to achieve. Nevertheless, the fact that a system fairly reflects commercial reality is just as important as ensuring fair treatment for the budgetee. These considerations lead us to the principles of responsibility accounting.

ORGANIZATIONAL AND BEHAVIOURAL IMPLICATIONS

A financial reporting system is a means of bringing information to each level of management in order that responsibilities to the organization may be fulfilled. It follows that accounting figures should be compiled so that the results may be considered attributable to one person's performance. This requirement causes accounting to cross the threshold into behavioural science (especially the areas of motivation and human relations), which forms the basis for management control.

Responsibility accounting

Each responsible individual should prepare his budget on the basis of controllable costs (and revenues, where appropriate) at his level of authority. Essentially the responsibility centre is a personalized concept, whereas the notion of cost centres may well be impersonal. For example, a machine shop in an engineering company will be composed of several cost centres — milling machines, turret lathes, auto-robots, and so on — but the whole shop is under the authority of the foreman. This is his responsibility centre for which he is the responsible individual.

Responsibility accounting changes the emphasis of cost and management accounting from products, which are passive inanimate objects, to people who are led to participate in vigorous planning and cost control through the budgetary process.

Cost classification is a vital area of responsibility accounting, the aim being to assign costs to the individuals who are responsible for their incurrence. However, charging individuals with only those costs subject to their control has many attendant practical problems when joint costs are involved. The general rule is to charge the person who can bring the greatest influence to bear on cost incurrence with responsibility for any joint cost, rather than making some meaningless apportionment.

Responsibility centres as a basis for reporting

Accounting control reports should be fitted to the various areas of individual responsibility, and as one moves further up the managerial hierarchy, more cost items will be reported at each level, since more costs are controllable as the scope of managerial responsibility enlarges. Top management will therefore receive a summary of all costs, made up of summaries of controllable costs at each subordinate level, plus details of those relevant to the top level.

Such reports can do little to rectify previous mistakes, but by indicating exceptions to plan they ensure that causes are investigated and appropriate corrective action taken to prevent similar mistakes in the future. The orientation must clearly be towards the future rather than to the past.

A common weakness in many companies is an over-emphasis on

current profit performance. For example, return on capital by division, plant, or product line helps to explain changes in the rate of return for the company as a whole, as well as assisting in appraising the performance of individual managers. But two principal dangers exist in this approach. First, both profits and the capital base must be clearly defined to avoid misunderstanding; for example, whether profit is measured before tax, or the investment base is net of depreciation and other specific items. Secondly, sub-optimization through departmental orientation rather than corporate orientation on the part of individual managers can result from emphasizing the department to the exclusion of the company as a whole. In addition, there are more general problems of arbitrary cost allocations and holding individuals responsible for costs over which they have no control.

Adopting a systems approach should ensure the highest degree of consistency between departmental and corporate goals. However, divisional responsibilities must be specific, since control must be specific. An individual manager's budget should only be modified after negotiation between the manager and his superior together with the budget officer. The manager should accept the modification as reasonable and feel committed to the new target. If this practice is not followed, the manager may lose confidence in the attainability of the budget, no matter how specific it may be, and may fail to see how his budget fits into the overall corporate pattern. The guiding principle is that those charged with responsibility should be consulted on all matters relevant to it.

In summary, anyone fixing responsibility and implementing the control related to it should

1 Define clearly the organizational structure, and delegate responsibility so that each person knows his role.
2 Determine the extent and limits of functional control.
3 Ensure that responsible individuals are fully involved in preparing budget estimates, since they will be held liable for deviations.
4 Provide those responsible with means of exercising control, in the form of regular, relevant statements of cost and, where appropriate, of revenues.
5 Organize ways and means by which subordinates may report to superiors on significant variances and corrective action taken (or to be taken).
6 By the above procedure, confirm that every item of expense is the responsibility of some person within the organization and also that

every responsible individual knows for what expenditures he must account, and to whom.

The ability to delegate is one sign of a good manager, and the budgeting process enables the control of expenditure, segmental revenue-generation and profit responsibility to be delegated. Specifically charging managers with responsibilities forms an important way of ensuring that tasks are performed satisfactorily, since few people will reduce costs or otherwise seek to improve profitability unless responsibility has been specifically delegated to them.

Impact of control on individuals

As already noted, the design of planning and control systems takes us into the territory of the behavioural sciences. The question of motivation is particularly relevant. For control (as distinct from planning) purposes, the use of accurate calculations and their transmission (in the form of results) to others may be beneficial, harmful, or neutral, depending upon

1 The kind of persons and tasks involved.
2 The setting in which operations are conducted.
3 The vehicle, time sequence, etc., used for information transmittal.

Clearly, therefore, the effect of control on individuals can play a large part in the effective control of the company.

Budgets have been known to unite employees against management where reports show results rather than reasons, or are excessively historical in relation to future goals, or are prepared by inflexible and narrow-minded accountants.

One vital study in this area by Argyris[1] quotes the following statements about reports from supervisory management.

> I'm violently against the figures. I keep away from showing them to the workers. I know the boys are doing a good job. They're trying to do their best. If I give them the heat with this stuff they'll blow their top.

> You can't use budgets on people. Just can't do anything like that. People have to be handled carefully and in our plant carefully doesn't mean with budgets. Besides I don't think my people are lazy.

As a result of the pressure, tension and general mistrust of management controls, the above mentioned tendency of employees to unite against management may result. Such controls as budgets tend to make employees feel dependent and passive, which emphasizes their subordination to management – not only are they told what to do, but also how to do it. Consequently, a great care must be taken in administering management controls to ensure that employees do not experience excessive exposure to such factors as pressure, inter-departmental strife, barriers to communication, or inclinations to be department centred rather than organization centred. Such care will involve:

1 Reporting both results and (insofar as possible) reasons for those results.
2 Emphasizing both past and present performance.
3 Maintaining flexibility.
4 Stressing the established goals (and future expectations).

The problem of directing activities towards goals is one of motivation, which is often overlooked by conventional budgeting methods. The budget is not the goal, it is the plan that should aim to motivate goal attainment. As such, it should be based on realistic expectations, and this demands effective communications between the different operating levels of the company.

Good attitudes must provide the key to successful budgeting. This is facilitated by satisfactory relationships between subordinates and superiors, which rest on the existence of clear cut organizational lines and the disposition to delegate authority along with responsibility. Budgets should not be used as pressure devices, since this will prohibit the development of team spirit in striving to achieve planned goals. A budget should be seen as a yardstick – not an instrument of pressure.

By helping to clarify targets and by demonstrating the inter-dependence of the different sections of the business, budgets form a powerful means of motivation. If the budgetary process does not aid in motivating people in the right direction, then serious thought should be given to discounting or thoroughly revising the procedures practised. The ideal situation is that in which a control system is so designed that it leads people to take actions that are not only in their own best interests but are also in the best interests of the company.

It becomes necessary, therefore, to consider the aspiration levels of different individuals. This requires incorporating sufficient flexibility within the budgetary system to improve motivation by the upwards or downwards movement of targets in order to achieve continuous improvements in goal attainment. For example, an individual's aspiration level will tend to decrease following a failure in his goal striving behaviour. Similarly, his aspiration level will tend to increase following success. In addition, aspirations are affected by external events other than task performance (such as his relationship with his superior, his personal financial condition, his domestic situation, etc.), but these effects tend to decrease as experience with the task increases. Since each individual's aspiration level will be unique to him (and to his pattern of success/failure and non-task circumstances) it is necessary to reflect recent past performance levels with revised future target levels if positive motivation is to be ensured.

Weaknesses of budgetary control

From the standpoint of internal financial reporting, the budget is an all-pervading consideration. We conclude this section by re-emphasizing the problems encountered in using budgets and describing an approach which will minimize these difficulties.

Four important problem areas are frequently encountered in the use of budget systems

1 They can grow to be so complex, detailed, cumbersome, meaningless and expensive that they become dangerous.
2 Budgetary goals may come to supersede organizational goals, requiring care in using budgets as a means and not an end.
3 Budgets may tend to hide inefficiencies by continuing initial expenditures in succeeding periods without proper evaluation. The budgetary system must contain provisions for re-examination of standards and other bases of planning, by which policies are translated into numerical terms.
4 The use of budgets as pressure devices defeats their basic purpose.

To allow for different levels of activity, and the inherent inaccuracies of forecasting in an uncertain world, budgets must be flexible.

The inability to forecast with total accuracy does not nullify the value of the budget as a managerial tool. It does mean, however, that the budget should not be a static device that is insensitive to changing conditions. Flexibility is an obvious necessity in providing meaningful current standards for guiding operations and judging performance.

Although cost – volume – profit analysis can be a useful adjunct to effective budgeting, it must be accepted as a relatively inflexible tool that hinders the comparison of alternatives on account of its static nature. In more detail, it fails to take account of

1 The dynamic nature of industrial activity.
2 The efficiency of management.
3 The efficiency of labour.
4 Technological progress.
5 The size of plant and resource limitations.
6 Price changes.
7 Varying product/sales mix.
8 Objectives other than profit (derived from specified cost and sales levels) such as the degree of consumer satisfaction to be achieved.

Even when budgets have been prepared, based on accurate, currently attainable and internally derived standards, the financial reporting system should have tolerance levels built into it. It cannot be expected that standards will be met perfectly, thereby requiring some measure of the significance of results *vis-à-vis* plans to be developed – results beyond this tolerance limit being the subject of control action, and results within this limit being accepted as random variations.

The tolerance range should not be so broad as to excuse all levels of performance, nor so narrow as to cause control action and investigation to be applied too frequently.

The statistical control chart in Figure 6.2 allows successive levels of performance for a particular factor to be observed in relation to standards, and tolerance limits set accordingly.

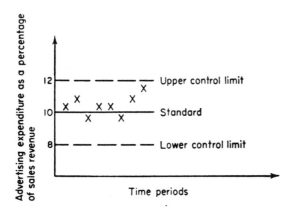

Figure 6.2 Statistical control chart

CRITERIA FOR INFORMATION USEFULNESS

How effective a manager is in his job will tend to depend upon his general ability; his knowledge of what he is seeking to achieve; and how much, how relevant and how good his information is, along with how well he interprets and acts upon it.

Management information needs

Nevertheless, one hears frequent complaints from managers that information is too late, of the wrong type, unverified or even suppressed. It is evident, therefore, that if information is to be of value, it must be clear, detailed, timely, accurate and complete – not merely some vague figures thrown out by an unplanned system. Management information and its presentation must observe the important concepts of control, namely: accountability, controllability and selectivity. In addition, data should be checked for the important qualities of impartiality, reliability and internal consistency.

Basically, the manager needs information to

1 Help him in making plans and setting standards (to indicate what is expected of him).
2 Indicate his performance and achievement in executing those plans.
3 Assist him in decision making (to bring 1 and 2 closer together).

As frequently happens, the manager may not know the precise information he needs (or, alternatively, what information is available). The systems designer can help by observing the types of decisions made, testing the adequacy of existing information, suggesting alternate data flows, determining what information is available and indicating the means and costs of providing it.

The process of specifying, collecting, analysing, reporting and using information is essentially the same in any size of business, whether for routine purposes or for special projects. Methods of collection and analysis do vary, however. The differences lie in the relative employment of manual as opposed to mechanical or electronic methods. The increasing adoption of electronic data-processing should ensure that fewer managers will have cause to complain about insufficient, inaccurate or delayed information – provided that systems designers ensure that relevance, reliability, and timeliness are taken into account. The danger, rather, is that they may be inundated with data which is too

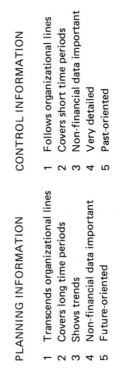

INFORMATION

A ENVIRONMENTAL DATA
1 Social
2 Economic
3 Political

B COMPETITIVE.DATA
1 Past performance
2 Present activity
3 Future plans

C INTERNAL OPERATING DATA
1 Quantitative financial
2 Quantitative physical
3 Non-quantitative

MANAGEMENT FUNCTIONS

PLANNING → EXECUTION → CONTROL

PLANNING
1 Set objectives
2 Formulate strategy
3 Decide amongst alternatives

CONTROL
1 Measure performance
2 Isolate variances
3 Aid in re-planning

FEEDBACK

INFORMATION

A NON-FINANCIAL DATA
1 Market
2 Manufacturing
3 R and D
4 Personnel

B FINANCIAL DATA
1 Market
2 Manufacturing
3 R and D
4 Personnel

INFORMATION SYSTEM CHARACTERISTICS

PLANNING INFORMATION
1 Transcends organizational lines
2 Covers long time periods
3 Shows trends
4 Non-financial data important
5 Future-oriented

CONTROL INFORMATION
1 Follows organizational lines
2 Covers short time periods
3 Non-financial data important
4 Very detailed
5 Past-oriented

Figure 6.3 Anatomy of management information

113

voluminous and poorly formulated for them to use.

In aiming to provide the right information to the right people at the right time and at low cost, the financial reporting systems should, ideally, be designed as part of a total systems framework such as that portrayed in Figure 6.3, which is derived from Daniel[2].

Uses of financial information

A great deal of information, although useful for planning and control, is generated primarily for some other purpose that is only tangentially related to planning and control purposes.

In most companies the accounting routine provides the bulk of data which are derived from

1 Payroll procedures.
2 The order processing cycle, beginning with the receipt of an order and ending with the issue of invoices and the collection of accounts receivable.
3 The procurement and accounts payable cycle.

Since so much information is within the accounting sphere, the accountant will play a most important role in reporting on accomplishments.

Financial reports are essentially statistical tables, the brevity, arrangement and content of which should all be subject to the prime test of usefulness. However, accounting statements generally describe what has already happened within the company, and omit such items as

1 Information about the future.
2 Data expressed in non-financial terms, such as that concerning market share, productivity, quality levels and adequacy of customer service, etc.
3 Information dealing with external conditions as they might bear on a particular company's operations.

Given that all these elements are essential to the intelligent management of a business, the key to the development of a dynamic and usable system of management information is to move beyond the limits of conventional accounting reports and to conceive of information as it relates to the vital areas of planning and control.

The organizational structure of a company and its managers' information requirements are inextricably linked. In order to translate a statement of his duties into action a manager must use, as well as receive, relevant information. This involves considering all the data and intelligence — financial and non-financial — that are available, rather than relying wholly on the accounting system and the reports it produces, to satisfy a particular manager's information requirements.

A structured approach to reporting

To achieve the aim of successfully communicating the essential facts about the business to its managers, the accountant, as systems designer and operator, must have a clear conception of the purposes, possibilities and limitations of the many different types of statements and reports. Also, he must understand the problems and viewpoints of their users in order to ensure that they, in turn, appreciate the true meaning, and limitations, of the reports that he prepares for them.

At each level of management, and especially at the lower levels of the hierarchy, the accountant should pose two questions

1   What are the necessary and controllable factors pertinent to the level of authority in question?
2   In what form are they best presented to aid in decision making at this level?

At this stage, the two complementary forms of controlling corporate activities must also be considered. They are

1   Control against long range objectives or plans.
2   Control against standards, representing short-term goals or targets.

Both forms are essential to effective overall control, but top management is more interested in the former, and supervisory management in the latter, for obvious reasons.

A structured approach to reporting by areas of responsibility will enable top management to view the results and efficiencies of individual departments in the light of their contributions to overall objectives. If corrective action is required from the top, this may well indicate a failure to achieve control at a lower level.

Similarly, the existence of a time lag between actual events and the reporting of these events, through the top management control system, may create the need for corrective action that is more drastic than if such action had been instituted at a lower level of control which could be associated more closely with the actual events.

This requires that the interface of top management with subordinate management control systems should provide a rapid feedback of financial data to the former. Without this rapid feedback, when top management is obliged to instigate corrective action it is often found that this action is delayed, that it becomes more complex and that more people become involved. This is not the most favourable setting for effective control.

Within the control framework, the characteristics of good reports are that they should

1 Be oriented towards the user, considering both his level and function.
2 Give as much information as possible in quantitative terms and flow both ways in the organization.
3 Be based on a flexible system that allows quick changes to meet new conditions.

On a tangible plane, succinctness is a great virtue in reporting, whereas on an intangible plane, one major advantage of an adequate reporting system is that the mere act of reporting requires a manager to pause and think.

INTERNAL FINANCIAL REPORTING AND MANAGEMENT CONTROL

Definition and distinctions

Management control can be defined as the use of a reliable, readily understood and sensitive system of information and standards which ensures that resources are obtained and used effectively and efficiently in the accomplishment of the company's objectives.

Clear distinctions should be drawn between

1 Strategic planning, which is concerned with overall policies and objectives.
2 Management control (as defined above, which has a month by month focus).
3 Operational control (relating to day to day tasks).

To illustrate these different activities we can consider the setting of financial policies as a strategic planning activity, whereas planning and reporting on working capital requirements is a management control matter. At a more detailed level, the control of credit extension falls within the sphere of operational control.

Financial reporting subsystems within managerial accounting are therefore an important element of management control, which should be their primary focus. Management control has the following characteristics

1 It is complex because it is concerned with the total organization.
2 The information within it tends to be precise, integrated, and developed within a prescribed set of procedures.
3 Although communication is difficult, it aims to lead to desired results by catering for the needs of many personnel, especially line and top management.
4 It has its roots in social psychology and the mental activities involved are those of persuasion and motivation over a relatively short time span.

Accounting systems themselves cannot be the starting point in constructing an overall system, since it is management control rather than pure accounting that deals with the on-going operation of the whole enterprise. Internal financial reporting systems are systems of both the management control system and the financial accounting system, but in the case of conflict, the needs of the former should predominate. In turn, however, since management control is the system around which others should be constructed, this system must itself be predominantly financial. Only in this way can it encompass all the parts of the company in common terms so as to assist management in determining that the parts are in balance.

Management control systems

In terms of management control, a suitable system may be defined as a set of policies, procedures, and associated information processing designed to give direction to corporate activities. This direction results from a knowledge of the objectives sought, the progress made towards them and the need for corrective action (if any).

While a control system is able to exercise a positive influence on events, the system alone cannot control; it can only help the manager to achieve control.

This he will seek to do by, first, using information and knowledge to explain the behaviour of phenomena making up the processes that are of interest to him. Such an understanding will enable him to predict future outcomes from those behaviour patterns. As a consequence of explanation and predictive ability, the manager will be able to adapt his decision making in order to achieve the outcomes desired, or, to put it another way, he will be able to exercise control.

Feedback and effective systems

The information link between output and input (or, strictly, revised input) is the feedback channel (see Figure 6.4). For control to be effective, information must pass along this channel rapidly. In a dynamic environment, the time interval between deviation and correction must be kept to a minimum.

FEEDBACK CHANNEL

Figure 6.4   Basic system with feedback loop

In the psychology field, and especially in learning theory, it has been shown that motivation is maintained at a high level when the time lag between action and knowledge of results is minimized. This emphasizes the need for a system to supply feedback information as rapidly as possible. Furthermore, it must be designed to report to those responsible for taking corrective action and not to intermediaries in the information networks of the company.

The danger exists that feedback carrying messages of failure may tempt the recipient to attack the control system rather than take corrective action. The concept of individual aspiration levels is especially relevant in this context. Furthermore, feedback may show that objectives are unattainable in terms of corporate, as distinct from individual, aspiration levels, in which case corrective action should take the form of a search for alternative objectives that are attainable.

It should always be recognized that systems and feedback seldom operate perfectly. In addition, people and equipment (as facilitating agents) are usually far from perfect and, even when constrained by a system, frequently produce peculiar problems and situations.

Characteristics of cybernetic systems

When the input-output model of a system is fully developed with feedback loops, one enters the domain of self-regulating or cybernetic models. (This type of system is illustrated in Figure 6.5.)

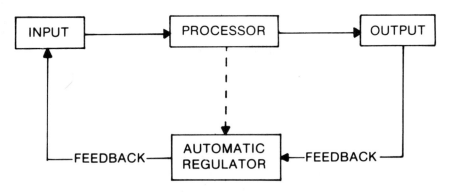

Figure 6.5   Basic cybernetic system

Such systems are closed rather than open; they operate independently of the human factor once established. The best example is, perhaps, a simple thermostat. The computer (suitably programmed with decision rules) is the analogous business example.

Complexity characterizes cybernetic systems, with the proliferation of variety characterizing the control problem. ('Variety' in this context relates to the number of distinguishable elements or variables in the business situation.)

Cybernetics, described as the science of control and communication in the animal and the machine, specifically sets out to recognize, describe and handle (through feedback principles) the complexities of the real world. By considering 'viable' systems (that is, those that exist beyond a certain complexity barrier), it never errs by treating systems in an over simplified way.

STAFFING AND OPERATING THE MANAGEMENT CONTROL SYSTEM

The organizational implications of the systems approach are not such as to require wholesale changes in the organizational structure, or in administrative behaviour. Although some would suggest significant (and commendable) changes, from the financial point of view it is mainly necessary to ensure that accountants take a company-wide view in discharging their duties.

Accounting department

The size of the company will determine the degree of specialization and exact staffing requirements. However, the starting point will be the statement of objectives, from which the organizational plan for the accounting department can be derived by

1 Preparing an organizational chart with job specifications for all accounting posts.
2 Appointing suitably qualified people to these posts.
3 Instituting effective methods of controlling these persons once in post.

In a company of any size, the dichotomy between reporting on stewardship (to shareholders, bankers, etc.) and to management will be recognized by the appointment of a financial accountant with responsibility for the former, and a management accountant with responsibility for the latter.

Together with the duties of the internal auditor, these functions will typically be co-ordinated by the chief accountant (or financial controller). In a similar manner, the management accountant will co-ordinate the duties of the budget officer and the cost accountant along with their staff, whereas the financial accountant will co-ordinate the payroll, bought ledger, sales ledger, cashiers and general sections of his department.

Budget committee

The budget committee is responsible, on a consultative basis, for overseeing the preparation of budgets. It usually consists of several members of the top management group, together with the budget officer who will act as convenor and secretary to the committee.

This committee establishes the general guidelines to be followed in budget preparation, and subsequently exists to

1 Resolve inter-departmental differences in preparing budgets.
2 Offer general advice on the preparation of budgets.
3 Co-ordinate the preparation of budgets.
4 Scrutinize budget reports, comparing results with the plan and submitting appropriate recommendations upwards or downwards as the situation demands.

It is emphasized that budget proposals should be made by the line organization (subject to modification and approval from above), with the budget committee forming an advisory group responsible for the consolidation of the budget and the speed and accuracy of the budgetary process, rather than for the detailed content of the budget.

Management control/systems committee

The establishment of a management control committee, composed of senior executives from all functions, should increase the probability of success in adopting systematic control procedures.

As with the budget committee, it should not be responsible for designing or imposing systems upon the organization, but should play a role of guidance, leadership and co-ordination. Its particular aims may be

1 Welding the whole company into a team, working continually towards systems improvement.
2 Aiding this team by providing technical assistance.
3 Both controlling and evaluating the results of system development from a managerial point of view.

CONCLUSION

An effective reporting and control system must be based on personalized organizational centres of responsibility, and be sufficiently flexible to maintain a high level of motivation. Within this framework, usefulness must always be the overriding consideration.

REFERENCES

1 Argyris, C., *Personality and Organization,* Harper Brothers, (New York, 1957)
2 Daniel, D. R., 'Management Information Crisis', *Harvard Business Review,* (Cambridge, Massachusetts, 1961)

7

Budgets and budgetary control

Alan R. Leaper

All businesses have some form of budgetary control in existence whether or not they recognize it or call it by that name. Someone in the organization co-ordinates the resources of the business in some degree to achieve some sort of plan, but whether they examine alternative plans, ideal criteria and harmony of objectives is possibly another question.

There are many benefits to be derived from the introduction of a formalized budgetary control system, among which are the following

1   It defines the objectives of an organization as a whole and in financial terms.
2   It provides yardsticks by which to measure efficiency for various parts of the organization.
3   It reveals the extent by which actual results have varied from the defined objective.
4   It provides a guide for corrective action.
5   It facilitates centralized control with delegated responsibility.

The disadvantages of a formalized procedure are by no means so readily identifiable; in general terms they usually concern the following

1   The additional costs/personnel necessary to perform the function.
2   The suspicions aroused by its introduction, that it is merely another vehicle to implement cost reduction programmes.
3   The complacency of paper work becoming routine with the eventual possibility that little notice or action is taken.

Immediate benefits should not be expected from the introduction of a budget procedure; it may take a year or two to educate those concerned in the proper compilation of the data required and in the proper application of the data subsequently made available.

WHAT IS A BUDGET?

A budget in business planning is the expression in financial (and rather summarized) terms of a comprehensive short-term operational plan for a business entity. The financial numbers relate to specific action programmes which give rise to asset acquisitions and disposals, earning of revenues and incurring expenses. A budget in which the financial numbers have been 'pulled out of the air' is worse than useless.

Many alternative plans may be considered before the final one showing the most practical profit is chosen. Executives and other responsible officials from all functions of the company must contribute towards the plan. Data in the unit terms of each of the functions concerned must be collected and translated into monetary terms. For example, the sales manager is primarily concerned with units of the finished article or service and would therefore contribute the volume and models to be included in the plan. The production manager talks in standard hours and efficiencies. The personnel manager will be responsible for the levels of wage rates, absenteeism factors, welfare schemes, etc. The chief executive must be fully convinced of the benefits to be derived from the plan and really believe in it.

Budgetary control is the process of managing these facets − planning and co-ordinating all functions so that they work in harmony and control performances and costs. It establishes the responsiblity, throughout the corporate structure, of all managers for achieving the company's budgeted objectives. It entails measuring at suitable intervals how the plan is actually progressing and, if divergencies are occurring, taking the necessary corrective action to ensure that the company gets back on course again.

By having a budget built up in this manner it is possible to fix responsibility at every level of the organization − and this is important.

Most managements have found that it is not sufficient to face the problems of a business on a day to day basis or even on a year to year basis; medium-term operational (or programme) planning is therefore carried out over a time horizon of three to five years ahead. Generally, such planning involves a projection of the total market for the company's products and an assessment of what the company's share of that market should be, based on historical performance and management objectives. Obviously the degree of accuracy of the projections and plans varies with the period covered. In practice, in view of the many uncertainties involved in projecting activities over, say, a three-year period, the usual procedure is to prepare plans for the first year in considerable detail, and then to resort to summary projections for the remaining two years. As each year's plan is done, refinements are made on the basis of recent experience and a new third year is added.

BUDGET CENTRES

Efficient control requires acceptance that costs are best controlled at the point where they are incurred. The transport manager should therefore control the transport department's costs. The span of control of any one person should not be unduly large, however.

The area controlled by an individual is known as a budget centre. The Chartered Institute of Management Accountants has defined a budget centre as:

A section of the organisation of the undertaking defined for the purposes of budgetary control.

The budgets prepared at a given level of budget centre are then consolidated at the next level up (profit centre, division or company, as the case may be).

A substantial business organization will generally comprise a number of operating units, each of which has primary responsibility for its own profits and cash flow, (profit centres) as well, perhaps, as its capital investment (investment centres).

Thus, a business may comprise several profit centres, and in a larger organization these may be grouped into investment centres or divisions. Each division will normally have its own financial controller who will prepare the divisional master budget (see the following sections); larger profit centres may also have their own management accountants who prepare the draft profit and loss and cash budgets.

Within the budget centre there may be other smaller areas to which costs are attributable and for which it is deemed desirable to control a particular group of assets. For example, in the transport department fleet vehicles may be grouped by type or area. Each such smaller group may be defined as a cost centre.

The Chartered Institute of Management Accountants has defined a cost centre as being:

A location, person or item of equipment, or a group of these, in or connected with an undertaking in relation to which costs may be ascertained and used for purposes of cost control.

One person only should be responsible for incurring costs within the defined budget centre and the ultimate responsibility for budgetary control lies with the chief executive.

COMPILING A BUDGET

There is really no established order in which budgets should be prepared provided all parts are geared into a common factor. This is generally the principal limiting or bottleneck factor which varies for each individual company.

Most companies tend to establish a sales target determined by market potential and their share of the market: this can provide a basis for budgets. Many others prefer to establish their production capacity and plan a budget to ensure the full utilization of available equipment. The ideal, of course, is to achieve a harmony of both of these important items. However, many other factors may determine the level of activity to be budgeted, among which are insufficient cash to finance expansion, a scarce raw material, and a possible shortage of skilled labour.

Having established the basis for compiling the budget all known external factors which could have a bearing on its fulfilment must be examined – national wage awards, sales taxes, credit squeezes, the movement of purchase prices and so on.

In larger organizations a budget committee is usually formed to review these items and determine, as best it can, the likely effect they will have on business during the period to be used in the budget. Having determined these external factors, the budget accountant/committee will advise functional and departmental managers of their effects and provide guidelines for the compilation of the subsidiary departmental budgets, the main examples of which are considered below.

Sales budget

The sales budget should show total sales in quantity and value. It may be analysed further by product, by area, by customer and, of course, by seasonal pattern of expected sales.

The main problems arise in the determination of quantities and the calculation of standard prices.

Constraints such as competitive activity (new products and aggressive pricing policies) have to be borne in mind.

The budget should be compiled by the sales manager, who will seek the opinions of his salesmen and use any statistical forecasting techniques arising from market research. Other considerations include general business and economic conditions, company policies regarding advertising, new products, supplies, product demand and plant capacity.

A special pricing study is usually helpful at this stage. It should show the complete product range, the sector of the market involved, competitive models or products (both pricing and features available), introduction dates, discount structures and advertising strategy.

In some cases, when jobbing production is involved, budgets must be made in terms of the expected sales value only.

Production budget

The production budget is a statement of the output by product and is generally expressed in standard hours. It should take into consideration the sales budget, plant capacity, whether stocks are to be increased or decreased and outside purchases.

The form the budget will take depends upon circumstances. Usually the quantities are shown for each department (known as budget centres) and information is taken from machine loading charts, material specifications, time schedules and other production or time-study records.

When computing labour cost, the average labour rate to be used depends on the wage plan in effect. For hourly rated employees not on incentive bonuses, an overall plant rate may be sufficient. In other cases, departmental or labour grade rates may be used. When a straight piece rate plan is in effect, the labour cost is the amount paid per unit produced. When other types of incentive plans are used, average labour rates that include an estimated amount of bonus payments must be computed. In companies where standard costs are used, cost accounting records can be very useful in determining budget requirements for non-productive direct labour. Many cost accounting systems are sophisticated enough to indicate the extent to which direct labour is non-productive and involves down time, waiting time, changeover or set-up time and so on.

The production budget will be prepared by the plant manager in close co-operation and collaboration with accountants, production engineers, work study engineers and other key personnel. Adequate lead times for delivery of new equipment and/or development of new processes will be considered.

At this stage, the sales and production budgets should be compared to ensure the maximum utilization of capacity aligned to satisfactory sales growth. If the sales budget exceeds the production capacity, decisions on capital expenditure and new plant may be required before proceeding further. If significant under-utilization of existing capacity is denoted, examination of how best to use this spare capacity must be undertaken to determine, for instance, if sub-contract work is profitable, if a revised pricing structure could increase volume or if plant should be declared redundant and scrapped.

Production costs budget

This supplementary budget should determine the 'cost of sales' allied to the required production.

Generally, by far the largest element in cost terms is direct material. This part should be compiled by the chief buyer in conjunction with the production manager. Using the sales and production budgets, it will determine the requirements of raw material and piece-parts, period by period, to meet the output, and will be evaluated in cash cost terms. Considerations should take into account bulk buying, delivery periods, stock holding, suppliers' credit terms and trade discounts, as well as recognizing any changes in material specifications, new model introductions, etc. In timing such purchases as raw materials and piece-parts, consideration must be given to the necessity of keeping inventory levels to the very minimum and thereby not tying up valuable capital. Competitive pricing exercises should be undertaken with potential suppliers to ensure that costs are strictly controlled and keen.

Direct labour is another most important element of production costs. The work study department should be called upon to establish standard times for individual units. These may then be evaluated by the required volumes and converted into direct labour needs. The degree of labour efficiency must be determined, as must the type of employee necessary, that is, male/female; skilled/semi-skilled/unskilled.

Direct expense budgets covering warehousing, transport, warranty and special tools should be determined by the appropriate managers responsible for incurring or approving the respective expenses.

Factory overhead costs (burden) should be established by departmental foremen and consolidated by the production manager. Expenses of all types should be considered and some assistance may be necessary from the finance department in determining depreciation, insurance and other expenses possibly beyond the control of the local foremen.

Chapter 8 provides further guidance on establishing production cost standards.

Personnel budgets

This is a headcount schedule of the total labour requirements necessary to carry out the sales and production budgets and, in fact, run the whole business from managing director to office boy and production worker to office cleaner. It should be prepared by the personnel department in conjunction with all other functional department heads.

The schedule will show the number of personnel required, the hours to be worked, wage rates, salaries, etc., and should be built up by departments. The respective costs should, of course, be included in the applicable departmental budgets. The recruitment and training policies of the company will be incorporated in the budget and cognizance should be taken of all labour related costs, for example, national insurance and pension schemes.

Operating and service department budgets

The type of department falling into this category may be administration, finance, selling, advertising and service, and may also include warehousing and shipping.

The departmental head of each of these functions will be responsible for compiling his individual budgets. The data included will cover personnel requirements by number and grade and be cost-determined in conjunction with the personnel manager; it will cover departmental running costs detailed by account, namely, utilities operating expenses, depreciation, insurance, rates, and so on.

Special note should be taken of competitors' activity in determining the size and use of the advertising budget.

If raw material or bulk purchases are necessary, the usage and cost of these will be planned with the purchasing agent or chief buyer.

The basis of determining costs included in these budgets invariably depends on the established trend in previous years, adjusted for known changes. It should also be remembered that historical costs will include inefficiencies and these must be identified and determined if likely to continue. The considered effects of volume and activity should also be borne in mind.

Capital expenditure budget

This supplementary budget is usually compiled by senior management in conjunction with engineering and technical services.

The budget will show details of the capital expenditure proposals in the period of the master budget and will probably be prepared for a number of years ahead because of its longer term implications. Items included will be distinguished by the various types of assets – land, buildings, equipment, furniture, etc., and should also state the reasons for proposals – for example, replacement, new methods, capacity.

Back-up data should also accompany the proposals to justify the expenditures. This will take the usual forms of capital evaluations, such as return on investment and discounted cash flow analysis. The strain on cash resources should also be considered when compiling this budget.

Profit and loss account

The first component of the master budget is the budgeted profit and loss account. This budget will summarize the effects of all the relevant data contained in the supplementary operating and service department budgets, sales, purchasing, personnel and capital expenditure (depreciation, salvage receipts) budgets. It will be prepared in months or other chosen periods and be compiled by the financial controller. A sample profit and loss statement incorporating provisions for budget and standards is shown in Figure 7.1.

Cash budget

The second component of the master budget is the cash budget, which is critical in view of the possible constraints that an unsatisfactory cash position may have on the required expansion of a business and hence on the acceptability of the master budget as a whole.

	BUDGET	%	STANDARD	%	ACTUAL	%	VARIANCE
CURRENT MONTH							
Gross sales							
Less: Deductions from sales							
Total net sales							
Manufacturing standard costs							
Material							
Labour							
Burden							
Direct expense							
Total standard costs							
Standard manufacturing gross profit budget and volume variances							
Actual manufacturing gross profit							
Expenses							
Selling							
Advertising							
Administrative							
Engineering							
Total expenses							
Operating profit							
Other income and deductions							
Net profit before taxes							
Income tax provision							
Net profit							

Figure 7.1 Example of a profit and loss statement

The financial controller, with the assistance of all other management, should determine the timing by period, usually monthly, of production, sales, fixed asset purchases, etc., and then calculate the effects on the cash balance. The reason for this budget is to determine by period where additional cash may be required or where surplus cash may be available for short-term investment.

The income side is built up from the sales and debtors budget plus any other miscellaneous receipts, such as loans, new capital, sale of assets, grants, interest. The expenditure side will show the incurred expenses of the production and service department budgets, purchasing and capital expenditure budgets plus other payments relating to the distribution of profits, such as dividends and income taxes.

Balance sheet

The third component of the master budget is the projected balance sheet which will show the net effect of the budgets on the financial position of the company. Again, being compiled by the financial controller, it will consider information contained in the budgeted profit and loss account, capital expenditures and cash and the related movement of the working capital and financing.

Management must examine the implications of the profit and loss, cash and balance sheet master budgets that result from consolidating the subsidiary budgets and determine if they are acceptable. Do they show the most practicable overall profit to be accepted as a plan for the ensuing year or period to be budgeted? If the answer is negative then the problem areas should be determined and the departments concerned advised specifically of their shortcomings. As all the budgets are mainly inter-related, such a change generally entails resubmission of all the subsidiary budgets. This exercise may appear to be rather long-winded and even time wasting, but one of the real values of preparing budgets in this manner is that the consideration, discussion and communication of the short-term profit objective of the company involves all levels of management in its achievement, and by this process is most likely to reveal the maximum practicable profit objective for the company.

In practice, a lot of companies tend to take either sales or production in isolation and agree independently what the level of activity should be in these fields; once decided on, they proceed to build all the other budgets around them. If the resultant profit is in excess of the outlook for the current year, they are happy to leave it as such. However, assuming that the job is to be tackled properly, it is at this stage of review that any attempts at over budgeting or, worse still, conservative budgeting, should be weeded out. The level of responsibility for performance of the plan from each manager should be agreed upon, so that he fully commits himself to its attainment.

When the master budgets have been finally agreed and accepted, they should be adopted formally by management as its policy and plan for the forthcoming year or period and thereby provide a budget against which performance or achievement will be measured.

CONTROLLING THE PLAN

As indicated, the budgets are built up by progressive areas of responsibllity. It follows, therefore, that operating statements will be prepared for each of the budget centres involved. These should form part of the management information system used to control actual performance against the budget plan.

Good budgetary control follows the management theory of 'management by exception'. While management is given full details of expenditure, sales, production, etc., under its functional control, reports and information should be focused on matters that are adverse, or that show an unusually favourable variance, so that its energy is concentrated in the right direction and its effort is not diluted by a lot of information which merely indicates that things are going as planned.

There are differing schools of thought on the amount of detail that should be provided to management. Some management accountants prefer to provide only data over which managers have some degree of control. For instance, if depreciation policy is decided by the board, there is no point in giving an operational manager a depreciation charge for, say, the machine shop. He has no control over what that charge will be; according to this theory, this information is unnecessary and does not help him to perform his part of the plan under normal conditions. This theory does not give management the full picture and lacks the important benefit of enabling management to see the overall effect and contribution of its department to the business as a whole. The statement may be broken down into two sections labelled 'controllable' and 'uncontrollable'. Just what is controllable or uncontrollable can be surprising. For example, if a shop foreman is shown a list of fixed assets in his area on which there is a depreciation charge he may well indicate items of equipment which are surplus to his requirements but for which he has not bothered to raise a disposal request. These items can then be removed from the department and sold at good salvage prices, releasing valuable floor space, eliminating routine maintenance checks and saving administration time and effort searching for and identifying equipment at physical inventory time.

Timing of feedback

When considering the subject of control the question of timing is of great importance. When should the measurement of control be effected and over what period? Having decided the period the budget is to cover, which is usually annual (see the next section), the budget itself will be set out in terms of sub-periods: months and/or quarters, or perhaps a thirteen four-weekly basis for the subject year, depending on the type of business. In addition to the detailed annual budget, most companies have some form of long range plans for a number of years ahead, covering, for instance, the profit and loss account, balance sheet, cash flow and probably capital expenditures.

This longer term planning concerns itself primarily with determining whether or not the internal fund flow of the business will cover its commitments and capital expenditure programme, etc., but of course the longer term plans will not be prepared in anything like the same detail as the yearly short-term operating budget. It is a matter of individual company requirement to determine which data is best controlled on a quarterly, monthly, weekly or even daily basis.

An organization needs a fairly sophisticated accounting system to generate and disseminate information on a daily basis and this type of data is generally confined to production data. Standard hours produced, finished units, efficiencies, absenteeism, etc., all lend themselves to daily control. Billings in terms of unit sales and value would best be reviewed on a weekly basis, although for local consumption this, again, may be preferred on a rough daily basis. All other profit and loss cash flow data would be embodied in monthly financial statements and a balance sheet could be prepared on a quarterly basis.

The best system for a business must be determined by the constraints within which it works and what is needed to control the situation. Normally, data of a daily and weekly nature is restricted to middle management to facilitate operational control and is not fed through the pyramid of top management unless a special situation demands such close control. As a general rule, the lower down the management line one goes, the sooner information should be in management's hands. The foreman should have his output in standard hours measured against budget and his material usage for his batch of machines during the following morning so that he can take the necessary action to correct any deviation from his target.

Thus it has been said that this first-line information is the life blood of the business, and the accounting results which follow at the end of the month confirm and quantify an already known situation.

FLEXIBLE BUDGETS

One criticism of budgetary control which is sometimes raised is its rigidity, where actual results may be the outcome of circumstances which have changed since the budget was originally prepared.

Budgets, when set and agreed upon, can only take into consideration one set of circumstances. As actual conditions seldom equate with budgeted conditions, the difference between actual costs and budgeted costs must be demonstrated. Information should, therefore, be available to suggest the appropriate level of expenses generally known as budget standards, which fluctuate at varying levels of production activity or sales volume.

In order to achieve control of this situation, flexible budgetary control was introduced — as opposed to fixed budgets. Flexible budgeting is applied in businesses where it is impossible to make a firm forecast of the future conditions. Fixed budgeting should be satisfactory for the more stable industries; however, these are very few and far between and flexible budgeting is more widely applicable.

Flexible budgeting is designed to provide a more realistic picture of the variance between actual expenses and budgeted expenses. One expects to be able to distinguish that part of the variance which is due to volume and for which a manager will not have control, and that part of the variance over which the manager should have control. To achieve this, one must be in a position to calculate budget standards at varying levels of activity.

The application of this calculation is demonstrated below by considering first a report on the basis of fixed budgeting and then showing a similar report calculated on a flexible budgeting basis. Before looking at these reports, it must be clear that costs are classified for flexible budgeting purposes. This in itself is a most difficult task and one that may be tackled in many ways which cannot be amplified in this chapter. However, for the purpose of this exercise, the following broad categories are used

1 Fixed costs. Costs which do not vary in the short term with volume.
2 Variable costs. Costs which do so vary.
3 Semi-variable costs. Costs which will vary with volume but not in direct relationship.

Chapter 8 on costing provides detailed examples of these types of expenses; of course, if standard costing is already applied in the company, the setting of a flexible budget is rendered considerably easier. If standard costs are not available, the technique of marginal costing will need to be applied in dealing with individual costs to determine the degree of variability. Scatter graphs or the regression theory may be used. Table 7.1 is based on fixed budgeting and demonstrates how much the actual is off target. This type of measurement is an improvement on, say, measuring against last year's performance when circumstances may have been different. The report provides some conception of the amount by which actual experience varies from budgeted plans.

Table 7.1
Example of fixed budgeting

Expense type	Budget £	Actual £	Variance £
Material	10 000	12 500	+ 2 500
Labour	5 000	5 900	+ 900
Rent	3 000	3 000	—
Salaries	1 000	1 100	+ 100
	19 000	22 500	+ 3 500

However, if one is to adhere to one of the basic principles of budgetary control, that people should be responsible for costs over which they have control, this report may not provide the solution.

Table 7.2 applies similar information but is calculated on the basis of flexible budgeting. Thus, clearly, the advantages of flexible budgeting are demonstrated by the second report. It shows in reality that instead of the manager being responsible for an adverse variance of £3500 as he was in the first report, he is, in fact, only responsible for the adverse variance of £500, the remaining £3000 being due to increased volume in production which may be the result of conservative sales forecasting, or some other factor which must be taken up with a different department in the organization.

Flexible budgeting is thus extremely useful for getting behind the causes of variances, particularly if quantities, as well as costs, have been budgeted. For example, with sales variances one can determine whether the variance is due to prices, volume outlet mixture, product mixture or a combination of all these elements.

Table 7.2
Example of flexible budgeting

| | BUDGET | | | ACTUAL | VARIANCE ANALYSIS | |
	Standard per unit	Fixed budget	Flexed budget		Controll-able	Volume
Output in units		10 000	12 000	12 000	—	+ 2000
% of original budget		100%	120%	120%	—	+ 20%
		£	£	£	£	£
Variable costs						
Material	£1.00	10 000	12 000	12 500	+ 500	+ 2000
Labour	£0.50	5000	6000	5900	− 100	+ 1000
Fixed costs						
Rent		3000	3000	3000	—	—
Salaries		1000	1000	1100	+ 100	—
Total		19 000	22 000	22 500	+ 500	+ 3000

USE OF COMPUTERS

Generally, manual methods of making the planning computations are time consuming, with the result that only a few alternative plans of operation can be fully evaluated when setting a budget and analysis of variances may be limited by time constraints. Computerized financial models have been developed to assist in simulating the results under many different assumptions as to volume, products and plans of operation. Most steps in budgeting involve some alternative assumptions or decisions, and the final outcome of the budget process can vary greatly in terms of the profits and resources which will result from each assumption or decision. As a practical matter, the burden of making the planning and budgeting computations under even one set of assumptions is generally considered to be all that a company can expect its people to carry in addition to their other operating responsibilities. Very often the work is such that deadlines are missed and budgets for the new year are not available on time. The computerized financial model takes the drudgery out of the calculations, once the computer programs are prepared, by applying the given relationships to different sets of assumptions and conditions. This process of simulating different methods of operations is a big help in exploring the alternatives available in the planning process.

ZERO-BASE BUDGETING

Zero-base budgeting is a technique for short-term operational planning, whereby existing levels of expenditure on ongoing activities are systematically questioned. This is in contrast to the more common 'incremental' approach. In incremental budgeting, the benchmark tends to be the level of activity and expenditure in the immediate past, budget proposals being related to this in terms of 'more' or 'less'. In zero-base budgeting, the benchmark is the 'minimum survival' level of activity and expenditure as seen by the manager of the activity in question. If the budget proposal is only to maintain the existing level of activity, assuming this to be above the 'minimum survival' level, the proposal must explain why the additional expenditure involved over and above the 'minimum survival' level is justified. A manager in charge of several activities will be required to state which level of expenditure on each of these activities he would choose if he could only spend, say, 80 per cent of his budget. The point of this approach is to squeeze out 'budget slack' at the lower levels of decision making and to allow the senior levels to decide how, if at all, the balance of the budget will be spent.

INSTALLING THE SYSTEM

The organizational chart should be examined with a view to determining where the responsibility for sales, costs and profits really lies. Revisions, where appropriate, may be considered at this time. The organization structure should be so developed as to fix responsibility right down the line. There must be an organization chart which clearly defines the levels of responsibility and the chain of command, setting out who is responsible for what and to whom. It is desirable to support each functional position with a job description defining the function, duty and responsibility. Tradition must be ignored, responsibility and control being given to those who are responsible for taking the decisions, but care must be taken to preserve the 'business flair' of an organization, and those given the responsibility should be placed where their individual resources can be used best.

However, if one is to adhere to one of the basic principles of budgetary control, that people should be responsible for costs over which they have control, this report may not provide the solution.

The key factors should then be determined before designing the system most suitable to the company's needs. The system design should cover flow diagrams of the information generated, collection of data necessary for budget preparation and for control reports to be subsequently prepared. During this period consideration should be given to the level of sophistication of the existing information system, whether the proposed system will provide an improvement and also the level of human resources with which one has to work the new system.

Having obtained a positive reaction to these considerations, the next step is to test the initial design with various personnel at all levels in order to determine its suitability to meet their requirements for management information.

Once initial design is finalized, the next step is to prepare a series of seminars and teach-ins to explain the thinking behind the purpose and operation of the system. Questions, constructive criticisms and improvements should be invited so that all are involved and communicate at all levels.

A timetable for installation of the programme should be established. A critical path analysis is the ideal basis for identifying the order in which the budget data should be collected and which information is to be cross-referred to two or more departments.

Now is the time for the collection of information for the 'first budget'. Considerable time, assistance and guidance should be made available to staff at this stage, and perseverance on behalf of those taking responsibility for the installation of the system will be required. It is vital that all levels of management go through the discipline of thinking through and preparing their portion of the budgets. Miracles should not be expected from the first results. It is not unusual for a company to take two or three years to get a control system of this nature fully operational. However, at each stage one should expect to produce some results which are usable even in the first year. What these results will be may differ from company to company but initially they usually provide a good insight to sales and cash flow data. An important by-product is management education and awareness of what the business is all about.

Budget period

There is no general rule governing the selection of a period of time for a budget. This will be decided by the particular circumstances of the business. For instance, the fashion industry must, of necessity, have a very short budget period, sometimes of three or four months duration, whereas in the shipbuilding industry a budget may range over three or four years. For most businesses, however, the calendar year is normally the accepted period: it is broken down into twelve monthly periods and the information is complementary to the published accounts.

However, if there is a strong seasonal influence affecting sales, it is sometimes prudent to have a 'model year' upon which to base the budget and this usually starts just ahead of the main selling period. Businesses which rely mainly on the summer or Christmas trade may well justify a model year. Model years, as the name implies, usually commence with the introduction of new models. A car manufacturer, for example, may run its model year from September to the following August in order to have a good start to the year following the autumn motor shows and new year car registrations. The motive behind this is that if business has not gone as well as expected there is still sufficent time before the end of the model year to curtail activity, restrict costs and reconsider expansion programmes or introduce special promotions in order to keep profits in line with, or better than, budget.

Budget manual

It is helpful to have such a document available within the company so that there is no ambiguity about what is required of each individual in relation to budgets. The type of information one might expect the budget manual to contain is a brief explanation of the purposes of budgetary control as practised within the company and organization charts and job descriptions showing the specific budget responsibilities for each function; routing of budgetary control forms for collection and control documentation; timetables or programmes for completion of budgets and control data feedback; budget periods; samples of reports and statements to be employed and accounts classification and coding data.

Budget committees

The question of who should control the preparation of the budgets and who should review these controls is one that each organization arrives at during some stage of the budget preparation.

It is desirable that top and middle management contribute to and agree levels of activity to be budgeted, although it must be recognized that the human factor involved makes this difficult to achieve. A keen manager, anxious to please at a budget review meeting, will possibly incorporate a stretch element to his plan. Another manager setting his own targets against which his performance will be measured may be inclined to be over cautious (particularly if an achievement bonus is paid). Investigations have been made in this area and the results carry important lessons for the businessman interested in making the most of his budget system. One conclusion is that the budgets studied were used as pressure devices for constantly increasing efficiency, but because of the effects on people, the budgets tended to generate a long run result of decreased efficiency. Naturally enough, this is attributed to the lack of participation in the budget preparation phase by those being budgeted and to the lack of sales ability on the part of accounting personnel. Another study concludes that successful budgeting is more concerned with human relationships than with accounting techniques and that if good principles of human relationships are applied, successful budget practices will be inevitable. Yet another appraisal of current business budgeting indicates that important weaknesses in practice are the result of superficial appreciation of budget concepts by management, inadequate techniques, and the absence of a disciplined environment in many organizations. Upon reflection, it becomes apparent that the requirements for a successful budget operation are not restricted to accounting or finance planning techniques but that successful managers are those who keep wider considerations in mind while executing the more mechanical aspects of the budget process.

Various views are held on this point of responsibility. If operating managements are made responsible for profits, then one of the objectives of budgetary control, that is, the proper co-ordination of the organization, is achieved.

The same processes should be involved as with the control aspect. What an organization should attempt to achieve is the total commitment of all levels of management to the plan. Each level of management should review its plans and performances through the usual management committees, be they formal or informal groupings, right up to the chief executive, and the overall objective should be clear and unambiguous at each stage.

However, one person will be responsible for pulling together the various parts of the master budget. This job usually falls on the chief accountant or financial controller or his department. Larger companies employ a budget manager and, of course, this co-ordinating exercise naturally falls into his lap. He may be called upon to undertake a number of exercises to determine what the various results thrown up mean within the overall company objectives, but it must be emphasized that his role is one of support. The responsibility is fixed upon the persons committing and accepting stewardship over resources.

The budget organization can be regarded as analogous to a telephone company operating an important communications system; it is responsible for the speed, accuracy and clarity with which the messages flow through the system, but not for the content of the messages themselves.

Information codes

Budgetary control has extended control information beyond the more traditional accounting information to broader aspects of control, setting out data in terms of hours worked, ouput of production in standard hours, information on market share, quality of product, etc. This is all necessary for the achievement of the plan. However, looking at the pure accounting contribution to budgetary control, a suitable system of accounts coding should be designed so that the information is collected and analysed within the budget and cost centres.

The accounting code should be what is commonly called a subjective/objective system. The subjective part of the code should qualify information into its primary or traditional classification, that is, the nature of the expense, for example wages, fuel, rent, etc. The objective part of the code will be used to analyse the expenditure to the cost and burden centres, that is, machine X in the machine shop.

It is important to give considerable thought to the design of the coding system, as it should not only allow for coping with existing needs for information, but also have the flexibility to be expanded to meet future demands. A system of this sort should enable a company, using the subjective code, to produce information necessary for the preparation of the traditional statutory accounts. And by going through the objective section of the code, the information required for budgetary control and management accounting can be produced which should be made available to those drawing up the budgets as appropriate.

CONCLUSIONS

Budgetary control often strikes apprehension or fear into non-financial people. People tend to be sceptical or mistrust having their performances measured against a standard. This is a human and understandable response. Most people, at some time during their careers, have had budgetary control used against them as a cost reduction tool.

It is up to finance managers to clarify and emphasize that budget flexing and control is an essential and deliberate need of modern day management. It is a management tool designed as a fair basis upon which to measure performance against a predetermined plan, and conduct business in the most efficient manner possible, thereby improving profitability.

8

Costing and internal pricing

H. W. Calvert and Simon Archer

The purpose of costing is generally to find out the cost of an organization's outputs. These can be either its final outputs (products or services made available to the outside world) or intermediate outputs used within the organization in the production of its final outputs. Costing therefore involves two phases of fact finding activities

1 Finding out the quantities of inputs required or used in the production of outputs.
2 Finding out the cost of those quantities of inputs.

Internal pricing refers to the situation where one organizational sub-unit produces an output which is used as an input by another sub-unit of the same organization, and it is desired to charge the second sub-unit with a transferred-in cost.

Apart from its purely fact finding aspects, a major problem in costing arises when a number of outputs are joint products of some input. Typically this is the case with those inputs of an organization we generally call 'overheads'. The problem here is that the determination of exactly how much of these inputs has gone into any given quantity of outputs is arbitrary. This problem occurs in a severe form in many transport businesses: how to deal with overheads or 'system costs' in working out, say, the cost per passenger mile or tonne mile. A similar difficulty arises in businesses such as petrochemicals, where a given quantity of a particular raw material is turned into a number of joint products within a sequence of processes. The problem here is how to allocate the cost of the raw material to the various joint products derived from it. Again, any such allocation is arbitrary. These kinds of *ad hoc* allocations can be misleading if they are used as data for a decision (such as product pricing) without their arbitrariness being recognized. This problem poses a particular challenge to management accountants working within the kinds of industries mentioned, but they are liable to arise to some extent in almost any kind of organization.

The information provided by costing is clearly among the most vital to any organization. The production and marketing activities cannot proceed in a rational manner without it. Good costing presupposes an accurate and detailed knowledge of how outputs are produced, and typically requires co-operation between accountants on the one hand and engineers or others having the required knowledge of the product on the other. Depending on the complexity of the product, good costing may also require the application of well-developed data processing capabilities, for example computerized bill of materials systems. Often, therefore, it is best to regard costing as a co-operative effort between accountants and other colleagues having the necessary knowledge and skills.

The need for co-operation with engineers or production people is particularly evident where a standard costing approach is adopted. In standard costing, a cost is developed for each output, intermediate or final, so as to act as a norm or guideline for the purpose of cost control. Costs actually incurred can then be compared against the standards, and the differences or variances can be analysed in a number of ways so that requirements or opportunities for cost improvements can be identified. Standard costs may also be useful for internal pricing and as a check on prices charged for final outputs.

STANDARD COSTING

Standard costing has much in common with budgetary control, which was considered in Chapter 7. On the one hand, standard cost data can be extremely useful in compiling budgets, particularly for such items as raw material costs; on the other hand, budget data may be required to establish the standard cost allowances for overhead items. We return to these matters later in this chapter. Since costs are built up on the basis of the determination of input quantities followed by the determination of the costs of those quantities, a full standard costing approach involves standards both for the input quantities and for the unit costs applicable to those quantities. In certain cases, however, it may be possible to establish standard data for quantities but not for unit costs, or vice versa. For example, an important raw material may be subject to extreme price volatility so that the usefulness of a standard cost may be questionable; nevertheless it may be perfectly feasible and useful to establish standard quantities. Alternatively, the products may be essentially of a non-standard nature, made to customer order, so that the establishment of standard quantities may be possible only for a limited number of inputs, while the establishment of standard unit prices for those inputs may not be difficult at all.

Apart from their use in cost control, standard cost data are often more convenient to use than 'actual' cost data. For example, if a stock of raw materials is accounted for using standard costs, variances from standard purchase prices (material purchase price variances) are isolated when the materials are purchased. Thus, the raw materials may be held in stock at standard cost, and any subsequent movements of the materials out of stores and through work in progress into finished goods stock will be likewise accounted for at standard costs. This avoids the need to establish 'actual' costs for materials subsequent to purchase, whether on a first-in-first-out, weighted-average or other conventional basis.

In costing, the original or prime inputs are conventionally divided into three categories of cost elements

1 Materials – these are the materials which go physically into the final output in some shape or form, and this is emphasized by the frequently used term, 'direct materials'.
2 Labour – again, this category normally includes only the labour which is a direct physical input to the product, and excludes the work of supervisors, etc. It is likewise frequently referred to as direct labour.
3 Overheads – which are any cost elements not falling into either of the two previously mentioned categories.

FIXING A STANDARD

Standard costing being a technique of comparisons – the actual with the standard – the first problem is to fix the standard. Three types of standard are generally considered.

Historical

This is based on costs previously achieved and may easily be ascertained, but it has two principal defects. Standard costing will be of no value when applied to an industrial unit where control has been inadequate. In such an organization the past performance may provide a weak standard which could be easily attained and so give little incentive to management and factory supervision. Also, if standard costs based on such a foundation are used as a guide to price fixing, then either prices may be fixed at an uncompetitive level or the sales department may consider that many lines cannot be remunerative.

Ideal

This is based on the assumptions that plant will always work at full available capacity; there will be no unavoidable loss of material; the highest grade of labour will be available and there will be no lost time. Such a standard would present a target which the most energetic supervisor would not attempt to attain and a cost which could never be achieved in practice. The result might be that the sales department would be tempted to offer products at unremunerative prices.

Normal or expected

This is based, probably after work study, on agreement between the management functions concerned – production, personnel, purchasing and costing – on the levels which could be attained under normal working conditions. For most purposes this type of standard is to be preferred.

Revision of standards

In conditions of inflation, and generally when prices are unstable, it is most important that standards be kept up to date. How frequently it may be possible to revise the standards at an acceptable cost depends both on the complexity of the product involved and on the extent to which the required product information is available in an appropriate form for computerized updating of standard costs. It is not uncommon for standards to be updated more than once a year, say, six-months or even quarterly. On the other hand, in some industries the complexity of the product is such that a high degree of data processing sophistication is necessary for thorough updating to be feasible at all. In the absence of such a capability, reliance has to be placed upon approximate methods such as the application of indices on an 'across the board' basis rather than on updating the costs of individual cost elements. The problem with this latter approach is that the revised standards progressively lose their character as cost norms which can be used for control purposes. Variances are as much a function of the indices being used as of cost abnormality which requires follow-up action.

In addition to updating prices or unit costs, standards must be revised whenever there is a change in the technical specification of a product. This requires co-operation between the engineering section where specification changes are worked out, the purchasing and production sections whose actions govern the introduction of the revised items, and the costing section. Lack of co-ordination often leads to a situation where inputs are being accounted for on the basis of one set of standards (typically, the new standards), while the outputs are being accounted for on the basis of another set of standards (typically, the old or unrevised standards). This discrepancy leads to an accumulation of erroneous charges or credits in the accounts for stock or work in progress.

Direct materials

The standard cost of direct materials will depend on the standard quantity of material to be used per unit produced and the standard price of that material. The quantity will be based on the specification of the product and the process losses and rejects which are agreed as the standard between production management and the cost department. The standard price will be based on the average price which should be paid over the period under consideration, taking into account that a material may have to be purchased from several suppliers.

Direct labour

Where possible the standard cost of direct labour should be based on a work study of the operations involved. This will fix the standard times for each process and, where an incentive scheme is in operation, the standard hourly rate will be that which would be payable at the standard efficiency.

Conventionally, the standard cost of direct labour tends to be considered in a manner analogous to the standard cost of direct materials, that is, as a straightforward multiple of the units of output. In many circumstances, however, the cost of direct labour may be relatively invariable with respect to the level of output in the short term. In other words, the cost of direct labour may behave in a manner much closer to that of overheads than to that of direct materials. In such circumstances, it may be advisable to abandon or modify the conventional treatment of direct labour; for example, by treating it similarly to a semi-variable overhead as described below.

Overheads

For the purpose of standard costing, three elements of overhead costs need to be distinguished

1 Fixed costs — costs which do not vary in the short term with volume.
2 Variable costs — costs which do so vary.
3 Semi-variable costs — costs which will vary with volume but not in direct relationship.

In determining standard unit costs of outputs, it might appear obvious that only the variable overheads can properly be taken into account. It is not possible to establish the amount of fixed or semi-variable costs at the unit level, since the amounts of such costs do not vary proportionately with the number of units. The most logical approach is to integrate the standard costs per unit with a system of flexible budgets as described in Chapter 7. With such an approach, variances with respect to unit standard costs can be identified separately from variances with respect to the budget allowances for fixed and semi-variable costs. The standard or allowed cost per unit will vary according to the level of output achieved: it is equal to the standard variable cost per unit as shown in Table 7.3 in Chapter 7 plus the total budget allowance for fixed and semi-variable costs at the relevant level of output divided by the number of units produced.

An alternative, but less satisfactory, approach is to assume a normal level of production or output, and to calculate the standard overhead cost per unit by taking the total overhead budget allowance at that level of output and dividing it by the number of units to be produced at that level. This approach gives rise to 'volume variances' whenever the level of output is different from the pre-established normal level. Given the inherent uncertainties of most business activities, however, it is questionable how informative such 'volume variances' are for control purposes. Certainly, the flexible budget approach is far more powerful for cost control purposes. Moreover, it is probably misleading to speak of a 'normal level' of output rather than a 'normal range' which will correspond to, or fall within the range of outputs allowed for in the flexible budget. Where the 'normal level' approach is adopted, however, one of the three bases mentioned above (historical, ideal or expected) will be used for fixing the standard unit overhead cost. The appropriate procedures for dealing with overhead costs on this basis are described in the relevant sections below.

One significant advantage of the flexible budget approach is that it can be used to give guidance on what is often a very important piece of information: the additional cost, at a given level of output, of producing one or more additional units (or the costs avoided if one or more fewer units are produced). This is known as the differential or marginal cost of the units in question. The topic of marginal costing is explored later in this chapter.

COST CONTROL THROUGH VARIANCE ANALYSIS

The most important service which standard costing can give to management is information for the control of costs through variance analysis. The difference between the variation of the production for a period at standard cost and the actual cost for that period is of great use to management, but even greater is the consideration of changes in this variance from one period to another. This shows how efficiency is moving.

The standard cost of production of each section for the period under consideration will be calculated first. This will be the quantity of each item actually produced, multiplied by its standard cost in that process. It will represent the cost which should have been incurred under standard conditions. The actual cost incurred will be available from the records kept in the financial and cost accounting departments. As already noted, it is common to account for raw materials held in stock and their subsequent movements at standard cost, the material purchase price variance being isolated upon purchase. Variances in the quantities of raw materials used will, however, be identified in production; these materials' usage variances will be expressed in money using the standard prices of the materials concerned. They will be identified for particular production cost centres and perhaps, in job order type businesses, by customer order as well. Moreover, in a job order kind of business, it may be important to identify also the material purchase price variances associated with particular customer orders, and in that case actual material costs will be made available from the store issues and invoices for materials charged direct to individual orders.

The direct and indirect labour costs of production will be available from the wages analysis. Again, the labour cost variance typically comprises a price (or rate) variance and a quantity (or efficiency) variance. These variances will be calculated for each production cost centre, and in addition, as in the case of materials, it may be necessary to identify the variances at the level of particular customer orders. Other items of overheads can be obtained from suppliers' invoices and from the apportionment of whole items of expense to the various production cost centres. The latter will apply to service charges, electricity, insurance, rates, and similar items which are not allocated in the original charge.

Direct materials

The analysis of direct material costs can be obtained in the following manner. If the standard for producing one unit of product Z is, say, 10 lb of material XY at a standard price of 20 pence per pound, that is £2.00 per unit, and if the production in week eight is 2000 units, the standard cost of material for the week will be

$$£2.00 \times 2000 = £4000$$

If the actual consumption of material has been 20 500 lb which has cost £4260, there will have been an adverse direct material cost variance of £260(A), where (A) stands for 'adverse'. This information is useful to management as £260 is a significant amount which must be investigated. The variance may be due to a number of factors which must be isolated. The most important are the price and usage variances into which the direct material cost variance is usually analysed.

The direct material price variance is the difference between what the material used should have cost and what it actually cost. In this case the material used should have cost

$$£0.20 \times 20\ 500 = £4100$$

As the actual cost was £4260, the direct material price variance is £160(A). The quantity of material which should have been used was

$$2000 \times 10 \text{ lb} = 20\ 000 \text{ lb}$$

so there is an excess usage of 500 lb which at the standard price of 20 pence, costs £100. This is the direct material usage variance which, again, is adverse. Note that the price and usage variances together make up the total direct material cost variance, that is

$$£160(A) + £100(A) = £260(A)$$

Where more than one material is used in making a product the price variance is generally shown in respect of each material. The usage variance can be calculated for each material, but in cases where the proportions of certain materials may vary, if there is a difference in the price of the materials, a cost variance will arise from any variation in the composition of the mixture.

If an alloy is made of 70 per cent of 'X' and 30 per cent of 'B' which cost, at standard prices, £200 per ton and £300 per ton, respectively, and a batch of metal is made up from 600 ton of 'x' and 400 ton of 'y', there will be a materials mixture variance. At standard prices the 1000 tons should have cost

$$£(700 \times 200) + £(300 \times 300) = £230\ 000$$

whereas the cost was

$$£(600 \times 200) + £(400 \times 300) = £240\ 000$$

giving a material mixture variance of £100(A).

The material mixture variance is always calculated on the standard prices after the price variance has been taken on the actual material used. The fact that the proportions of the materials in a mixture are not as standard is no guarantee that a mixture variance presents reliable information. The use of an excess of one or more of the materials may be due to process technicalities.

The direct material usage variance is defined as that portion of the direct materials cost variance which is due to the difference between the standard quantity specified and the actual quantity used. Where there is a mixture variance, the difference from standard due to the total quantity of materials used is referred to as the direct materials yield variance. The mixture and yield variances will together equal the usage variance so that where there is no mixture variance shown, the usage variance and the yield variance will be the same.

Labour

The analysis of cost variances for labour is similar to that of materials, except that the major sub-variances are referred to as rate and efficiency instead of price and usage. Each production manager will require a further analysis of the efficiency variance according to the techniques of the operations and the relative significance of the individual variances.

If, in the above mentioned case, the labour cost had been set at a standard of production of five units per labour hour with an hourly wage rate at this level of productivity of 60 pence per hour, that is, 12 pence per unit, and the wages cost of production in week eight had been 420 hours, which cost £246, there would be a direct wages variance of £6(A) because the standard wages cost was

$$2000 \times £0.12 = £240$$

The analysis of this variance would be direct wages rate variance

$$420 \times £0.60 - £246 = £6(F)$$

The variance is favourable, (F), because the actual cost was less than the hours worked at the standard rate.

The direct labour efficiency variance will be

$$(420 - 400) \times £0.60 = £12(A)$$

— adverse because the actual hours worked exceeded the standard hours for the actual production.

Where a financial incentive scheme is in operation, it is generally found that an adverse efficiency variance will result in a favourable rate variance owing to the average rate earned being less than the standard. Conversely, if there is a favourable efficiency variance, the bonus will be high and there will be an adverse rate variance.

Overheads

For the purpose of variance analysis it is advisable to have the overheads divided into variable and fixed costs. A standard having been agreed for the variable overhead, the variable overhead variance can be calculated by multiplying the production for the period by this unit standard cost and comparing the result with the actual expenditure on account of the relative indirect costs. These items can be obtained from the stores requisitions, wages analysis, etc. A more detailed analysis of variable overhead variance may not be justified on account of the expense, but, if required, that part which is due to prices can be calculated, as can variances in the quantities of the items utilized.

As mentioned earlier, fixed overheads are a 'period' cost so that the unit cost must be compiled from the expenditure, production and working hours budgeted for the same period. In the case of product XYZ, assuming that the budget for the year is a production of 110 000 units to be produced in 50 working weeks of 440 hours each at a fixed overhead cost of £5500, the unit cost of fixed overheads will thus be 5 pence, and the rate per hours worked 25 pence. If the actual fixed overhead is recorded as £122 for week eight, the standard cost of the production is

$$2000 \times £0.05 = £100$$

so the fixed overhead cost variance is £22(A). This variance arises from two factors; the difference between the actual expenditure (£122) and the budget amount allowed for the period (£110) which gives a fixed overhead expenditure variance of £12(A), and the difference between the actual production for the week (2000 units) and the budgeted production (2200 units) which gives the overhead volume variance

$$(2200 - 2000) \times £0.05 = £10(A)$$

Again, the expenditure variance and the volume variance add up to the fixed overhead cost variance

$$£12(A) + £10(A) = £22(A)$$

The expenditure variance arises from the prices of the items included in the fixed overhead and the utilization of the factors employed — higher wattage lamps being used in corridors, extra security staff being required. The volume variance is due to the production being above or below the budgeted figure, the result of the number of hours worked being above or below the budget, and the labour efficiency being favourable or adverse.

The capacity usage variance is favourable if more hours than the budgeted number have been worked. This can cause some difficulty unless it is remembered that the more hours worked, the more should be produced, other things being equal. In week eight, 420 hours were worked against a budget of 440, so there was a loss of twenty working hours which, at the fixed overhead cost of 25 pence per hour, is a variance of £5(A).

The volume efficiency variance is related to the labour efficiency variance if the former has been based on labour hours. In some cases it may be based on machine hours. As the production is equal to 4000 standard hours there is again a loss

$$(420 - 400) \times £0.25 = £5(A)$$

The capacity usage variance and the volume efficiency variance are together equal to the volume variance.

Where the fixed overhead is budgeted on a monthly basis and the number of working days in the month varies, the volume variance may include a calendar variance. This will be favourable when the number of working days in a month exceeds the average, and adverse when it is less. The greater the number of days in the month, the higher the production should be, thus tending to improve variances. The sum of the calendar variance for the year will always be nil.

It has been shown how the total production cost variance can be analysed so as to give more accurate information regarding the cause of excesses and savings. A chart of this analysis, such as that shown in Figure 8.1 may be useful. It is not exhaustive and further analysis can be made to suit individual requirements.

Figure 8.1   Chart of production cost variance

Table 8.1
Example of a cost report

DEPARTMENT X   OPERATION X12A   PRODUCT XYZ

Report for week no. 8, ending 2 May 19. . Standard cost per unit: £2.22

		Budget	Standard	Actual	Variance	Analysis
Production	units	2200		2000	200 (A)	
Materials	lb	22 000	20 000	20 500	500 (A)	
Labour hours		440	400	420	20 (A)	
Costs						
Direct materials	£	4400	4000	4260	260 (A)	
Price						160 (A)
Usage						100 (A)
Direct labour		264	240	246	6 (A)	
Rate						6 (F)
Efficiency						12 (A)
Overhead variable		110	100	106	6 (A)	
Price						8 (A)
Utilization						2 (F)
Overhead fixed		110	100	122	22 (A)	
Price						10 (A)
Utilization						2 (A)
= Expenditure						12 (A)
Calendar						—
Capacity usage						5 (A)
Volume efficiency						5 (A)
= Volume						10 (A)
Totals	£	4884	4440	4734	294 (A)	

Note: The standard cost for the period will bear the same ratio to the budgeted cost as the *actual* production bears to the budgeted production.

Presentation

The presentation of the analysis of the cost variances is very important; it should be prepared so as to show the maximum information in the minimum space and with economy of figures. A cost report on week eight from the figures previously quoted might appear as shown in Table 8.1.

MARGINAL COSTING

As mentioned earlier, the differential or marginal cost of one or more units of output is equal to the change in the total cost of output dependent on whether or not a company produces that unit or those units. In the case of one marginal unit, marginal cost is equal to the standard unit cost plus the change in the total semi-variable costs. The latter may be zero or may be relatively large depending on whether the change in output level encounters a capacity constraint and, if so, the financial implications of that constraint.

One possible capacity constraint relates to direct labour. The decision to produce the marginal unit or marginal lot of units may or may not saturate the capacity of normal shift working and give rise to overtime payments or shift premium payments which exceed the basic standard direct labour cost per unit. Such overtime or additional shift work may also call for an increase in supervisory labour expense, and so forth. In this connection, the warning given earlier about the treatment of direct labour as an element of standard variable cost per unit needs to be recalled. Direct labour used to be considered a variable cost because, if trade was slack, workers were discharged or stood off without pay. More recently, the cost of training labour, periodic difficulty in obtaining even untrained labour and the economic consequences of the guaranteed working week and redundancy provisions have tended to make labour costs a fixed expense which only changes with large and prolonged variations in the volume of production.

Marginal production cost should not, however, be taken to be identical to standard variable unit production cost. To equate these is to ignore the kinds of production capacity constraints referred to earlier. The technique of direct costing (sometimes erroneously called marginal costing or, more correctly, variable costing) involves the use of the standard variable unit cost as the basis for keeping the accounts for finished stock and work in progress. In addition, production cost variances are related either to the standard variable cost per unit on the one hand, or to the flexible budget for semi-variable and fixed expenses on the other.

Moreover, the use of flexible budgets does not concern production costs alone. It also relates to the costs of selling and distributing output. Here too, some costs may vary directly with the level of sales, others may be fixed in regard to that level and others may be semi-variable. Thus, a profit and loss statement based on a marginal costing approach will generally show a 'contribution margin' which is equal to sales less total directly variable costs. This contribution margin can also be calculated at the unit level for individual products.

The term 'contribution margin' is, perhaps, somewhat misleading insofar as the amount calculated as just described is not identical with the true marginal contribution to profit of the unit or units in question. This is because no account has been taken of possible changes in the level of the semi-variable expenses. Nevertheless, the standard contribution margin and variances from it have proved to be useful control tools, especially in high volume consumer product businesses where marketing activities are organized on a product management basis. For this reason, and for the sake of simplicity, the behaviour of semi-variable expenses is ignored in the following example.

The first applications of marginal costing were as a technique for use in times of trade recession when plant was under utilized and business could not be obtained at prices which would cover the total unit costs, that is,

Table 8.2
Marginal costing in a time of trade recession

Plant capacity	100 000 units
Cost of 100 000 units	£
Direct materials	300 000
Direct labour	100 000
Variable production overhead	10 000
Fixed production overhead	150 000
Administration expenses	80 000
Variable selling expenses	10 000
Fixed selling expenses	50 000
	£700 000 = £7 per unit

the variable unit cost plus the total fixed expenses divided by the number of units produced. The simple example contained in Table 8.2 illustrates such as situation.

At a sales price of £8 per unit a profit of £100 000 will be made, and this may be a fair return on the capital employed in the business. However, if the plant is working at only 80 per cent of capacity the variable cost will be 80 per cent of £420 000 or £336 000. The fixed expenses will remain at £280 000, giving a total cost of £616 000. The sales at £8 per unit will be £640 000 giving a net profit of only £24 000. The sales department is unable to obtain any further business at £8 to fill the vacant capacity, but a customer can be found for 10 000 units at £6.50. This business appears to be unremunerative as the total cost is £7.00 per unit. However, on a marginal cost basis the unit cost is £4.20, so that the price of £6.50 will show a contribution of £2.30 per unit and this will increase the net profit by £23 000, nearly doubling that important figure.

Useful as the marginal costing technique is, certain precautions must be observed when using it and there are certain restrictions on its use. The most significant of these are

1   Business at such cut prices must not be taken on long term contracts where there is a chance that before the contract is completed trade may improve and orders at more remunerative prices could be booked.

2   Business must not be taken on a marginal cost basis in the same market where more normal prices are being obtained. This policy might offend established customers and, in the case of overseas business, care must be taken that the low price exports do not come back into this country in competition with the company's own sales in the home market.

BREAK EVEN GRAPHS

On the assumption that no significant distortion will occur if costs are divided into directly variable and fixed, so that variable cost is a good approximation of marginal cost, it is possible to draw simple break even graphs or profit charts. Assuming that all expenses other than directly variable costs are stable throughout the probable range of sales, the marginal cost aspect can be presented in the following manner.

A graph is drawn taking the horizontal axis as the amount of the sales, either in quantity or in value; if a number of items are sold the total figure must be expressed in value. The sales figure will start at zero and cover the maximum range of the sales. The vertical axis will represent the receipts from sales and the expenses incurred, both fixed and variable.

Having estimated the fixed expenses for the period under review, this point is located on the vertical axis and from it a line is drawn parallel to the horizontal axis. From the production cost budget and the selling cost budget the marginal cost of the budgeted sales can be ascertained. A line can now be drawn from the point on the vertical axis from which the fixed

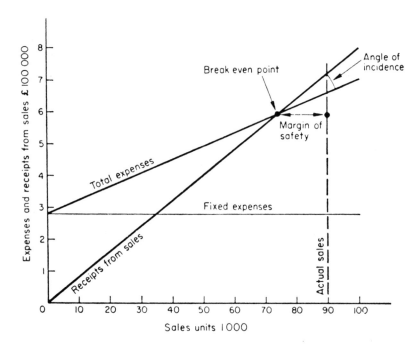

Figure 8.2 **Example of an orthodox break even graph**

cost line started so as to show at the budgeted sales the total expenses of the organization for that level of sales. In the graph in Figure 8.2 the fixed expenses have been taken as £280 000 per annum, and the variable costs of £100 000 units as $420 000.

The 'receipts from sales' line can now be drawn, commencing from the origin where the vertical and horizontal axes meet to show sales of

£800 000 for £100 000 units. Assuming that there is a contribution, that is, that the sales price exceeds the variable cost, this line will cut the line of total cost at a point where the receipt from sales equals the total cost. This junction is called the break even point, the level of activity at which there is neither profit nor loss. The distance of the receipt from sales line above or below the total cost line will show the net profit at the relative level of sales.

Profit/volume (P/V) ratio

The break even graph will show at a glance the sales which must be achieved to obtain any required net profit, and also the effect on the profit potential of variations in the fixed expenses and the profit volume ratio. The P/V ratio is an important factor in planning the profitability of an enterprise; it is the relation of the contribution to the net sales expressed as a percentage. A trading concern will aim to concentrate its business on the products which offer the highest P/V ratio, subject to factors which will be considered later.

The greater the P/V ratio the wider will be the angle at which the receipt from sales line cuts the line of total cost. This angle is known as the angle of incidence and it should be watched carefully.

Another important feature of the break even graph is the excess of the sales for any period over the sales for the same period at the break even point. The difference, which is known as the margin of safety, should also be watched carefully as it indicates the amount by which the sales can fall before the profit made will be reduced to zero and losses will start to be incurred.

In drawing a break even graph it must be remembered that in practice the fixed expenses are not constant for all levels of activity; they tend to increase in stages as the activity rises, but they do not fall so quickly when there is a recession in trade. Account must also be taken of the tendency for sales prices to fall if sales are pushed beyond a certain point. This may be due to larger trade discounts being granted. Variable costs may be reduced by bulk buying when trade expands, but higher rates may have to be paid for skilled labour if the demand increases. These factors must be considered when the line of total cost is drawn; in practice it will not be straight but may curve upwards or downwards.

The break even graph may be used for other purposes as well as showing the effect of varying levels of sales on the net profit. Other applications include the evaluation of different methods of distribution.

Should the company run its own van or send its goods by carrier? Here the comparison is that of a fixed cost per article or per tonne mile (the total cost depending on the quantity carried) with the fixed cost of a van (tax, insurance, depreciation, garage and driver's costs) plus a running cost per mile or tonne mile. The break even graph may be used to show the amount of traffic which must be handled to make the introduction of the van an economic project.

The graph in Figure 8.2 shows a break even chart based on the figures given earlier. The graph in Figure 8.3 gives an indication of the effect of allowing for the behaviour of the semi-variable expenses which have been included with the fixed expenses. The effect of the capacity constraints which determine the behaviour of the semi-variable expenses is shown in the characteristic step function of the latter.

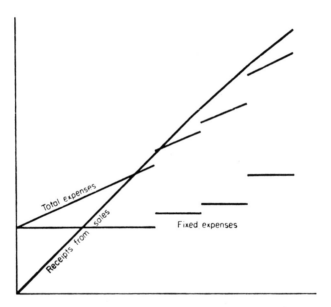

Figure 8.3   Example of a modified break even graph

'Profit' or 'contribution' chart

The break even graph is fairly well known in industry, but for most purposes the profit chart will present the same information in a simpler manner, with less probability of errors in drafting, and in a way which often displays the effect of a policy more clearly. In the profit chart the horizontal axis can be drawn as for the break even graph, but to obtain the best effect, the way this is positioned on the page is most important. The vertical axis will be drawn below, as well as above, the horizontal axis. It will be graded in values but, instead of showing costs and receipts from sales, it will show profits above the horizontal axis and losses below the horizontal axis.

Taking the case previously quoted, if there were no sales there would be a loss equal to the fixed expenses of £280 000. This fixes one point on the profit line; zero on the sales line and minus £280 on the profit axis. As there is a contribution of £3.80 per unit until, at sales of 100 000 units, the loss of £280 is converted into a profit of £100 000.

The graph thus drawn is that not of cost and sales but of the contribution. This line will cut the horizontal axis at the break even point; the horizontal axis is therefore sometimes called the break even line. To

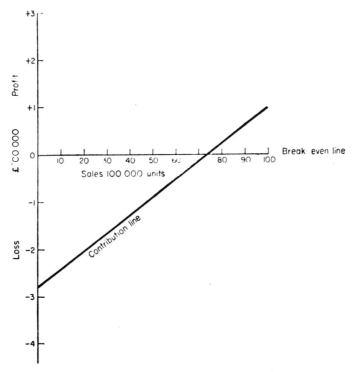

Figure 8.4   Example of a profit or contribution chart

obtain the best use of the page an estimate should be made of the highest figure which the fixed expenses are likely to reach and also the net profit. The break even line can then be placed so that a scale can be used which will make full use of the page. Figure 8.4 shows the information used for the graph in Figure 8.2 in the form of a profit chart.

Limiting factor

The P/V ratio is of great value to management, but the product which shows the highest P/V ratio may not always provide the maximum profit. Some factor limits the activity of every business; it may be sales, finance or one element of production, plant capacity, labour or materials. Shortage of one item of material or one grade of labour may be the limiting factor. If the plant is not fully occupied and there is no shortage of the labour and materials required, then provided the company has the financial resources, sales will be the limiting factor. The sales department will push the sales of the items with the highest P/V ratios.

Where, however, the plant can be fully employed, the use of restricted facilities must be taken into consideration. In Table 8.3 it is assumed that the sales department has ample orders to employ the factory at the prices quoted.

Table 8.3
Comparisons of P/V ratios and profit contributions

Product	A	B
Units produced per hour	10	20
	£	£
Direct materials	4.00	8.00
Direct labour	0.08	0.04
Variable production overhead	0.16	0.08
Variable selling overhead	0.40	0.60
Total marginal cost	4.64	8.72
Selling price	5.80	10.17
Contribution	£1.16	1.45
P/V ratio per cent	20	14

Although the P/V ratio of A is much higher than B, the contribution per unit of B is greater than for A, and the contribution per hour will be £29 for B against £11.60 for product A, because twice as many units of B can be produced as units of A. Where products have to pass through several processes, the planning of production and sales to obtain the optimum product mixture is most important. It is not always best to concentrate on the products which show the highest P/V ratio or even the highest contribution per unit. Sometimes a product mixture which leaves certain units of the plant underemployed will yield the highest contribution and profit.

This example shows the danger of a sales department fixing selling prices on the basis of costs, total or marginal, without understanding the implication of limiting factors which may operate with regard to certain processes.

MAKE OR BUY?

An important decision may often face the management when the plant is fully occupied and components are required which could be made in the factory or purchased from outside sources. Apart from considerations of quality, reliability of delivery and credit terms, the profit position can be assessed by the application of marginal costing. The following simple example will demonstrate the basis for a management decision.

Table 8.4
Cost comparisons between manufactured and bought-in components

Component units produced per hour	X 20	Z 30
Direct labour	£0.05	0.033
Direct materials	4.00	3.00
Other variable costs	0.45	0.167
Total marginal cost	4.50	3.20
Purchase price outside	5.50	4.00
Saving per unit if made in the factory	1.00	0.80
Saving per hour if made in the factory	20.00	24.00

If there is not sufficient plant capacity to produce the requirements of both components, it will pay to make Z and buy X, for although the saving on Z is only £0.80 per unit as compared with £1.00 per unit for X, the saving per machine hour is £24 for Z against £20 for X. Assuming fixed overhead on the machine will be the same in each case, an apportionment of this cost to the two components is unnecessary and has therefore been ignored.

The application of marginal costing may highlight important factors when a decision has to be made as to which of two or more factories should be closed because capacity exceeds needs.

Opportunity costs

The example just given is also helpful in illustrating the concept of opportunity cost which is often highly relevant to management decisions. The saving per hour if component Z is made in the factory can also be described as the opportunity cost of transferring one hour's worth of production of Z to outside purchase. The corresponding opportunity cost of relieving in-house production of one hour's production of X is £20. An opportunity cost of £20 is clearly more acceptable than an opportunity cost of £24, so that it is preferable to transfer the production of X to outside purchase.

TREATMENT OF FIXED PRODUCTION EXPENSES FOR FINANCIAL STATEMENTS PREPARATION

Generally accepted accounting principles for external financial reporting purposes, as well as the Inland Revenue, require stock and profit figures to be calculated on the basis that the value of stock includes an allowance for fixed costs per unit. Thus, where marginal or variable costing is used for management accounting purposes, it will be necessary to make a calculation at the end of each major financial reporting period (that is, yearly, quarterly or even monthly) of the amount of fixed overhead to be included in the closing stock and work in progress figure for that period. Since any such allocation of fixed expenses to individual units is arbitrary, there would seem to be no point in seeking an elaborate and cumbersome solution to this problem. For example, a relationship can be established between standard variable cost and the total of fixed and semi-variable costs per period so that for the purpose of calculating stock and cost of goods sold a percentage is added to the standard directly variable costs in respect of the fixed and semi-variable cost elements.

Suppose that for the period in question the total fixed and semi-variable costs of production amounted to three times the total standard directly variable costs of production. Then it would be reasonable to add a three hundred per cent overhead burden to the standard variable cost of stock to arrive at the balance sheet figure. This figure would therefore be entered in the stock account and a corresponding credit would be made to the account for cost of goods sold. At the beginning of the ensuing period, these entries would be reversed, thus reducing stock to standard variable cost and charging the same amount back to the account for the cost of goods sold. The same procedure would be followed at the end of the ensuing period, using the appropriate corresponding data. Thus, the figure of cost of goods sold for this period will be reduced by the additional overheads applied to stock at the end of the period but also increased by the amount of additional overheads which had been applied to stock at the end of the previous period.

In certain cases, it may be thought desirable to sub-divide stock in the various categories so as to establish more detailed figures for the fixed overhead applied. However, it is difficult to see the point of this unless the business in question is faced with a situation where the concept of 'full cost per unit' has a particularly important significance. Businesses which work extensively on contracts established on the basis of 'full cost plus' are a case in point; however, such businesses do not generally find it so useful to employ variable or marginal costing in the first place.

INTERNAL PRICING

When considering the issues of internal pricing, it is necessary to recall what was said in Chapter 6 about responsibility centres. The issue here is somewhat different, depending on whether the goods or services transferred internally pass between two cost centres or two profit centres.

Transfers between cost centres

The obvious basis for making transfers between two cost centres is to use the standard cost of the goods or services transferred. This would be a standard 'full' cost or a standard variable cost depending on the type of costing system in use. However, this approach can be used only when a standard cost for the goods or services transferred has been established. In addition, there are circumstances when the inclusion of an element of fixed cost may have a counter-productive effect on the decisions made by the people involved.

To deal with the first point, it will generally be possible to arrive at a standard, or at least at a budgeted, cost per unit of the transferred goods or service (provided, in the case of services, a convenient measuring unit is available). But whether this standard or budget allowance per unit should be so calculated as to include a unit fixed cost element is a more delicate issue. Under the internal pricing mechanism, the standard cost per unit is used to charge the transferee cost centre for each unit it uses, and to credit the transferor cost centre for each unit it transfers. Where the use of the transferred good or service represents a discretionary cost to the transferee cost centre, the situation is similar to a transfer between two profit centres.

A fairly familiar example is the use of the services of a duplicating department by other departments in an organization. The duplicating department establishes a standard cost per page for various types of duplicating work, and these costs are used as transfer prices to charge the various user departments for the work done on their behalf. The calculation of unit fixed costs and the inclusion of these in the standard costs used as transfer prices mean that costs which are fixed to the duplicating department appear as variable costs in the accounts of the user departments, since, of course, they vary according to the amount of duplicating work done for them. Increased use of the duplicating facility, therefore, will cause an apparent cost increase in the accounts of the user department or departments concerned in excess of the increased cost to the organization as a whole. (The latter, of course, is equal to the marginal cost of the additional work, not the so called 'full' cost.) This may lead to wrong decisions, as discussed in the next section.

Transfers between profit centres

The appropriate way to account for transfers between profit centres depends on two factors

1 Whether or not the goods or services transferred are of a kind for which an external market exists, so that arms length market prices can be determined.
2 Whether or not it is the organization's policy to allow the goods or

services in question to be sold and/or bought in such an external market, if it exists.

Where an external market exists and the organization's policy allows the profit centres to buy and sell in that market, arms length market price is clearly the logical basis on which to account for transfers between them. Even where the level of an arms length market price can vary, there is nothing to prevent profit centres negotiating with each other to establish transfer prices which are mutually satisfactory.

The problem is not so simple if, for one reason or another, the organization wishes to restrict the right of profit centres to buy the goods or services in question from the external market. This might be the case because the profit centre producing the goods or organization wishes to restrict the right of profit centres to buy the goods or service in question from the external market. This might be the case because the profit centre producing the goods or service within the organization has excess capacity. The converse situation arises when the organization wishes to restrict the right of the transferor (or up-stream) profit centre to sell the goods or service on the open market. This might be the case when one or more of the transferee (or down-stream) profit centres are particularly dependent on supplies of the product in question, and the latter is scarce. In such cases, although it is still appropriate to use market based transfer prices, friction may arise because either the transferee or the transferor may find a more advantageous price externally, or may claim to have done so as a bargaining tactic. Where the bulk of a profit centre's output, or its input, is sold or procured within the organization as a matter of policy, the existence of such a policy is, in fact, a denial of the true profit centre status of the 'profit centre' involved. In such circumstances the existence of external market prices for the goods or services transferred is somewhat irrelevant, and the situation is analogous to that described in the next paragraph.

Where the bulk of the profit centre's outputs or inputs is sold or procured within the organization and is such that arms length external market prices do not exist, then it is more appropriate to speak of a 'pseudo profit centre'. Opinions differ as to whether it is worthwhile having pseudo profit centres rather than designating the responsibility centres in question as straight forward cost centres. On the other hand, a situation may exist where the bulk of the responsibility centre's outputs or inputs relate to products for which the arms length external market price can be ascertained, but it is also involved with a certain quantity of transfers for which no arms length market prices exist. In these circumstances, the responsibility centre is not a 'pseudo profit centre', and it is desirable to find a method of accounting for the latter category of transfers in a way which is consistent with its profit centre status.

Two part and three part transfer price systems

Where market based transfer prices are either unavailable or inappropriate for the reasons mentioned above, the most effective approach is to use a multi-part transfer price system. In such a system, transfers are accounted for on a unit basis at standard variable cost plus a lump sum per period in respect of fixed costs. Where the transferor is a profit centre, but not when it is a cost centre, a further lump sum is added which is calculated as an allowed rate of return on the assets employed in producing the transferred outputs.

The advantage of treating the fixed overhead and profit elements as lump sums rather than as an amount per unit transferred is that decisions regarding the quantities to be transferred can be taken on the basis of what is most profitable for the organization as a whole. The lump sum allowances for fixed costs and return on assets employed are agreed as part of the budget; they represent the cost of committed capacity and do not alter as a function of the number of units actually transferred during the budget period. Thus, the down-stream responsibility centre perceives the economics of the situation as it affects the organization as a whole. This is not the case when the fixed costs of the up-stream responsibility centre are made to look like variable costs to the down-stream responsibility centre by being included as an element in the unit transfer price.

Where the semi-variable costs are an important element of the cost of the transferred items, it may be preferable not to treat them in the same way as the fixed costs. Rather, the transfer price may be obtained by consulting a previously agreed flexible budget schedule, so that the changes in the level of the semi-variable costs are reflected, the fixed cost and return on asset elements being dealt with as previously described.

To sum up, in situations where it is not feasible or appropriate to use arms length market transfer prices, it is important that the responsibility centres involved are presented with the accounting information regarding the transfers in a manner which reflects their impact on the economics of the business as a whole. This is not achieved when the transfer pricing system ignores the differences between variable costs and fixed costs, or between these categories and semi-variable costs where the latter are a significant element.

Where the transferred items cross an international or other fiscal border, the multi-part transfer pricing approach described above will not generally be satisfactory for customs duty purposes. It may therefore be necessary to use unit transfer prices incorporating a fixed cost element for invoicing purposes in order to satisfy the requirements of the customs or other fiscal authorities. There is no obligation to use these invoice transfer prices, however, for management accounting purposes and, for the reasons described above, it will generally be better not to do so.

9

Cash forecasting and control

R. L. Mansbridge

This chapter concentrates on how to plan and control that very necessary resource in every company — money. Effective financial planning is essential to company survival. It is important not only to managers and employees whose jobs are at stake in the event of financial distress, but also to shareholders, banks and others who finance the company. Financial managers must understand the cash implications of various future possible contingencies, in order to know the types and amounts of funding which may be required, well in advance of actual needs. Financial planning provides the framework guiding the company's relationships to providers of funds. Therefore, systematic financial planning and forecasting should play a central role in the managerial process.

TIMING OF CASH PLANS

There are essentially three time spans which a financial manager should cover in cash planning and control. Planning is mentioned first but the control is equally important.

Plans are of no use unless there is a good control mechanism to highlight when, where and how events are off plan. This probably applies more in cash planning than in profit planning. If a company makes an unplanned loss one month or one year, the effect is less devastating than not being able to pay the wages on a Friday.

The three time spans are

1 Monthly cash forecasts for, say, the next three months.
2 Short-term cash forecasts of, say, one or two years, probably by month.
3 Long-term cash forecasts for five to ten years, usually by year.

The day to day planning and control of cash is omitted here as this is purely arithmetic and the checking of bank statements.

The timings of the cash plans are dictated mainly by the budgeting or planning cycle of the operation. It is essential that the cash plans lock into profit and balance sheet planning.

MONTHLY CASH FORECAST AND CONTROL

Assuming that the company's planning and reporting system runs by calendar month, this forecast should be produced as near the beginning of the month as possible. It shows

1 Actuals for the last month, over/under plan and over/under last month's forecast.
2 Forecast for next month, over/under plan.
3 Forecast for month two, etc., over/under plan.

A schedule of this is shown in Figure 9.1. This is a simple statement of money received and paid, showing how last month compared to the plan and prior forecast. Similarly, it shows forecasts for months one, two, three, etc. against the plan. The length of the forecast is determined by the urgency of the cash position. Thus, if the overdraft is right up to the limit in a tight money situation and there are large seasonal payments, the forecast will go further than three months to cover this.

The plan column mentioned will be the short-term forecast showing the month by month movement of cash which links in with the budget of profits.

The forecast for next month will be those figures which the financial manager is planning to pay and receive next month. To do this he will use the following sources of information

1 Calendarized profit and cash plan.
2 Short-term profit outlook for next month (if this is done month by month).
3 Debtors' and creditors' ledger.
4 Information on taxes, loans, etc.

	LAST MONTH			MONTH 1		MONTH 2		MONTH 3 ETC.	
	Actual	o/u Plan	o/u Fore-cast	Fore-cast	o/u Plan	Fore-cast	o/u Plan	Fore-cast	o/u Plan

Receipts
 Trade debtors
 Investment income
 Receipts from
   Overseas sub-
     sidiaries
 Loans or financing
   received									

Total receipts									

Payments
 Stock purchases
 Salaries and costs of
   employment
 Other overheads
 Capital expenditure
 Interest
 Tax
 Payment to
   Overseas sub-
     sidiaries
 Repayments of loans
 Other									

Total payments									
Surplus (deficit)									
Opening cash/ (overdraft)									
Closing cash/ (overdraft)									
Overdraft facility									

Figure 9.1   Monthly cash forecast and control

5   Capital expenditure authorizations.
6   Last month's actuals.

Thus, the short-term forecast should accurately give the money movements picture for the next two or three months. It will also be closely locked in with the activities of the company, that is, production, sales costs, and so forth.

The variance from plan will be analysed in conjunction with the profit and cost variance statement. Variances will highlight some of the questions itemized below

1   *Trade debtors*
    Is this due to lower turnover or late payment by debtors? Is the number of days outstanding on the debtors' ledger increasing?
    Is this seasonal or is a trend developing which may need more financing in future?

2   *Investment income*
    Does the company still own the investments as planned?
    Should future income be adjusted?

3   *Receipts/payments − overseas subsidiaries*
    Is this lower business activity or are international money transactions being blocked or restricted?

4   *Loans or financing received*
    Is this due to a change in capital spending?
    Are planned loans not forthcoming?

5   *Purchases, salaries and overheads*
    Is this due to operating volume, price variations or late payment of creditors?

6   *Capital expenditure*
    Is planned spending cancelled or delayed?
    Are costs different from plan due to price only or has there been any change in specification?

7   *Interest*
    Is the rate of interest different from the plan or is the overdraft size different?

8   *Tax*
    Is this due to a change in rates or in taxable profits?

The purpose of showing over/under forecast is to see

(a) How good a forecast was done one month prior to events.
(b) What changes have happened in one month which could not have been forecast.

The immediate object of (a) is not to see whether the financial manager is a good forecaster, although over a series of forecasts an opinion can be formed, but to judge how accurate the next few months' forecasts are likely to be.

Total receipts less total payments equal the surplus (or deficit) each month. Hence the running balance for the next three months is forecast. Specific decisions which should be made are

1 If there is a cash balance, should this be invested? For what period can this be done (30 days, 90 days, etc.)?
2 If there is an overdraft, what items of payment can be delayed? Can the overdraft facility be increased?

SHORT-TERM CASH FORECAST

This forecast links in with the budget or operating plan for the next financial year. Its timing should be on the same basis; for example, if the plan is by month, then the cash forecast will be monthly. Many companies now plan two years ahead in their short-term planning cycle, the second year in less detail and without such a commitment as the first. This avoids the cliff-hanging situation in which, at the close of the company's fiscal year, the world stops on one day and starts again on the next.

Cash is simply one of the resources which go to make the budget work. Within the budget all resources must be planned – manning, facilities and money.

The main objective of the short-term cash forecast is to see how the cash balances move, if the company does what it is planning to do. This forecast must highlight, on a phased basis, the need for any short-term borrowing. This is particularly relevant in a seasonal business, even if high profits are being made. Long-term borrowing should be decided from the figures in the long-term forecast (see later in this chapter).

It is obviously better to plan in advance for any overdraft requirements than to borrow on an emergency basis. When a request to borrow is made, a profit budget and cash forecast is often required by a potential lender.

Cash forecasts can be produced either by converting the profit budget into receipts and payments or from the budgeted balance sheets. The latter method is probably more appropriate for long-term forecasts. Basically the end result is the same in that the movement of the cash balance from one balance sheet to the next is shown.

As already indicated, the cash forecast must lock into the company's profit plan. The first cycle is to agree a marketing/sales plan and production plan. This is merged with the overhead plan to produce a profit plan. This and the capital expenditure plan are the necessary tools for the cash forecast.

Because all the work in producing a budget must be done before the financial year commences, an up-to-date forecast for the current year must also be calculated. The cash forecast must obviously start from a factual balance, progress to the year end and then be calculated for the next year. This means that not only does the cash balance have to be known at the last month end or quarter date, but a balance sheet must be prepared also so that the outstandings are correctly brought into account.

Assuming that there is a profit forecast for the current year and that the profit and capital budgets for the next two years are agreed, the cash forecast using the receipts and payments method would show similar headings to Figure 9.2.

If the balance sheet forecast method is used, a source and application of funds statement would be produced as shown later. This statement traces the items in the profit statement and any extraneous items which cause a cash movement for both receipts and payments. This facilitates a quick check of the numbers against the profit budget. It is particularly valuable on the payments side where items such as salary costs and overheads are specifically identifiable.

The opening balance each month (or quarter) plus the surplus (or minus the deficit) gives the closing balance before any borrowings or loans which have not yet been agreed. This immediately shows whether loans are required. By studying the phasing it can be seen whether this is a seasonal dip or whether it looks like a permanent borrowing requirement. The correct overdraft facility is the amount up to which the bank has agreed to pass cheques.

Headings on the cash forecast shown in Figure 9.2 could be calculated on the basis set out below.

Quarter/Month	1	2	3	4, etc.	Total
Receipts Trade debtors Investment income Loans/financing arranged Other					
Total Receipts					
Payments Stock purchases Salaries and costs of employment Other overheads Capital expenditure Interest Tax Repayment of loans Dividends Other					
Total payments					
Surplus/(deficit)					
Opening cash/(deficit)					
Closing cash/(deficit)					
Current overdraft facility					

Figure 9.2   Short-term cash forecast

Receipts from debtors

By reference to the debt collection department, the forecast of number of days outstanding for the average debtor will be made for the next year. Receipts from debtors will be calculated on the basis of the current situation and the budgeted turnover. The financial manager should question precisely how debt collection will be speeded up. This is a good objective, but as the cash forecast is always very sensitive to changes in the payment profile, it must not be over-optimistic. With most companies debtors provide the only receipt of any size, so there is no compensation if an error in forecasting is made.

Investment income

The investment income credited to the phased profit statement will be used after allowing for the receipt of cash.

Loans/financing arranged

This heading will only include financing which has been arranged prior to the budget. It does not include overdraft facilities as these will be shown at the bottom of the forecast. The object of the forecast is to see how the cash deficit measures against the current overdraft facility. The types of financing entered on this line will be mortgage money which will be received against capital expenditure, or a fixed loan or debenture of which the proceeds have not yet been received.

Other receipts

These receipts are essentially non-trading cash receipts and would include items such as the sale of fixed assets. These are sometimes accounted for by reducing the capital expenditure but unless a simultaneous purchase and trade-in (as with motor vehicles) is involved it is better to separate the receipt from the payment.

Stock purchases

The payments side of the forecast follows the logic of splitting expenditure as it appears in the profit budget. In a trading company, stock purchases equals the charge in the profit budget plus opening creditors less closing creditors.

To determine the closing creditors, an assumption will be made as to whether the company wishes to, or has to, pay creditors more quickly or slowly than at present. Stock purchases in many companies represent a large portion of total payments and can be a useful form of financing. The ethics of this must be carefully weighed, especially for large companies which have a monopsonistic buying power over small suppliers. The problem for a small company trying to finance itself out of creditors is (short of being sued) whether it obtains a name for being a bad payer and whether this affects business.

Salaries and costs of employment

Net salaries and wages in the profit budget are usually phased in line with the cash payments. The only items to be allowed for would be commissions or bonuses which are paid at a later date. Deducted tax and costs of employment as charged to the profit statement should be adjusted for creditors at the beginning and end of the period, as for stock purchases.

Other overheads

These consist of all items of cost (other than purchases and salary costs) between turnover and profit before depreciation. On the working papers it is easiest to run through the calculation from the charge by item to the profit budget, adding opening creditors and deducting opening preparements. With expenses which are the normal invoice and payment type, the same logic applies as for stock purchases. With cash items such as travelling, etc., the profit charge needs no adjustment for the cash budget. Items such as rent and rates are usually paid in advance on specific days and this determines the phasing in the cash budget.

Capital expenditure

The capital plan must be produced alongside the profit plan, which in turn incorporates the production and sales plans. Plant to produce the end product is as much a plannable item as the purchase of raw material. Usually, it is more important to plan capital, especially facilities which have a long lead-time. For each item of capital expenditure in the plan, the phases of management approval, commitment and cash spending should be specified, with dates and amounts. In the smaller business, management approval is basically when the owner says that a certain asset must be purchased. In many companies commitment is synonymous with approval. The date of commitment is important, however, as once a commitment is made it will cost the company money to reverse its decision.

At the time of capital budget the dates of the cash spending should be forecast. This forecast would be based on experience. With capital items having long lead-times from order to delivery (for instance a factory or specially designed machine tools), the capital requisition and management approval have probably taken place before the budget. In this case the cash budget is dictated by the pre-calculated figures. For short lead-time items, the capital budget should operate from the date the asset is required. It must be determined whether payment will be made on the delivery invoice or by stage payments.

Interest

The interest charge in the profit budget is calculated from the result of the cash forecast. The apparent problem of putting the cart before the horse can be resolved in one of two ways: either by calculating all items in the cash forecast (except interest), completing this before finishing the profit budget; or by using the last cash forecast with a rough adjustment for known large changes to produce the interest charge (the same logic applies to interest receivables) in the profit budget. The latter would appear easier in most cases.

Payment of interest on fixed loans and mortgages would be determined by the agreements.

Tax

Many companies end their formal planning at the profit before tax level, on the premise that as tax is unavoidable and uncontrollable it is not worth planning. This thinking is erroneous because the payment of tax is a significant item for a profitable company.

Tax planning is essential for a company based in the UK. It is even more vital if the company has overseas investments.

The payment of tax in the cash forecast is based on the rates and rules current at the time of the budget. The only deviation from this would be when a government has made a firm commitment to change the mechanics or rates of corporation tax.

Repayment of loans

This item will include those repayments to which the company is committed. It is an item easily overlooked and could lead the company into serious legal problems if it is unable to repay loans or mortgages on time. Before completing the cash forecast the finance manager should check the last balance sheet published, and any loans received since, with the loan agreements to ensure that he is planning repayment at the correct time.

Dividends

These payments will consist of the final dividend on the current year's trading and probably an interim based on the first half of the budget year's trading. The amount of the dividend on preference shares is pre-determined. The ordinary dividend forecast would be based on the company's dividend policy.

Dates of payment would be similar to the prior year unless circumstances have changed.

Other payments

This covers any payments not itemized above. These would include non-trading or extraneous loss items and would be shown in the cash forecast as circumstances might dictate.

SOURCE AND APPLICATION OF FUNDS

This statement requires the prior production of the profit budget and forecast balance sheets. There must be a balance sheet at the end of each period for which the cash forecast is required.

Many companies budget profit on a monthly basis but balance sheets are only budgeted quarterly or annually. This makes a monthly source and application of funds statement more difficult to produce.

Figure 9.3 gives a possible layout for the source and application of funds statement.

This statement links into the profit figure then adds back all the items in the profit budget which are non-cash. This is mainly depreciation, but 'other' would include provisions for bad debts, stock, and writing off patents, etc. The total of these line items represents the cash inflow due to trading.

The outflow of cash is shown by balance sheet heading. The gross increase in fixed and current assets is deducted. This is calculated by reference to the balance sheets at the beginning and end of the forecast period.

Quarter/Month	1	2	3	4, etc.	Total
Profit before tax Depreciation Other non-cash items in profit statement					

Increase/decrease in:
  Fixed assets
  Stocks
  Debtors
  Creditors					

Tax payment Dividends paid Loans received Loans repaid					
Net movement in cash					

Opening cash surplus/
  (deficit)
Closing cash surplus/
  (deficit)					

Current overdraft facility					

Figure 9.3   Source and application of funds statement

The cash movement section will show tax and dividend payments. These figures will be opening creditor plus profit charge less closing creditor.

Loans received will be only those which have been arranged prior to the budget being prepared. Loan repayments will be repayments of existing loans.

The net movement in cash will, accordingly, be the change between opening and closing cash balances.

SHORT-TERM CASH CONTROL

Most companies segregate their cash control away from the profit performance control. Concentration is nearly always on the latter until cash problems arise. The statement that a company has 'got to make money' is heard frequently, but money in this sense is profit and not specifically cash. Many businessmen equate profit with cash, but unless the two are linked it does not always happen that one follows the other.

The reporting of cash to central management should be at least as often as the profit reporting and could be on formats similar to Figures 9.2 or 9.3. The line narrative would be the same as the plans and the headings could be

This month
Actual | Plan | Variance

Year to date
Actual | Plan | Variance

A facing page would explain variances which would correlate with the profit variance statement.

In this way there would be two types of variance – those related to profit performance, that is, volume or cost variances on production, sales or overheads, and those related to cash management. These would include such items as

1 Improvement in debtor collection.
2 Delay in payment of creditors.
3 Early repayment of loans.
4 Changes in tax or dividend payments.

Control of the accuracy of forecasts is exercised by the comparison of actuals to budget. But the effect of any variance is as important as knowing what the variances are. If a variance is caused by a large payment being made one day late, and therefore included in the next month's figures, this must be highlighted so that the short-term forecast, which gives a picture of the cash for the next two or three months, can pick it up.

LONG-TERM CASH FORECASTS

The basic principles of forecasting over a period longer than two years are essentially the same as for the short-term but the process and style of approach are different. The figures tend to be less accurate, of course, and the interest lies more in long-term trends than short-term fluctuations.

Objective

The objective of a long-term cash forecast is to see the cash flows which will be generated by the company's long-term profit plan and to assess the capital expenditure needed to attain that plan. The borrowing requirements of the company will be seen from the cash flows and a decision can be made as to how the finance can be raised. Alternatively, if cash surpluses build up, decisions can be made whether to increase dividends, to invest the cash outside the company, or invest in more assets within the company.

If the forecast shows up a short-term requirement for finance, this could be covered by borrowing from the bank. Alternatively, a decision could be made to slow down or delay expansion.

A long-term requirement for cash would initiate a study into how that cash should be raised – by share capital increase, debenture issue or mortgage of property. This would depend on a lot of factors but quite a number of these could be decided by figures in the long-term forecast. The balance sheets would show the fixed asset movements, the unmortgaged fixed assets, the debt/equity ratio, and the current asset situation. Outside factors, such as the general business climate and likely movement of interest rates, would be part of the basic assumptions behind the long-range plan.

Format

The format of the long-term cash forecast could be almost identical to the short-term source and application of funds. As a balance sheet would be produced (probably yearly) for the long-range forecast, this document would be used to produce the cash forecast; the cash forecast really becomes an integral part of the creation of the long-range plan, and is produced at the same time as the balance sheet.

The cash forecast in the short term is a fairly self-contained exercise, but the long-range cash forecast covers a lot of corporate activities.

The profit before tax will be calculated from the profit forecast. This is determined by the forecast of new products, the costs and volumes, the marketing policy and the trend of overheads.

Depreciation will be based on the current policy with respect to the assets as forecast in the capital plan. This creates a problem as the capital plan is based on the facilities required to manufacture and sell the forecast products. One way to get round this is to assume a certain depreciation content in the unit manufacturing cost and the overheads.

The fixed assets increase is calculated from a facilities plan. This plan, basically, starts from the production and marketing plan to determine the facilities in terms of factories, offices and training centres that are required, and from this the space requirement is calculated. This can then be costed and plant, vehicles and furniture are added to produce the forecast of capital expenditure. As this is one of the major long-term decisions made in any company it is a vital part of the long-term plan.

The stock levels would be based on historical trends of the ratio to cost of sales, updated by the marketing strategy which could specify a stock build-up just prior to launch of a new product.

Debtors and creditors would also be based on trends. Debtors bear a direct relationship to turnover and creditors to purchases and overheads.

The tax payment will be based on the profits after calculating capital allowances. Normally, the current rates and timings of tax would be used, unless there is firm evidence that these will change.

The dividend payment requires a corporate decision as to the company's dividend policy. Failing a policy, the current rate as a percentage of distributable profit would be used.

It is unlikely that any loans arranged at the present time would be received more than two years ahead, that is, after the period covered by the short-term cash forecast. But the repayment of existing loans must be covered.

From this it will be seen that overlapping decisions and calculations are required for the balance sheets and cash forecasts. In the same way as the long-range profit forecast locks into each yearly balance sheet and shows the performance of the business as planned in terms of turnover and costs, so also does the long-range forecast in terms of where the money comes from and where it goes.

By definition, all forecasts are inaccurate as they are calculated from what the company planners think at one point in time. Tomorrow the strategy could be completely different. The cash forecaster has two problems here: first, how uncertain is the profit statement, and second, how uncertain are the other assumptions concerning cash?

Many companies now use a computer to produce the profit effect of various strategies, and having homed in on a politically and commercially acceptable profit figure, proceed to calculate the cash forecast in a deterministic way with just one set of rules. It is just as important to see a best and worst case for cash as it is for profit — in fact, more so if the company is in a capital – restricted situation. The calculations discussed earlier should therefore each be examined to see what chances there are of the situation being better or worse. Areas of specific flexibility would be

1 The length of credit affecting debtors and creditors.
2 Any significant change in interest rates.
3 Changes in the tax laws affecting the rate of tax, calculations of capital allowances, tax on interest and dividends or the time of payment.
4 Changes in national dividend policies.
5 Changes in the international situation affecting remittances, blocked currencies, overseas borrowings and exchange rates.

Without a computer program it would be impossible to flex the above without vast manual calculations. Obviously, it would be impossible ever to finish a forecast if every contingency were to be thought of and evaluated. But it is important to look at the risks and opportunities as far as they can be foreseen at the present time. This determines the areas of the company's operation which should be analysed more closely. Very often the original policies which were used at the start of the long-range cash forecast have to be changed.

DYNAMIC ASPECT

The actual cash movements change from plan in the same way as the actual profits. It is therefore essential to update forecasts continuously.

In the long term the frequency with which forecasts are updated should be the same as for profit. This would be determined by the frequency of changed strategies and markets, and the effect of these on the resources of the company.

In the short term the cash situation of the company and the significance of changes from the year's plan should dictate the frequency of reviews of the cash forecast. It is useless to update a no-change cash forecast where there is plenty of cash available. However, where cash is the restraining item in the company's policies, more frequent review than monthly may be required. It is most important to differentiate between trends and random daily variations.

INTERNATIONAL ASPECTS

An international company's objective for cash does not necessarily correlate exactly with the policy for profits. Whereas the profit objective could be to maximise after tax profit so that on consolidation the group shows the best earnings per share situation, cash does not necessarily show this.

The cash policy should be determined by what the cash is to be used for. This is usually a mixture of paying the dividend of the holding company and ploughing back for internally financed expansion.

The methods of getting cash into the holding company from overseas subsidiaries are

1 Dividends.
2 Repayment of loans or share capital.
3 Payment for goods exported by the holding company to a subsidiary.
4 Payment by a subsidiary of management fees, fees for technological know how or royalties.

All these cash transactions are subject to the rules of each country's national bank. They change frequently and are designed to guard the balance of payments positions. This often runs contrary to a company's policy of trying to reduce its exposure to parity changes. That is, money is borrowed in a country likely to devalue and held in a country likely to revalue. Against this, of course, interest rates tend to be high in the former countries and low in the latter. This produces a compensating effect.

It is the financial manager's responsibility to safeguard company assets and take reasonable precautions against currency risks — not to play the money market.

International cash management is dealt with in more detail in Chapter 17.

FURTHER READING

Garbutt, D., *How to Budget and Control Cash*, Gower, (Aldershot, 1985)

10

Internal auditing

Harry H. Scholefield and P. C. Elliott*

In a small business consisting of an owner/manager and a small number of employees the owner will be able to keep in close touch with all activities. However, as the size of the business increases this becomes more and more difficult. The statutory auditors will assist management to ensure that financial records, accounts and other statements are kept correctly and drawn up to reflect the progress of the business; but in addition, management needs to know that controls are operating satisfactorily in all activities. Typically, management establishes its control systems using two basic approaches corresponding to two different levels of control.

On-line controls (first level)

The on-line control function consists of on-going measures and procedures designed to provide reasonable assurance that all significant actions of the company are taken in accordance with company policies and with appropriate regard for efficiency and the protection of corporate assets.

Off-line controls (second level)

The off-line control function is an appraisal activity designed to evaluate

---

*The authors wish to thank B. J. B. Driver, P. J. Henry and A. J. Somers for their valuable comments on an earlier draft of this chapter.

the adequacy, efficiency and effectiveness of the company's on-line controls and to promote more efficient and effective controls through constructive recommendations.

The off-line control function is performed by internal auditors. The modern internal auditor appraises controls rather than acting as the control and his activity is not confined to data records. The efforts of the Institute of Internal Auditors have done much to ensure that the responsibilities of an internal auditor are more fully understood and practised.

ORGANIZATION

If the chief internal auditor reports directly to top management, he will be independent and will carry, without question, the appropriate status to review controls over all activities. In a smaller company he will probably report to the chief executive. However, in larger organizations, partly for historical reasons, he may report to the financial director or comptroller.

The financial function also provides a service to other functions and there is no reason why a chief internal auditor reporting within finance should be hampered in reviewing activities of other functions provided that he is given the full support of top management. It is therefore important that the internal auditor reports to a strong corporate officer who can guarantee his independence, his access to all company records, and also shield him from internal pressure to alter or suppress his findings. Moreover, the executive to whom the internal auditor reports must be in a position to assure that the internal auditor's reports are read by every level of management concerned.

If the internal auditor reports to the financial director or comptroller there is, however, a danger that he may not be free, then, to express himself fully on financial activities. A necessary safeguard against such an impediment is for it to be agreed, and included in his terms of reference, that the internal auditor has the right of direct access to top management should he feel that this is warranted. In the USA, and to a lesser extent in the UK, this safeguard is extended further in some companies where he has access as a final resort to the Board Audit Committee, which is typically composed of non-executive directors.

TERMS OF REFERENCE

The internal audit function helps senior management to attain corporate objectives and seeks to protect shareholders' interests. In the final analysis it is this latter role which predominates; even senior management can be corrupt. Recommended responsibilities of the internal auditor were set out in a statement approved by the Institute of Internal Auditors' Board of Directors in 1947 and revised in 1957, 1971 and 1976. The revised statement is included in Appendix 1 to this chapter.

Every management must decide on the particular terms of reference which it proposes to give its internal audit department. After agreement, terms of reference should be produced in writing giving a firm base for planning, staffing and carrying out internal audit work without objection and resentment from those responsible for activities to be audited. Senior management should make clear throughout the organization the importance they attach to the internal audit function.

The work of internal audit is not easy. It is, after all, an inspection, and people normally resent being inspected. A very careful path has to be trodden, to ensure that controls are reviewed and that the organization's policies are being carried out without giving the impression that the internal audit department is either criticizing policy or that it will be making adverse criticisms on decisions taken, when those decisions could have been proved wrong only after the event.

STAFFING

It will be clear from the preceding sections that internal auditing is a responsible job, involving contact with senior staff and requiring skill and tact in personal relationships. Having decided to establish such a department, it would be folly to staff it with people incapable of the performance required.

Opinions differ as to whether internal auditing is a profession in itself or whether it is a useful step in the career development of those with management potential. Whether the more senior positions of the internal audit department are filled with those having a career in internal auditing or not, it is generally agreed that this department affords an excellent early training ground for those with management potential. Because of the department's interest in all activities, shorter-term recruitment for the lower levels should encompass not only those employees with financial backgrounds but also those from other disciplines. The perfect internal auditor will, perhaps, possess both financial and applied science qualifications, but such staff are not plentiful. A balance can be achieved by a mixture of staff from different functions in appropriate proportions.

Criteria for selection of staff should encompass education, experience, performance and potential. A points system can be developed for each area of selection so that only in exceptional circumstances would audit candidates be accepted who did not meet an overall minimum points requirement. In addition to 'control mindedness' and the usual virtues, the internal auditor needs perseverance, empathy and a logical approach with analytical ability. Given staff who have satisfied the above requirements, internal auditing has the best opportunity to meet and maintain its objectives.

Those employed on internal auditing early in their careers should not serve too long; say, up to 4 years. This time is sufficient for them to gain an insight into many aspects of the organization, to learn and carry with them throughout their careers the value and basic requirements of good control, and to contribute significantly to the work of the department. A longer term may lessen their enthusiasm, with the exception of those internal auditors envisaged as career audit specialists. The movement of good staff into internal auditing together with promotion of many on leaving it, will be an excellent advertisement and will banish any earlier images of internal auditing as a department where finance staff finish their working years.

PLANNING

All business activities require a plan, a budget and a stewardship review, and internal auditing is no exception.

Audit plan

The list of activities to be covered should be separated into auditable units. These units should be of such a size that the chief executive does not receive too many reports and that the time spent on auditing each unit is not excessive. A broad guideline would be 100–150 man-days per audit.

The review of all activities every year, regardless of the stability of organization, adequacy of controls or chance of loss or profit improvement, is wasteful and a decision should be made regarding the time cycle over which activities are to be reviewed.

It may be considered appropriate to audit every 2–3 years those activities with major financial or other potentially harmful exposure. The period will depend on relative exposure, on-line controls and strength of management. Where audit evaluation indicates weak or inadequate controls, or where for other reasons financial exposure or risks due to non-compliance with company policies are particularly high, the interval should be reduced to less than 2 years. Intervals between audits for activities which do not have major financial exposure may be greater than 3 years and will vary according to the relative exposure as judged by management and the internal audit manager involved.

The above approach to planning is appropriate in an organization where internal auditing has been conducted for some time and experience gained in the activity. How can an audit plan be developed, based on a systematic approach to risk measurement, for an internal audit group in its infancy or for one which is extending its activities?

Let us consider the relationship between risk and internal audit as depicted in Figure 10.1.

Potential risk minus on-line control = Overall risk

Figure 10.1   Relationship between risk and internal audit

The greater the overall risk, the greater the need for off-line reviews; these in turn should contribute to the effectiveness of on-line control and hence reduce the overall risk. Thus the extent of off-line reviews needed should, other things being equal, diminish over time. An assessment of potential risk is derived from a good knowledge of an area and could be provided by internal audit management in those areas where they possess considerable experience. However, in those areas where they lack experience, discussions would have to take place with line management. Similarly, in the case of on-line control effectiveness in a previously unaudited area, line management's input will have to be sought, since the audit function will be able to make an evaluation only after audit. A possible approach to allocating risk to auditable units by line management is outlined in Appendix 2.

Calculation of staff numbers

An assessment of the plan must be made in terms of audit man-days, including travelling time, in order to determine staff requirements. Initially, timing is rather difficult to assess but, as experience is gained on actual audit timing, estimates will improve. After adding the man-days audit effort for each year in the time cycle, some adjustments to allocation of audits within the year may be necessary to give a more even distribution of effort. Staff requirements can then be estimated: an allowance for leave, sickness, training courses, *ad hoc* requirements and public holidays is needed. In a later section it is recommended that internal audit staff keep timesheets; timesheets summarized for previous years will help when estimating both audit time and the additional allowance, as well as providing input for allocation of costs. An example of a 5-year internal audit plan is shown in Appendix 3. There will, of course, be some trade-off between audit frequency and manpower, despite the evaluation of risk. An overall 2-year interval extended to a 3-year interval would reduce required manpower by a third.

The budget

Based on the plan, the budget for the coming year can now be prepared and will include

1 Salaries (plus on-cost to pension schemes, etc.).
2 Travelling and accommodation expenses.
3 Training courses.
4 Computer time.
5 General share of overheads.

Management agreement and stewardship

The next requirement is management's approval of the budgeted cost of the department and of the broad plan within the agreed terms of reference. The budget may be the particular responsibility of one member of management, but the plan needs to be discussed with management as a whole if controls on all activities are subject to review.

It is recommended that the chief internal auditor should meet periodically with senior management to review audit effort and progress against the plan. Such a meeting can be used to review each year's new plan. Copies of the plan should be circulated before the meeting, giving management the opportunity to review the list of activities to be covered and the proposed timing, possibly leading to adjustments in timing, staffing and costs. It also allows the chief internal auditor to obtain input from senior management and to discover their concerns.

After approval of both the plan and the budget, the chief internal auditor is in a position to adjust staffing ready for the coming year. He is also in a position to calculate the estimated average cost of an audit man-day, by dividing the budgeted cost of the department by the planned audit man-days. This figure is very significant. It can be used to assess the limit of time that can reasonably be spent on audits, having regard to the possibility of benefits that may arise, either from preventing loss or improving profit in other ways.

AUDIT PROGRAMMES

It is a sound approach for the senior auditor and audit manager to meet before the review to prepare an audit programme. The programme will set down the audit objectives, followed by the detailed steps designed to achieve them, leaving room for adjustments as the audit progresses.

Auditing of financial controls

This type of auditing verifies the existence of both a strong system of internal control, and of the corporation's assets. It involves review of the general accounting function, debtors and creditors, receipts and payments of cash, payrolls, banking transactions, and materials and equipment purchasing. In addition, it involves the verification of fixed assets and stocks. The financial audit also includes an assessment of adherence to management policies, procedures and guidelines which include such matters as contracting, the adequacy and accuracy of cost reporting systems, budget systems and compliance with laws.

Operational auditing

Operational auditing involves the extension of internal auditing to all operations of the business. The principal objects of such audits are to assist the management in the effective discharge of their responsibilities by furnishing them with objective analyses, appraisals and recommendations designed to improve profits, and to protect the corporation from losses of all kinds.

The operational audit is a comprehensive examination of an organizational structure (or one of its components), of policies and objectives, mode of operations, and stewardship of human and physical resources. It can be said that operational auditing is characterized by the approach and the state of mind of the auditor – not by distinctive methods. Operational audits are seldom undertaken as special and distinct audits; instead they complement and augment the scope of appraisal systems by applying the talents, background and techniques of the internal auditor to the operating controls which exist in a business. The operational audit provides an independent appraisal of all activities within the company performed in such a manner as to serve all levels of management and to obtain the most profitable results.

Examples of internal audit extensions into operational areas during the course of the audit are

1 An appraisal of a company's inventory levels (including, for example, a review of order quantities), the adequacy of warehousing facilities and staffing at the same time as the accuracy of inventory is verified.

2 An appraisal of alternative methods of transport and possible savings at the same time that rates and services received are verified against payments made.

3 A review of policies relating to the maintenance of plant and equipment at the same time that contract payments for repair services are verified.

4 A determination of the quality of materials and services received as well as the quantity when payments for them are being verified.

Audits, however, do not fall neatly into one of the two categories, financial and operational. Rather, they involve a difference in approach and no internal auditor should proceed with any type of audit without an operational approach.

It is emphasized that the internal audit is an appraisal of controls and not the control itself. For example, stock checking should not be carried out by staff from the internal audit department. The internal auditor will, however, appraise the controls by reviewing the work of the checkers and by carrying out spot tests.

AUDIT REVIEW

Normally, prior notification is given of an audit. However, when fraud is suspected, an investigation must be carried out without warning. The overall plan is agreed with management but the actual date of the audit will not be known until close to the time. Notice of the date should be given to management and there should be sufficient tolerance in the plan to avoid descending on an activity at peak periods or at a time of emergency. The auditor, or audit team, will outline the nature of the work to be conducted with the senior management of the area to be reviewed as well as inquiring whether there are any management, financial, operational, or other controls with which senior management is not entirely satisfied. Such concerns should be incorporated into the programme. In addition, the most recent reports of the statutory accountants, the last internal audit report and working papers should be obtained for review; follow-up items should be noted.

The auditor, or audit team, will then start discussions with the appropriate level of management supervising the activity, having obtained the necessary introductions via senior levels of management. The auditor will ask for the relevant organization charts and main job descriptions of the personnel in the area covered by the audit and request a quick review of the department, thus, becoming aware of organizational and other changes since the last audit and gaining some knowledge of proposed changes. He or she should ask for introductions to those people he expects to contact during the investigation.

Controls cannot be appraised without knowledge of the activity. The auditor will, therefore, gather the facts and ask questions of the appropriate personnel in the area being audited to obtain a good understanding of the activities. A complex operation is better understood if it is flow charted. Flow charts should be kept as simple as possible, using symbols with the minimum of narration, produced as useful working papers rather than works of art involving the cost of several man-days or weeks.

The activity may involve the use of land, buildings, plant, equipment or people to move or change physical things or data. When the movements or changes are understood, the established controls can be reviewed to see that they are working as intended. In clerical operations it was once the fashion to select a week's or month's transactions which were checked in detail. Recently the fashion has changed to the use of statistical sampling techniques, on the theory that a random sample of calculated size taken over a whole period gives a sample more truly representative of the whole and, therefore, gives a better test than one of a block period selected at random.

Audit in depth

Before discussing the comparative merits of these methods, mention should be made of another internal audit technique known as audit in depth. In this technique a record or voucher is selected, not merely to test the authorization and accuracy of the supporting documentation, but to carry out an investigation of one item right through the organization.

The vouching technique compares with an audit in depth as follows, where there is an item of cash expenditure of £750 (for example, the cost of photographing a piece of equipment).

1. Vouching technique. Find the original invoice supporting this payment, check that it is made out in the name of the organization, is properly authorized, currently dated, cancelled, and that appropriate discounts have been taken.

2. Audit in depth technique. Carry out vouching technique; check expense account to which it is carried; ascertain the budget unit (or cost centre) bearing the charge; visit the budget unit to discover the purpose of the expense (for example, advertising), whether it is within the approved budget (for example, was this within the province of the budget unit?), how the photographer was selected (possibly the charge includes unnecessary travel and accommodation), how the photograph was used; review the controls operating along the route.

Such audit in depth may open up areas for future investigation of considerably more importance than the item of £750, for example, clarification of departmental responsibilities, the existence of an advertising policy, procedures and the general cost consciousness of the departments concerned. These are the type of questions that the owner of the business would want answered if he had time, and a report on these aspects is of much more interest to management than trivial errors arising in recording the item of expense.

The internal auditor cannot carry out such an investigation while sitting at his desk or within the accounting department. He should use the calculations and supporting documents as a record of something real that has happened and should go to the point of activity to further his investigations. Worthwhile investigations often start from trivial items of expenditure or income and to review only items exceeding a certain figure can be shortsighted. It will be appreciated that auditing in depth is a time consuming activity.

Sampling methods

Let us now consider the comparative merits of block period, statistical or other random sampling methods for testing established controls. All three methods have their uses.

Selecting a block period has the advantage of covering all items for a period; it is simple and vouchers are normally easier to find.

The statistical sample gives a random and representative review of the whole period but the method is not so simple and vouchers are harder to find.

Neither of these methods lends itself to audit in depth because transactions are too numerous. The best method for this technique is a truly random sample but restricted to a much smaller number than the statistical sample.

The small random sample is also of value in testing non-clerical controls. For example, an employee may be checking weights of filled packages; the random selection of a few items by the internal auditor for re-checking will indicate the value of this control.

The internal auditor should be aware of all these techniques and select the one, or combination, appropriate to the job in hand.

REPORTING

Some managements prefer verbal reports. It is recommended, however, that written reports are always produced following an internal audit review. These lead to better disciplines in the audit department; no opportunity arises for argument about the recommendations made, and there is a greater likelihood of success in follow-up. In addition, in the event of litigation against the company, written reports may assist the company's defence.

A sound overall reporting procedure would provide

1   Draft audit memos for discussion with the first-line management of operations being audited, followed by formal audit memos.
2   A draft report to the next superior in line for discussion, and incorporation of replies.

3 A final report to the chief executive, with a covering letter highlighting major findings.

The main purpose of producing the draft audit memos for discussion with the first-line management of the department being audited is to ascertain their actual validity. The audit memos and draft report allow management to provide input to the final report from all levels in the area being audited. They are an added check that the facts have been gathered properly, that the emphasis is right and recommendations are sensible. Statements dealing with each area of concern in the final report should outline the problem, its magnitude, its cause and audit recommendations, and should incorporate management's comments. In addition, an overall comment on control adequacy should be made in the covering letter and in this regard it is helpful if a standard terminology is laid down so that management understand clearly what the control assessment means.

The report should be completed as rapidly as possible so that it is still fresh and relevant when presented. It is usually accepted that the report should be distributed to the department or section head audited and the next superior in-line and the chief executive. The internal auditor should appraise controls on behalf of top management and his independence can be reinforced by the chief internal auditor making a presentation to management at least annually. He can then offer a brief review of his investigations, prompt action where follow-up of the recommendations has been unnecessarily delayed, report on his performance compared with the plan and review future plans as necessary.

An important part of any internal audit is the preparation and filing of working papers. 'Working papers' is the term applied to all schedules, memoranda, check lists, questionnaires and other papers assembled during an audit. The purposes of working papers are to provide a record of work performed, to substantiate the auditor's findings, to record his discussions with management, to serve as a base for review of the auditor's work and to act as a guide for subsequent audits.

The essentials of good working papers are completeness, neatness, legibility and indexation. Completeness should not be attained at the expense of preparing voluminous papers with information which could be included in the working papers by mere reference to company records. However, working papers should be prepared so that a comprehensive review can be made of them in a minimum of time and with a minimum of recourse to the auditor who prepared them.

Working papers should be indexed as they are prepared to facilitate cross referencing. On completion of the audit an index summary of the working papers should be prepared which would typically include

1 Final report and follow-up correspondence to report.
2 Audit memoranda and replies and cross reference to working papers.
3 Administration and general correspondence, time budget, job critique.
4 Background – organization charts, authority levels, flow charts, etc.
5 Audit programme.
6 Detailed working papers by subject.

As mentioned, working papers are an important part of an internal audit and minimum standards need to be agreed and laid down by audit management. Clearly, preparing and indexing working papers is time consuming and it would be reasonable to spend 5 per cent of total audit time on this activity.

AUDITING OF COMPUTING SYSTEMS

Internal audit is responsible for all activities and reviews controls on both efficiency and data. The internal auditor, therefore, is interested in the controls on all systems. He will pay greater regard to data processing systems than to mathematical systems because, apart from the smaller chance of his making an effective contribution, mathematical systems are, generally speaking, conceived by employees already organizationally independent of the executive function.

Auditing computing systems includes auditing the general controls operating in the computing department as well as in the systems themselves. The lack of elementary precautions to safeguard equipment and information can jeopardize the best of systems and, in any case, the computing department, as a budget unit, needs to be reviewed as much as any other activity.

Systems are created, *inter alia*, to control assets outside the computing department. Thus, the issues to be examined will be, first, the effectiveness of the controls created by the system to operate on those assets and, secondly, the effectiveness of the controls built into the system, whether manual, mechanical or electronic, to ensure proper processing of data within the system.

Systems are expensive to create and expensive to alter. It is therefore good common sense for the internal auditor to involve himself in, and comment on, systems during development as well as systems that are operational. This is sometimes referred to as 'pre-audit'. Important though pre-audit is, however, it is vital that the auditor maintains his off-line role.

The internal audit review of computing systems falls into three parts

1 Review of the computing department as a budget unit, and of the general controls operating in relation to staff, equipment and information.
2 Review of systems under development, examining the effectiveness of the proposals and the controls envisaged within them.
3 Review of operational systems for accuracy and effectiveness

Significantly, external auditors are coming much nearer to an effiency audit in their reviews of the first part than they have thought appropriate for any other activity. Some external auditors, however, have so far restricted their investigations to the third part, and have then carried out these reviews only on financial projects. Internal auditors should complement rather than duplicate the work of external auditing and a considerable contribution from the internal audit department can come from the review of the controls in the computing department and in new systems. It is, therefore, important to have a combination of data processing and audit specialists to conduct the internal auditing of computer systems. Good controls and disciplines in the computing department not only lead to efficient safeguards on and usage of, staff, equipment and information, but also to effective systems development and their subsequent operation.

Audit of computing department

Controls to be reviewed will include those on

1 Division of responsibilities.
2 Purchase and hire of equipment.
3 Fire precautions and general security.
4 Stand-by equipment.
5 Fall-back procedures.
6 Usage of equipment and information.
7 Acceptance of systems for development (for example, feasibility studies and justification statements).

8   Standards of documentation.
9   Testing of new systems and subsequent amendments.
10 Training.
11 Normal administrative responsibilities.

Audit of systems under development (pre audit)

After the new system has been thought out, but before detailed programming and testing begin, the project leader in charge of the systems development should prepare documentation in accordance with laid down standards and send copies to the user department and internal auditing function. A meeting should be held soon afterwards to review the system and its proposed controls and the internal auditor should include consideration of the impact of the system on the business environment and the surrounding control needs.

The internal auditing department will examine the system, consider its effectiveness and, after breaking it down into its different sections of activity, review the controls helping to ensure that only accurate, properly authorized input is accepted for processing, that no information can be added or lost after acceptance, that master files and amendments are authorized, that the processing is correct and that the output, whether visible or invisible, is correctly distributed.

With knowledge of other facets of the organization, the internal auditor may be able to suggest further integration to satisfy other requirements. The internal auditor will also review the statement of justification for the development.

Audit of operational systems

Errors in programs are either accidental or made with intent to defraud. If accidental, the application of proper testing routines or the controls built into the operational system will discover them. If made with intent (which will be more difficult if there is proper segregation of duties and good supervision) errors will not be documented and will remain undetected if the normal controls are not sound. The job of the internal auditor, as for other activities, is to appraise controls, not to act as the control. He will appraise controls by reviewing the organization and the system, selecting items for following through the system, using, perhaps, test-decks to compare results with those expected, and using the computer itself for random selection of items from master files and so on.

As with manual systems, he will choose the technique most suitable to the requirements. Various audit packages now exist to help select random items from master files, to sort and compare information and to prepare reports. Nearly all commentaries of so-called computer frauds indicate the absence of basic controls, so that, had the systems been manual, similar frauds could have been perpetrated even more easily.

Wherever possible, for efficiency reasons, audits of operational systems should be incorporated with the audit of the function concerned.

BENEFITS VERSUS COSTS

Internal auditors should keep timesheets to the nearest day or half-day. Timesheets provide audit job times and records of training leave, sickness and other absences. As such they are also control documents.

The audit job-time in man-days can be multiplied by the average cost per audit man-day to arrive at a job cost. The cost side is thus relatively easy to determine. The benefits side is impossible to quantify in total: it consists of losses discovered and recovered that would not otherwise have been found, of reductions in costs or improvements in income as a direct result of recommendations made, of losses that would have occurred if it were known that there would not be an internal audit appraisal, and finally, of the value in training staff for a future career in the organization. Even if it were possible to quantify all the benefits, the audit department should not be judged on the surplus or deficit of benefits versus costs. If on-line controls were operating perfectly, most managements would have an off-line function, and it is on this basis that internal auditing should be justified.

APPENDIX 1

The Statement of Responsibilities of Internal Auditors issued by the Institute of Internal Auditors is as follows

Internal auditing is an independent appraisal activity within an organization for the review of operations as a service to management. It is managerial control which functions by measuring and evaluating the effectiveness of other controls.

Objectives and scope

The objective of internal auditing is to assist all members of management in the effective discharge of their responsibilities, by furnishing them with analyses, appraisals, recommendations and pertinent comments concerning the activities reviewed. Internal auditors are concerned with any phase of business activity in which they may be of service to management. This involves going beyond the accounting and financial records to obtain a full understanding of the operations under review. The attainment of this overall objective involves such activities as

1 Reviewing and appraising the soundness, adequacy and application of accounting, financial and other operating controls, and promoting effective control at reasonable cost.
2 Ascertaining the extent of compliance with established policies, plans and procedures.
3 Ascertaining the extent to which company assets are accounted for and safeguarded from losses of all kinds.
4 Ascertaining the reliability of management data developed within the organization.
5 Appraising the quality of performance in carrying out assigned responsibilities.
6 Recommending operating improvements.

Responsibility and authority

The responsibilities of internal auditing in the organization should be clearly established by management policy. The related authority should provide the internal auditor full access to all of the organization's records, properties and personnel relevant to the subject under review. The internal auditor should be free to review and appraise policies, plans, procedures and records.

This internal auditor's responsibilities should be

1 To inform and advise management, and to discharge this responsibility in a manner that is consistent with the *Code of Ethics of the Institute of Internal Auditors.*
2 To co-ordinate internal audit activities with others so as best to achieve the audit objectives and the objectives of the organization.

In performing their functions, internal auditors have no direct responsibilities for, nor authority over, any of the activities reviewed.

Therefore, the internal audit review and appraisal does not in any way relieve other persons in the organization of the responsibilities assigned to them.

Independence

Independence is essential to the effectiveness of internal auditing. This independence is obtained primarily through organizational status and objectivity.

1 The organizational status of the internal auditing function and the support accorded to it by management are major determinants of its range and value. The head of the internal auditing function, therefore, should be responsible to an officer whose authority is sufficient to assure both a broad range of audit coverage and the adequate consideration of and effective action on the audit findings and recommendations.

2 Objectivity is essential to the audit function. Therefore, internal auditors should not develop and install procedures, prepare records or engage in any other activity which they would normally review and appraise and which could reasonably be construed to compromise the independence of the internal auditor. The internal auditor's objectivity need not be adversely affected, however, by determining and recommending standards of control to be applied in the development of systems and procedures being reviewed.

APPENDIX 2

Allocation of risk to auditable units

If an internal audit function is being set up or the existing function is being extended, the question to be answered is 'Who can identify the risk areas in the company and weight them between functions?'. The rational reply would appear to be that line managers are in the best position to do this. Line managers at each level are asked to allocate 100 points on a risk basis to the activities for which the personnel reporting to them are responsible. This exercise is conducted for all levels of management from the Chief Executive to first-line management.

The next stage is to calculate the risk points applicable to each auditable unit dependent on the decisions made by line management starting with the Chief Executive. The result will be as shown in Table 10.1. If we then continue with the finance function we have, as an example, the points allocation as shown in Table 10.2

Table 10.1
Allocation of risk points to each auditable unit

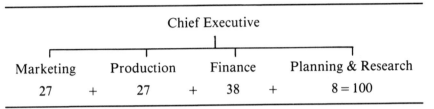

Table 10.2
Allocation of risk points to sections within the finance function

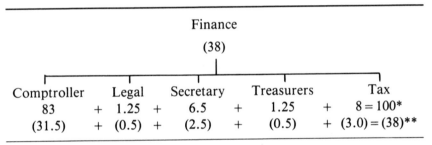

*Allocation of 100 risk points by Finance Director.

This procedure for allocating risk is continued to first-line management level so that each auditable unit has risk points associated with it. Risk point bands can then be decided for high, medium and low risk and each auditable unit can be classified by risk category. The next stage is to decide on the frequency of audit for each risk category.

APPENDIX 3

Example of a 5-year internal audit plan

The year of last audit, man-days of last audit, estimate man-days required for next audit, risk classification and frequency of audit are shown in Table 10.3 for the finance function of a company. An example

Table 10.3
Finance

	Last audit 1975–1979	Man-days	Estimated total man-days required	Risk*	Interval of coverage years	Annual equivalent audit man-days	Quarter	Audit plan man-days				
								1980	1981	1982	1983	1984
Computer systems & operations												
Computer operations	1975	130	150	H	3	50	1	150			150	
System development	1979	80	100	H	1	100	1–4	100	100	100	100	100
Other	1977	130	150	M	4	38			150			
Comptrollers – marketing												
Management accounting	1979	120	110	M	4	28				110		
Stocks	1976	60	90	H	3	30	2				90	
Sales accounting	1979	160	150	H	3	50		90		150		
Comptrollers – corporate												
Financial accounting	1975	60	80	M	5	16	3	80				
Purchases accounting	1977	138	140	H	3	47	3	140			140	
Capital budget & reporting	1979	80	90	M	4	22						90
Payroll	1979	90	80	H	3	27				80		
Treasurers												
	1978	170	150	H	3	50	3		150			
Secretaries, legal, tax												
	1978	105	120	L	5	24				120		
			1410			482		560	400	560	480	190

*H = High, M = Medium, L = Low

208

of an auditable unit summary for a company is shown in Table 10.4 consolidating information from the finance function in Table 10.3 with those of other functions. The annual manpower requirement is calculated on the basis of 210 working man-days per year derived as shown in Table 10.5.

Table 10.4
Auditable units summary

	Total man-days required	Annual equivalent audit	Audit plan 1980	1981	1982	1983	1984
Production	1885	599	615	630	680	455	750
Marketing	3350	981	890	1180	860	740	1410
Finance	1410	482	560	400	560	480	190
Other	820	287	350	240	220	360	450
	7465	2349	2415	2450	2320	2035	2800
Manpower	35.5	11.2	11.5	11.7	11.0	9.7	13.3

Table 10.5
Annual manpower requirement

Annual calendar days	365
Weekends	104
	261
Public holidays	11
	250
Annual leave	20
	230
Training, sickness, other	20
	210

Part III
FINANCIAL STRUCTURE

OVERVIEW

In Part III the conceptual and practical issues associated with raising finance are discussed. Finance can be classified under the headings of debt and equity although some financial instruments sit rather awkwardly between the two categories. Provided the financial manager understands the fundamental characteristics of competing financial instruments and appreciates the mechanics behind valuation of the composite features, the desirability of competing securities and shares quickly becomes apparent.

Raising funds from the sale of ordinary, preferred, cumulative, convertible, participating preferred, ordinary shares or from debentures, overdrafts or whatever, is not unlike raising revenue from the sale of a company's product. In raising funds, as opposed to revenue, the 'customer' of stocks and shares is known as the investor but in all other respects, customers and investors are similar. The financial manager is free to design whatever share or security is considered attractive to an investor. Not all investors have common preferences and there will be identifiable groups of investors to whom different instruments at different prices may be offered. Similarly, some investors are less inclined to experiment with new 'products' and will only consider orthodox instruments. It is the financial managers' job to know his market and to offer the most attractive package of shares and securities: the more attractive the product the better the price that can be achieved and ordinarily, this would be expressed as a reduced cost of capital. The lower the cost of capital the greater the rate of growth of the company.

The theory of perfect markets would suggest, however, that any gains an imaginative and enthusiastic financial manager might make for his company, resulting from the design and sale of 'tailored' securities, will be short lived. If the new instrument is popular with investors other companies will offer similar instruments and any price premium charged to investors will be competed away.

The first chapter of Part III considers the two generic forms of funding; debt and equity. Implications of gearing are examined together with the nature of financial risk, the tax shield and the option bonus. Ideas of perfect markets and arbitrage are introduced to explain why any gains from gearing are dependent upon imperfections in the market system, rather than the skills of a financial manager. In Chapter 12, James Thomson describes debt funding and considers borrower and lender requirements; the structuring of debt and all the major varieties of short-term, medium- and long-term debt. Like many decisions involving finance there is not a definitive formula for calculating the optimal debt structure. Companies are heterogeneous: unquoted companies do not have ready access to the domestic capital market or the eurobond market. The financial manager must analyse the state of the company, its future investment plans and the magnitude and timing of future cash flows and profits; this enables the selection of a sensible balance between short- and long-term debt, alongside the decisions on gearing.

Occasionally, a company may wish to make a public issue of debt securities. These may take the form of unsecured Loan stock or of Debentures which are secured on specific assets and therefore rank before unsecured loan stock in terms of entitlement to interest and repayment in liquidation. Interest on most corporate borrowing is allowable for tax, but the market for corporate debt is relatively inactive in the UK. The relative lack of corporate debt issues in the UK is often ascribed to vigorous competition from public sector borrowing, which makes the cost of debt issues relatively high compared to other forms of debt. Elroy Dimson in Chapter 13 describes the various methods of making a new issue of shares including public issues by prospectus, offer for sale, placings, offer for sale by tender, public issue by tender and a Stock Exchange introduction. Shares which might be issued are preference shares (often considered as a class of debt with fixed dividend payments but without the benefit of tax deductibility for the dividends), or various classes of equity or ordinary share capital. Finally, warrants can be issued (usually in conjunction with other securities) giving the holder the right to purchase a specified number of ordinary shares from the company at stated prices during specified periods of years.

Next to undistributed income and bank borrowing the largest single source of funds to quoted companies results from the issue to existing shareholders of 'rights' to subscribe to a specified number of additional ordinary shares at a stated price within a limited period of weeks. To help ensure that the issue will be fully subscribed the rights price is fixed below the current market price of the shares. Furthermore underwriters are usually employed, who effectively insure the success of the issue by agreeing to purchase any shares remaining unsold. Since the rights are issued to existing shareholders in proportion to the number of shares already held, existing shareholders can maintain the proportion of ownership that they have in the company simply by exercising their rights. Alternatively, they may sell the rights. Paul Marsh, Chapter 14, explains why rights issues do not dilute the value of existing shareholdings, why rights issues rarely fail and how to quantify the insurance benefits that underwriters provide.

Chapter 14 also indicates the likely flotation costs of rights issues including administrative, legal and underwriting costs. These costs undoubtedly explain why companies prefer to use internal sources of funds and bank borrowing when possible, and issue securities almost exclusively to raise large tranches of long term finance.

To summarize, the choice of financing is determined in practice by industry norms, limitations prescribed in a company's *Articles of Association*, convenience, term of requirement, taxes and flotation costs. The choice, amount and timing of funds raised from various sources must be planned within the context of projected sources and uses, indicating both the needs for funds and the ability to pay the cash costs of funds under various possible future business conditions. The chapters in Part III provide a comprehensive review of the main external sources of funds available to companies in the UK.

11

Capital structure

Philip A. Vale

Capital structure describes the mix of long-term funding used to finance the assets of a business. Conventionally 'long term', in this context, only excludes periods of less than 12 months. Discussions of capital structure, therefore, would ordinarily exclude any current liabilities used to finance a part of a firm's working capital requirement or to finance a particular asset. In this chapter, however, the discussion is restricted to the two principle generic funding instruments, debt and equity: a distinction is not made between current and long-term liabilities and, as a consequence, the principles outlined here can be considered to apply for financial structure in general.

The overriding objective for the financial manager must be to engineer the most efficent use of the business's funds. Efficiency in this context is usually described in terms of maximizing the value of the firm or maximizing the return on equity (ROE). Insofar as the value of an on-going business is the capitalized value of the earnings it generates in perpetuity, the two objectives are synonymous.

Decisions concerning capital structure need to be recognized as major strategic decisions that require considerable time and effort to formalize; they are an integral part of overall corporate strategy and can determine the success or otherwise of a business's trading plans. Major revisions to structure are expensive in terms of management time and administrative and legal fees incurred outwith the organization: the more urgent a requirement to alter structure becomes, the more expensive the operation tends to be and the more likely that new funds cannot be secured without incurring a cost penalty. For organizations not accustomed to the disciplines of external investors there is a tendency for the capital structure of a business to evolve in an *ad hoc* way that can constrain growth in a buoyant market: in a depressed market, an unnecessary capital burden may be carried. Incoming managers inheriting an *ad hoc* structure need to analyse alternative capital mixes in terms of the particular business, its stage of development, its long-term plan and its previous trading record. Competing structures that appear attractive in the intra company context can be compared with inter business comparisons taken from within the same industry. Finally, potential developments within the financial sector, the economy as a whole and any proposed legislation need to be investigated before a final proposal can be put to the board. Subject to acceptance in principle being received, the precise route and associated scheduling has to be prepared before the capital structure plan is complete.

PRIMARY CONSIDERATIONS

The orthodox academic treatment of capital structure takes as its starting place the economists' notion of perfect markets: in particular, it is assumed that some hypothetical firm to be analysed faces perfect markets for its shares and debt. The rather abstract but powerful tool of comparative statics can then be worked to establish equilibrium positions if only one variable is investigated in isolation. The assumption of *ceteris paribus* is central and the movement to a new equilibrium is instantaneous. 'Real-world' imperfections in the conceptual model can subsequently be considered individually to establish the nature and direction of any influence. The approach is rigorous and intellectually satisfying; simultaneously it can provide useful insights. For the majority of organizations, however, the initial assumptions of the academic treatment are too far removed from reality to produce conclusions that have immediate applicability. Unquoted firms do not have access to perfect markets for their shares or debt: the bulk of any debt requirement is ordinarily provided from institutional sources. The financial manager is more likely to encounter credit rationing in one form or another than a rising cost schedule for additional increments of debt. Similarly, the 'market price' of the company's shares will have to be derived from specific past, present and projected financial data: there will be no market for shares in the true sense. The majority of this chapter, therefore, approaches the subject of structure in a rather more pragmatic way, appropriate for many substantial but unquoted private companies. In the final section more formal wisdom of structure is outlined as appropriate to an environment where debt and equity are readily saleable: these principles are useful because they provide an insight to the rationale of 'competitive' investors.

FUNDAMENTALS OF STRUCTURE

Given the financial manager's objective to maximize the return on equity and accepting that the efficiency of a company's assets is unlikely to be dictated by the source of funds, there can only be scope for improving the performance of a company if different categories of funds carry with them different effective charges. Our discussion is restricted to just two types of fund, debt and equity. Debt can be thought of as a conventional, fixed-rate, term loan and equity as ordinary shares. Under such conditions and assuming no corporation tax, the point is very easily demonstrated.

Suppose a company employs assets with a gross worth of £1 million and the net trading profit generated before payments to either debt or shareholders is £0.12 million. The return on capital employed (ROCE) is 12 per cent. If the rate of interest on debt is also 12 per cent there is no immediate advantage, or disadvantage, in using either equity or debt funds. Earnings per share (EPS) will be constant.

Table 11.1
Equality between the cost of debt and equity with no corporation tax

Gross worth (£mill)	1	1	1	1
ROCE(%)	12	12	12	12
Shares @ £1 per share (mill)	1	0.75	0.5	0.25
Debt (£mill)	-	0.25	0.5	0.75
Interest @ 12% (£mill)	-	0.03	0.06	0.09
Profit after interest (£mill)	0.12	0.09	0.06	0.03
ROE (%)	12	12	12	12

Table 11.1 illustrates a very basic, but, central point. ROE, the maximand, is not affected by the level of debt if the cost of debt is equal to the return on capital employed. In short, the degree of financial gearing, the ratio of debt to equity, is irrelevant if the effective charges to debt and equity are the same. Intuitively this could be expected. Similarly, it can be inferred that if the rate of interest on debt is less than ROCE the use of debt will increase ROE whereas at rates of interest higher than ROCE additional debt will decrease ROE.

Substituting cheap money (debt) for expensive money (equity) will increase EPS if ROCE is unaffected.

DEBT AND EQUITY

The nature of debt and equity, and the fundamental differences between the two types of funds, allow us to guess that debt and equity are unlikely to cost the same.

Debt is an obligation taken by the organization to make repayments to the lender according to a prescribed and agreed schedule. Very often security/collateral is taken by the lender to guarantee, in part at least, the repayments. Default would occur if the firm did not make the repayments and the lender could then liquidate the collateral. In principle, the offer and acceptance of debt provides the lender with a more or less certain income stream. The capitalized value of that income stream provides adequate compensation for the lender's temporary loss of wealth. Clearly, if this were not the case no offer of debt would be forthcoming.

Equity, taken here to include only ordinary shareholders' funds, is very different. The offer of equity to a firm guarantees no income stream for the investor. The investor expects a return on the investment but has no recourse if the return is not forthcoming or if the return is made up of non-sequencial payments received at largely unpredictable points in the future.

At one extreme is the debt investor who is not involved with risk but with the conversion of present wealth into predictable amounts of future purchasing power; at the other extreme there is the equity investor who is prepared to gamble. The equity investor will require compensation not only for the loss of immediate purchasing power but also for the risk of losing the original investment or for receiving an uncertain return. The comment that clearing banks are not in the risk business and that venture and development capital funds are suppliers of risk capital must be clear.

Accepting the fundamental distinction between the two broad categories of finance and acknowledging the fact that equity will be more expensive than debt, it might be reasonable to expect firms to employ all debt and no equity. This should readily be seen as a nonsense. The intrinsic risk of business, resulting from the uncertainties of markets and the political, institutional and economic environments in which they operate, combined with exogenous factors such as Acts of God, do not disappear because a firm is exclusively debt financed. Furthermore, there must be a reasonable guarantee to the provider of debt if the nature of debt is not to become that of equity by default. In principle then, it might seem reasonable for an organization to borrow as much as the asset value of the firm – as assessed by the provider of debt. This valuation would usually reflect an expected sum of money that could be generated from the sale of a company's assets: the value will be less than the book value or replacement value of the assets and by a very considerable margin if the sale were to be organized by a liquidator. For very practical reasons equity is an inescapable source of funds if only to make good the difference between the security value of assets and the actual cost of those assets.

The assets of an organization can secure a loan but it is the future trading performance of the organization that services the debt. If a company cannot realistically demonstrate that it can achieve returns to finance debt, additional collateral will be required by an institutional lender. Thus the potential level of debt within an organization will be constrained by either the asset's security value or by the level of anticipated trading profits.

Finally, it must be recognized that if business risk is fixed for any given business at any given time and that debt is risk free whereas equity involves risk, then as the proportion of debt in the capital mix increases, so each £1 of equity must carry more risk. In a firm substituting debt for equity, shareholders would ordinarily require the prospect of higher returns. Certainly the possibility of an organization recording a loss increases with the level of gearing.

It is important to point out that so far we have only explicitly considered business risk associated with uncertain sales figures and gross profit margins. External equity investors may put restrictions on the level of gearing – irrespective of the availability of debt. In practice, these restrictions reflect the equity investors' perception of financial risk. Financial risk is an additional source of risk related directly to the level of gearing: the higher the gearing the greater the financial risk for any given business. Clearly the degree of financial risk associated with ordinary shares will have implications for the number of prospective shareholders. This is considered in more detail later.

The above is an explanation to suggest why a discussion of capital structure is never concerned exclusively with types and combinations of debt and why debt structure must be analysed as a sub-component of capital structure. It is only necessary for us to consider why capital structure rarely simplifies to a discussion of equity. In theory a firm can be exclusively financed by equity: in practice it is rarely the case, although some industrial sectors are characterized by a very major reliance on share capital.

TAX SHIELD

Very simply put, government provides a tax incentive for firms to employ debt. This arises from an allowance to charge interest against profits before taxation: any payment to shareholders is made after the payment of corporation tax. The higher the rate of corporation tax the more valuable the tax shield (see Figure 11.1 and Table 11.2).

If the contribution to gross worth from debt increases from zero to 50 per cent the tax bill is reduced by £37 500. This is the value of the tax shield and is equal to the rate of corporation tax multiplied by the debt interest; in this case $0.5 \times 75\,000$. Reductions in the rate of corporation tax reduce the value of the shield and will have implications for the appropriate level of gearing. For a stable company, generating adequate trading profits to finance a debt of £500 000 and facing a fixed interest rate of 15 per cent, the tax shield represents an effective flow of income to the company of £37 500 each year in perpetuity. If it is company policy to refinance the original debt with new debt of the same character at the end of the term, then the income stream can be capitalized to provide the present value of the tax shield. Present value of the Tax Shield = 37 500/0.15. Tax shield = 250 000.

The original loan benefiting from the shield was only £500 000. When the corporation tax rate is 50 per cent the government provides a 50 per cent subsidy to any debt a company accepts.

To capitalize the value of the tax shield we discounted at 15 per cent the interest charged on the loan. Clearly the lower the interest rate charged on debt the greater the present value of the tax shield. The annual value of the shield drops with lower interest rates, however, to restore the

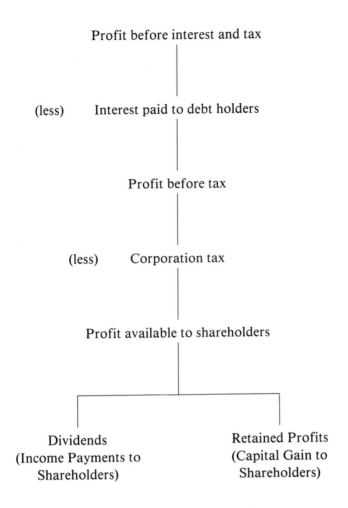

Profit before interest and tax

(less)   Interest paid to debt holders

Profit before tax

(less)   Corporation tax

Profit available to shareholders

Dividends
(Income Payments to
Shareholders)

Retained Profits
(Capital Gain to
Shareholders)

Figure 11.1   Payment to debt and share holders

capitalized value to the corporation tax rate multiplied by the loan
interest.

The full benefit to a company from using debt and securing the shield
will only be available if trading profits are adequate to service the debt:
accounting losses can be carried forward but the present value of the
shield will be reduced. Similarly, if the company does not effectively
borrow in perpetuity the capitalized value of the shield will be reduced.

Table 11.2
The value of the tax shield

Gross Worth (£mill)	1	1	1
ROCE	12%	12%	12%
Shares @ £1 per share(mill)	1	0.75	0.5
Debt (£mill)	–	0.25	0.5
Interest @ 15% (£000s) (Return to debt holders)	–	37.5	75.0
Profit before interest and tax (£000s)	120	120	120
Profits before tax (£000s)	120	82.5	45.0
Tax @ 50% (£000s)	60	41.25	22.5
Profit after tax and interest (£000s) (Return to shareholders)	60	41.25	22.5
Total income to share (£000s) and debt holders	60	78.75	97.5

Table 11.2 illustrates a firm with three possible gearing ratios: 0:1; 1:3; 1:1; Corporation tax payable reduces substantially in the illustration as the level of gearing increases: the corollary being that the total income available for both debt and shareholders increases.

Table 11.3 illustrates how the tax shield can be used to gear-up the earnings per share and, thus, increase the value of the company. In the case illustrated, the return on equity (ROE) rises from 6 per cent to 30 per cent for a given ROCE of 12 per cent.

Table 11.4 illustrates the disadvantage of debt if trading profits cannot be confidently expected to cover interest charges. Any short-fall between trading profit and interest charges can only be made good by a corresponding diminution of the company's net worth. Furthermore, Table 11.4 indicates that there is a minimum level of trading profit before interest and tax below which debt financing will reduce a company's net worth.

Table 11.3
Financial gearing and the tax shield

	£	£	£	£	£
Gross worth(£mill)	1	1	1	1	1
Profit before interest and tax (£mill)	0.12	0.12	0.12	0.12	0.12
Shares @ £1 per share (mill)	1	0.5	0.2	0.1	0.04
Debt (£mill)	–	0.5	0.8	0.9	0.96
Interest at 10% (£000s)	–	50	80	90	96
Profit before tax(£000s)	120	70	40	30	24
Tax @ 50% (£000s)	60	35	20	15	12
Profit after tax and interest (£000s)	60	35	20	15	12
Earnings per share (%)	6	7	10	15	30
Gearing Ratio	0 : 1	1 : 1	4 : 1	9 : 1	24 : 1

Table 11.4
Financial risk and gearing

	£	£	£	£	£
Gross worth (£mill)	1	1	1	1	1
Profit before interest and tax (£mill)	0.11	0.11	0.11	0.11	0.11
Shares @ £1 per share (mill)	1	0.5	0.45	0.1	0.04
Debt (£mill)	–	0.5	0.55	0.9	0.96
Interest at 20% (£000s)	–	100	110	180	192
Profit before tax (£000s)	110	10	0.00	(70)	(82)
Tax @ 50% (£000s)	55	5	–	–	–
Profit after tax and interest (£000s)	55	5	0.00	(70)	(82)
Gearing ratio	0:1	1:1	11:9	9:1	24:1

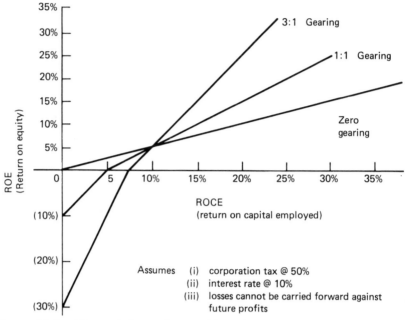

Figure 11.2   Financial gearing and break even

Figure 11.2 and Table 11.5 illustrate the effects of financial gearing more clearly. The key points may be summarized.

1   When the effective cost of debt, that is, after the tax shield, is the same as the return on capital employed (ROCE), the return on equity is unaffected by gearing.

2   When the effective cost of debt is less than the ROCE; substituting debt for equity increases ROE.

3   For any level of gearing there is a minimum, but positive, ROCE below which the ROE becomes negative and the net worth of the organization drops sharply. This is the source of financial risk and must be clearly differentiated from business risk discussed earlier.

Figure 11.2 illustrates one further point that needs to be made explicit. Debt as already discussed, is repaid and serviced according to an agreed, pre-arranged schedule. Ordinarily there would be no flexibility associated with this schedule and the commitment to make repayments would remain even if the fortunes of the indebted organization were to change

Table 11.5
Financial gearing and break even

Profit before interest & tax	0.0	0.5	1.0	1.5	2.09	2.5	3.0
Gross Worth	10.0	10.0	10.0	10.0	10.0	10.0	10.0
ROCE	0	5%	10%	15%	20%	25%	30%
Shares @ £1	5.0	5.0	5.0	5.0	5.0	5.0	5.0
Debt	5.0	5.0	5.0	5.0	5.0	5.0	5.0
Interest @ 10%	0.5	0.5	0.5	0.5	0.5	0.5	0.5
Profit before tax	(0.5)	0	0.5	1.0	1.5	2.0	2.5
Tax @ 50%	-	-	0.25	0.5	0.75	1.0	1.25
ROE	(10%)	0	5%	10%	15%	20%	25%
Shares @ £1	2.5	2.5	2.5	2.5	2.5	2.5	2.5
Debt	7.5	7.5	7.5	7.5	7.5	7.5	7.5
Interest @ 10%	0.75	0.75	0.75	0.75	0.75	0.75	0.75
Profit before tax	(0.75)	(0.25)	0.25	0.75	1.25	1.75	2.25
Tax @ 50%	-	-	0.125	0.375	0.625	0.876	1.125
ROE	(30%)	(10%)	5%	15%	25%	35%	45%
Shares @ £1	10.0	10.0	10.0	10.0	10.0	10.0	10.0
Profit before tax	0	0.5	1.0	1.5	2.0	2.5	3.0
Tax @ 50%	0	0.25	0.5	0.75	1.0	1.25	1.5
ROE	0	2.5%	5%	7.5%	10%	12.5%	15%

for the worse. Equity, on the other hand, affords the organization a certain degree of flexibility which has a real value to management. Dividends are paid out of post-tax profit, if the organization's performance does take an unexpected, temporary nose-dive and profits disappear, there is no obligation to pay ordinary shareholders. The net worth of the company is not affected provided all depreciation costs have been met and the company can work to restore performance with an unaffected asset base. There is a very clear trade-off for the private company: the advantage of issuing debt that arises from the tax treatment of interest must be considered in the light of the financial risk that gearing brings and the associated lack of flexibility in making payments for the use of funds.

OPTION BONUS

For rapidly growing companies with an impressive track record and the prospect of strong future growth, increasing the gearing ratio will raise the ROE and, provided that the profits are retained within the organization, contribute to the rapid buildup of ordinary shareholders funds. There can be the temptation to fully employ the debt capacity of the firm. That is, provided profits are large enough, the firm uses the full security value of its assets to generate debt. Such a strategy denies a firm the value of the option bonus and would not generally be considered prudent. If the debt capacity of an unlisted company is fully employed there is no scope, by definition, to raise further debt. Additional funds can only come from investment in equity. If the current holders of equity are not in a financial position to personally purchase additional shares external investors must be approached. Generally debt can be raised more swiftly than external equity: by retaining a level of surplus debt capacity a firm can generate funds that will allow it to respond quickly to an unanticipated but lucrative opportunity to invest. In short, surplus debt capacity can be used as a store of speculative liquidity. In this context 'speculative' does not necessarily carry with it connotations of risk. The option bonus is a store of purchasing power: in the extreme case this can be employed to make risk free, high yielding, opportunistic investments. With no surplus debt capacity such opportunities have to be foregone.

LIQUIDITY

A final point to consider when deciding the appropriate balance of the capital mix is more pragmatic. In the preceding discussion the appropriate level of debt was being prescribed by the organization's ability to provide security and its ability to service the debt. The ability to service debt was approached by the proxy of profit before interest and tax. In fact, profit does not service debt as defined here, debt is serviced with cash. If the liquidity position of an organization is poor, irrespective of its profitability, there is the possibility of default or expensive liquidation of certain assets to meet servicing charges. Equity on the other hand is financed by profits: the return to shareholders can take the form of capital gains if generated profits are retained within the company: there is no associated requirement for, or demands placed upon, liquid reserves.

COMPETITIVE MARKETS FOR DEBT AND EQUITY

No discussion of capital structure is complete without reference to Modigliani and Miller. In 1958 these authors presented the argument that the net worth of a business would be unaffected by the capital mix: this was the notion of the conservation of investment value. Because the value of any business is the capitalized income stream generated by its assets, reflecting the intrinsic profitability and risk of the organization, it is irrelevant how those assets are financed: whether the capital structure is made up of ordinary shares, debentures or other securities will not affect the performance of the assets. From the preceding sections such a proposition can only be supported if the effective cost of debt and equity are common. With perfectly competitive markets for a firm's shares and securities, with all participants in the markets being perfectly informed and with there being no distortion from the social and political systems, arbitrage will not be possible at equilibrium. If the gains from arbitrage have been traded away at the new equilibrium, the cost of debt and equity will be common for a given level of risk. The original proposition and subsequent modifications are described elsewhere but it is important that financial managers should not imagine that there are strong theoretical grounds for expecting a lasting advantage to be gained from financing decisions other than that engineered by the makers of fiscal policy.

WEIGHTED AVERAGE COST OF CAPITAL (WACC)

What is the implication of the equality of cost between debt and equity after tax for WACC? For the purpose of illustration suppose we begin with a company which has no debt. The cost of equity capital for such a company simply reflects the risk and required rate of return for the assets of the company (including its growth opportunities or goodwill). Now let us introduce some debt into the capital structure. The after-tax interest cost of the debt may appear low, but it does not alter the weighted average cost of capital according to the theoretical argument. The increased gearing increases the cost of equity (expected dividends and capital gains per pound of equity) just sufficiently to keep the weighted average cost of capital the same as it would have been if there had been no debt financing. In other words the cost of capital reflects only the required rate of return on the company's underlying operations and does not reflect the particular way those operations may have been financed. The financial community is not giving anything away and does not bless companies with extra debt any more than companies with less debt.

The theory is incomplete, however, as pointed out by Paul Marsh in Chapter 14. Other factors such as convenience, flotation costs and the costs of default must govern the balance between equity and debt in the capital structure of the company.

Unless one knows how to alter the cost of equity to reflect the extra cost per pound of equity due to gearing, one cannot calculate the weighted average cost of equity correctly. The purpose of obtaining the WACC is to try to determine a discount rate for an asset that is independent of the particular way the asset might be financed. A more useful way of determining this discount rate was discussed in Chapter 2. The required rate of return is merely the shareholder's personal rate of interest after tax plus a premium for the systematic risk of the individual asset.

CONCLUSIONS

Although the existing theory of finance provides little guidance as to the optimum capital structure of a company, many practical guidelines are available to help management maintain a sensible and prudent balance between equity and debt finance. Since borrowing entails legal obligations to pay interest and to repay principal, borrowing incurs a risk of reorganization or liquidation in the event of default. In an industry characterized by highly variable and uncertain cash flows, borrowing can entail greater financial risk than in less volatile industries. Thus a study of industry debt ratios can provide useful rules of thumb for the capital structure of a company including funds required for dividends, interest and repayment of debt. A sensitivity analysis of sales revenues, costs, working capital and capital investment requirements under alternative sets of business conditions can indicate the likelihood of default given a planned level of debt financing. Prudent financial managers keep the burden of interest payments and repayment of loan capital within the bounds of the company's expected ability to pay under a variety of possible conditions.

Arrangements for sufficient finance must be provided to ensure not only the continued financial viability of the firm under the most adverse circumstances but also to ensure that all likely options to invest in worthwhile growth can be exercised as profitable opportunities emerge.

12

Debt funding

James A. Thomson

In managing its finances, a company must establish an appropriate debt structure. It must select and maintain a balance between short- and long-term debt, fixed or variable interest rate borrowing; it must decide whether to raise finance in foreign currency and what security it is prepared to offer.

In present markets, the arrangement of debt finance should not be a constraint on an established management team. Finance for new ventures, or to back new technology, is available and in the past two years the number of Management Buy Outs successfully completed have demonstrated that debt can, in many cases, substitute for equity in the short term. That debt must be correctly structured. It is dictated by the needs of the business and the types of finance available.

BORROWER'S GOALS

The company's first aim will be to assure that the loan will be available for as long as it is required. The company does not wish to be faced with a request for repayment which it cannot meet. In other words the term of the borrowing should match the purpose for which the funds are to be used. A company which has succeeded in obtaining a large export order payable 180 days after shipment and needs the debt financing will turn first to its bank for a temporary increase in its overdraft. However, if the company plans a new factory then it will seek a commercial mortgage or long-term loan.

The difference between these two borrowing requirements lies in the source of funds to make repayment. The export order provides an assured source of repayment within six months so that a longer commitment from the bank is not required. Repayment of the finance for the new factory, on the other hand, can only be made incrementally over a period of years. The company would be unable to meet a demand for repayment after six months.

Cost is an important consideration. A fixed rate of interest may superficially be attractive since it assists in planning and project costing. However, a company may regret taking out a loan at a fixed rate if interest rates fall since lenders impose penalties for early repayment of fixed interest loans. In recent years, when interest levels have been high, borrowing on a variable rate, linked to base rate or money market rates, has provided both flexibility and protection against falls in rates.

Also lenders normally require security. A company must bear in mind that conceding security to one particular class of creditor, entitling him to the realization proceeds of that security in priority to other creditors may restrict other sources of finance. For this reason, finance which is secured specifically, such as a factory financed by commercial mortgage or equipment purchased on instalment credit, is generally preferable to borrowing against a more sweeping form of security such as a bank debenture.

The debenture is frequently taken as security for short-term bank facilities. It also constitutes a method of raising long-term secured finance in the capital markets. It combines fixed charges on property with a floating security over all other assets of the company, principally debtors and stocks. The debenture holder benefits from wide ranging powers in the event of a default by the borrower including the appointment of a Receiver, normally a chartered accountant, to manage the affairs of the company on the lender's behalf. The debenture is a simple form of security for both borrower and lender but, in view of the restrictions imposed, a company will seek to avoid debentures in order to retain freedom of action whenever possible.

SOURCE OF FINANCE

The principal sources of finance are a company's suppliers, the banks and the institutions. By institutions are meant insurance companies and pension funds for whom lending is another form of investing the funds entrusted to them on a long-term basis. A relatively small amount of finance is made available by government and similar agencies; for small and growing companies especially this is an important source of funds.

Although instalment credit, leasing, factoring and development loans are distinctive and important forms of finance, these areas are dominated by the subsidiary companies of the large banks. They can be arranged by consulting the company's bank.

Institutional funds are generally raised by smaller companies through intermediaries such as insurance and finance brokers since the insurance companies and pension funds do not have large lending departments. For large and multinational companies the funds are raised on the capital markets. The company issues an interest bearing security such as a Debenture Stock or a Eurobond which institutions can purchase and trade in a flexibile way.

LENDER'S REQUIREMENTS

A company seeking to raise finance would be well advised to think what a lender is looking for; these are the same considerations that the company itself has when it has surplus cash to invest.

The first consideration of a lender is for the safety of the investment. Banks are lending depositors' money and must ensure that their loans are repaid on the due date. This can be assured only by careful assessment of borrowers and ensuring that their capital and debt structure is suitable for the business they are engaged in.

Second, a bank or institution may be looking for liquidity; the ability to receive back at short notice any money it has lent. This was of special concern to banks which held substantial short-term customer deposits. In practice this requirement for liquidity has lost some of its significance although it provided justification for the traditional popularity among bankers for the 'working capital overdraft'. In the highly mobile financial markets of today, a liquidity crisis in the banking system is likely to arise so quickly that demanding repayment of such 'self-liquidating' overdrafts will serve little useful purpose. Also, in view of their greater reliance on term money market deposits, banks are more ready to provide medium-term lending commitments.

Finally, lending institutions are seeking a return on their funds. For an insurance company the benchmark is the return on gilts of similar term. A bank requires a margin between the cost of raising deposits and the rate at which money is lent.

The most important of these features is the lender's confidence that the borrower will be in a position to repay the loan on the due date. This confidence depends on the lender's assessment that the borrowing company both has an appropriate debt structure and has not exceeded its debt capacity.

DEBT STRUCTURE

The capacity of a company to raise finance is governed first by the level of shareholders' funds and second by its earnings from which interest and loan repayments are met. If borrowings are high compared to the company's capital and reserves, then the company can bear fewer losses before the lenders' principal is at risk: it has a high capital gearing. If the level of a company's profit, before interest and tax, does not exceed the annual interest charge by a reasonable margin then the company is vulnerable to any downturn in profitability or increase in interest rates: it has a high interest gearing.

A company which has raised medium- or long-term debt must also earn sufficient profit to meet the repayments on that debt. However, in assessing this aspect of the company's ability to raise finance, it is the gross cash flow generated by the company which is important. The cash flow is the measure of profit before interest and tax but also before depreciation of plant and other fixed assets. For it is from this figure that the company must meet loan repayments and interest as well as contribute to replacement investment.

The level of gearing which lenders will consider acceptable varies from industry to industry. Generally, capital intensive industries can carry only a low level of gearing. Their earnings, being sensitive to relatively small changes in capacity utilization, require a substantial part of the investment to be financed by equity rather than debt. As a rule of thumb, banks would not expect a company's debt to exceed 100 per cent of shareholders' funds with the figure for heavy industry being in the region of 25 – 50 per cent.

Management Buy Outs (MBOs) have been financed with a very much higher level of debt, with 300 per cent capital gearing not being uncommon. Does this not offend the above guidelines? An analysis of MBOs shows that the institutions financing them look for three features: asset backing, that is to say, a safety net in the form of assets or parts of the business which can be sold quickly to bring gearing down to more conventional levels; cash flow, so that in spite of high capital gearing the company has a more comfortable level of interest gearing; and a good management team which, highly motivated by running their own business, will rapidly bring down gearing levels by their actions. Moreover, although structured as long-term debt in the form of loan stock and redeemable preference shares, it is normally intended to replace such debt with equity from an issue of shares at an early stage. Finally, it must be appreciated that many venture capitalists – especially the so-called Growth Funds – look for a high compound rate of growth on their equity investment; this is achieved by including an exaggerated level of debt gearing in the finance package.

SHORT-TERM FINANCE

Trade credit

The principal source of a company's short-term finance is trade credit, the agreed payment period allowed to a company by its suppliers. A company buying goods on 30 day terms need issue its cheque only at the end of the month following that in which the goods were purchased. This represents finance for between 30 and 60 days, with an average credit period of 45 days. If the company purchases £1 million of goods and services each year on these terms then it is obtaining approximately £125 000 finance from this source alone.

Trade credit has a hidden cost. Most suppliers offer a discount for early settlement of invoices of up to 2.5 per cent for payment within seven days. This places an opportunity cost on the remaining five to seven weeks trade credit of up to 30 per cent per year. If the purchasing company can take advantage of such a discount, for example by borrowing from its bank at 12 per cent, then it may save up to 18 per cent per year in financing costs.

Trade credit in the UK is normally granted on open account terms, payment being requested by submission of a simple invoice. A company buying from abroad may be asked to sign a bill of exchange, thereby undertaking to pay on a specific date when the bill is presented to the company's bank for payment. Bills of exchange are used frequently in Europe, both as a means of payment and to obtain bank finance. The supplier may therefore be able to obtain advantageous financing terms to pass on to its UK buyer.

Trade credit differs from the other types of finance discussed in this chapter in two important respects. First, the company's credit standing will be kept under review both by suppliers, who set credit limits, and agencies such as Dun and Bradstreet. The financial management must bear in mind that the key factor in establishing a good trade credit rating is a satisfactory payments record.

Second, the amount of trade credit available to a company varies directly with the level of purchases, particularly if a company undertakes long-term contracts. It may overlook the extent to which it relies on trade credit. Lower purchases resulting from a declining order book may rapidly squeeze a company's finances, especially if the contracts were not profitable.

Bank overdrafts

Banks lend on overdraft to meet a company's requirement for short-term working capital to finance stocks of goods and to offer the payment terms normal in the trade to its customers. Overdrafts are made available on the company's current account and are used by the company drawing cheques up to the agreed overdraft limit.

Because overdrafts are used to finance sales, payment for which is subsequently credited to the account, banks regard such 'self liquidating' lending favourably since − at least in theory − they can call for repayment on demand at any time. If the company's current account does not swing into credit then the bank may seek to rearrange such 'hard core' borrowing into a medium-term loan with a repayment schedule.

Overdraft facilities offer a high degree of flexibility to a company. Funds received for the credit of the company's account are applied immediately in reduction of the company's borrowing rather than being held on deposit at a lower rate of interest. Interest is calculated on the day-to-day balance outstanding at a margin above the bank's published base rate. Interest is payable quarterly. Overdraft interest is no longer calculated by reference to an official rate, such as bank rate or its successor, minimum lending rate. However, market forces ensure that an individual bank's base rate does not long stay out of line.

The bank will wish to ensure that the overdraft facility is used for the self-liquidating purpose requested. It may require that drawings under the overdraft limit are matched by a minimum level of debtors and/or stocks, the level being established by reference to the borrowing company's published accounts.

Although banks provide overdraft facilities to large companies on an unsecured basis, they frequently seek security from their small- and medium-sized customers. The most usual form of bank security is a Debenture, which incorporates a mortgage over the borrower's premises, if owned, and a 'floating' charge over the company's stocks and debtors. The powers available to a bank which holds Debenture security are very wide-ranging. In particular, the bank is entitled to appoint a Receiver to the company if default becomes probable.

Short-term loans

Although banks obtain most of the funds they lend from deposits made directly with them, they also borrow from and lend to each other in the London money markets. The interest rates on loans and deposits in this 'wholesale' market for funds are determined by the rates at which funds are bid for or offered to banks at any time. In minimum amounts of £1 million, funds may be borrowed or lent at the London Interbank Offered Rate or 'LIBOR' for periods from overnight through one, three or six months up to five years.

For borrowing amounts in excess of £50 000, banks make available loans for fixed periods and at interest rates linked to LIBOR. Within an overall facility limit, a company can make drawings in multiples of £50 000 for periods of one, three or six months. The company selects the period of the advance according to its own funding requirements and also with a view to interest rates. Unlike an overdraft, the borrowing cost of each advance is fixed for the complete period of three or six months. Such a loan facility is particularly valuable during a period of rising interest rates.

Acceptance credits

A further source of funds for companies from the London money markets is an Acceptance Credit. Until 1981 this form of finance was provided only by the prime UK banks and merchant banks; it is now more freely available and, as a consequence of Bank of England monetary policy, is a very competitive form of short-term finance.

Against a company's undertaking to provide funds at maturity after a selected period of one, three or six months, a bank will accept bills of exchange in multiples of £50 000 drawn on it by that company. These bills, called Bank Acceptances, represent an unconditional promise by that bank to pay the face value to the holder of the bills when they mature after, say, three months. As such, the bills form readily marketable money market instruments which can be discounted in the London money markets.

Bank Acceptances are particularly attractive to banks and Discount Houses because they qualify as primary bank liquidity under Bank of England regulations. Indeed, the Bank of England will buy eligible Bank Acceptances from the market if there is a shortage in day-to-day liquidity. Accordingly the rates of interest available compare very favourably with the LIBOR rates for short-term loans. In comparing rates, however, it must be borne in mind that Bank Acceptances are bought and sold on a discount basis, that is, interest is deducted at the beginning. The true yield on a three month Bank Acceptance quoted at 10 per cent per year is therefore 10.25 per cent.

An Acceptance Credit facility is made available by a bank under a short agreement, the facility letter. The company deposits blank bills of exchange with the bank until it wishes to make a drawing. At the time of drawing the bank charges an acceptance commission, similar to its lending margin on a short-term loan or overdraft, which is paid by the company together with the costs of selling the Bank Acceptances into the market.

Factoring

Factoring of trade debts is a form of short-term finance which recognizes the liquidity of debtors. Instead of lending money, the factoring company is prepared to purchase up to 80 per cent of a company's approved debtors for cash, immediately copy invoices are submitted. The balance of 20 per cent is payable when the individual customer pays.

A distinction is drawn between non-recourse factoring, under which the factor assumes the risk of non-payment, and recourse factoring services which provide finance but leave that risk with the supplier: the supplier has to reimburse the factor if his customer does not pay.

The factoring company must ensure that the credit risk of the individual companies whose debts it is purchasing are acceptable. It will also wish to ensure that it has a security interest in the debts purchased. In practice, the factoring company is fulfilling the role of a company's credit control department. Full service factoring, indeed, incorporates a complete sales ledger service including book-keeping, administration and debtor collection.

To ensure that it has a proper claim to the debtors financed, the factoring company will normally notify those customers that it has purchased the debt and specify to which account and in what form payment should be made. However, factoring companies also operate factoring services which do not entail disclosure to the individual customers. Under these facilities, also known as confidential invoice discounting, the factor purchases the debts but appoints the supplier as its agent in collecting those debts. The factor incurs a greater degree of risk than with disclosed factoring; its assessment criteria will accordingly be higher.

Charges for factoring are calculated in a different way from bank overdraft and loan facilities. A financing charge is made equivalent to perhaps 2.5 per cent above bank base rate. In addition a charge is levied on turnover which, in the case of full service factoring, may amount to a further 2.5 per cent.

Factoring is available to companies with a wide spread of trade debtors: it is not a form of finance suited to all companies, such as retailers, selling direct to the public. Confidential invoice discounting can be particularly cost effective for companies selling to the public sector. In deciding whether to use a factoring service, a company will consider the savings from sub-contracting out the sales ledger administration. These may outweigh the loss of direct contact on payment matters with the company's customers. It must also be ensured that selling the company's most liquid asset, its debtor portfolio, does not restrict access to cheaper bank finance.

MEDIUM-TERM FINANCE

Sources of medium- and long-term finance divide into those which are asset related, for example, a lease on a machine or mortgage on a property and those which are structural and depend on the strength of a company's finances as reflected in its balance sheet, profit and loss account and cash flow. The principal source of medium-term funding of the second type is the banks; in many cases the lending bank will also take security.

Hire Purchase

Instalment credit, whether by hire purchase or lease, has increasingly been used by British companies to finance new plant and machinery. It is available from specialist Finance Houses, the largest of which are owned by the major banking groups. The Finance House makes funds available to the company investing in vehicles or machinery by itself purchasing the assets and then hiring them for an agreed monthly hire charge payable over the life of the agreement, usually five to seven years.

Legal ownership of the equipment remains with the Finance Company until all the rental instalments have been paid, the sum of those payments totalling the purchase cost of the machinery and interest over the period of the HP Agreement. However, the borrowing company is responsible for maintenance of the equipment, can use any capital allowances available as taxation relief and has the right to purchase it for a small fee at the end of the agreement period.

Instalment credit bears a rate of interest either linked to Finance House Base Rate or fixed for the term of the agreement and built into the monthly instalment. A deposit of 10 per cent to 25 per cent will be required, depending on the type of equipment. HP is more expensive than bank finance, although when interest rates are falling, finance companies offer very competitive fixed interest rate finance.

However, in spite of the cost, instalment credit offers a useful source of finance with interest and repayments spread equally over the useful life of the equipment purchased. It is a significant source of funding for newly established small companies, especially for vehicles and − due to the high second-hand value of the machinery − the graphics and printing industry.

Leasing

Both banks and finance companies provide lease finance. A lease is also instalment credit, offering variable or fixed rate finance repayable by monthly or quarterly instalments over the life of the equipment acquired. Leasing differs from Hire Purchase in various respects. First, the lease agreement does not incorporate an option for the company to purchase the machine at the end of the period; instead the equipment is leased for a further term, the secondary lease period, at a nominal rental.

Leasing has a second attraction for larger groups: it enables both the equipment and the related finance to be kept off-Balance Sheet; that is to say, that when analysts assess the published accounts the apparent performance is enhanced. Changes in accounting standards lead to leases being capitalized and shown in the accounts.

Off-Balance Sheet status is available for Operating Leases: these differ from a finance lease in that the lease does not pay back the equipment cost and finance costs during the primary lease period. The lessor, taking a view on the residual value of the equipment, is prepared to calculate lease payments on the basis that the equipment will still be worth, say 20 per cent of the purchase price and could be sold to realize that amount if necessary. In the USA, the expansion of operating leasing is assisted by a system of residual value insurance which enables lessors to predetermine the remaining value of the equipment leased.

Bank loans

Until 15 to 20 years ago, bank lending was made available on overdraft with the facility technically repayable on demand. In practice, overdrafts were used to finance a wide variety of investment and expansion projects undertaken by the borrowing companies. Any medium-term financing was provided by instalment credit and leasing subsidiaries who could look to the security of the equipment financed. Then, stimulated by the opening of the eurocurrency market, banks started to make loan facilities available for periods up to five years on a rollover basis.

Banks are prepared to commit funds for five, seven or ten years under the terms of a loan agreement or facility letter. The funds lent under this agreement are wholesale deposits drawn from the London money markets for periods of one, three or six months. Interest is charged at a margin above the LIBOR rate for the relative period. Such medium-term loans are called rollover loans because they are, in effect, a series of short-term advances of the type described earlier. When a loan drawing, or advance, taken under the facility matures after, say, three months it is replaced by a further drawing; the advance is rolled over.

Under certain circumstances the bank can call for repayment prior to the maturity date. Repayment is accelerated should the borrower breach certain undertakings such as granting security to other lenders or failing to repay other indebtedness on its due date. The loan agreement may also contain financial ratios with which the borrower must comply, typically maintenance of a minimum level of net assets and compliance with limitations on total debt.

Eurocurrency loans

Short-term advances or medium-term rollover credits can be made available by all banks in currencies other than sterling. The most common currencies are the USA Dollar and the Deutschmark.

These loans are funded with foreign currency deposits from the wholesale markets in a way which mirrors the Sterling money market in London. To enable foreign currency payments to be made, the interest rate is fixed two days prior to the funds being made available or rolled over under the facility. The interest rate is agreed by reference to the market rate in London.

The name eurocurrency loan in the context of today's markets is misleading. It simply denotes the pool of loans and deposits made by banks in currencies other than their own; the principal importance being that they fall outside the bank's domestic monetary system with its Central Bank Reserve requirements for the control of liquidity and money supply.

LONG-TERM LOANS

Long-term loans are those granted for periods of between 15 and 30 years, periods which are attractive to institutional investors. Banks are increasingly prepared to provide commercial mortgages and 20 year business loans, especially to small- and medium-sized companies. This area of provision, however, is the traditional territory of insurance companies and pension funds.

Mortgage finance

Mortgage loans are provided to finance the purchase of specific properties with the land and buildings providing security for the loan. Lenders are prepared to lend about two-thirds of an independent professional valuation of the property.

Finance is available on a fixed or floating interest rate, the fixed interest rate being set at an initial level of 1.5 − 2 per cent above the yield on a gilt edged security of comparable term. The costs of the valuation, together with legal costs may amount to as much as 2 per cent flat of the loan amount. Insurance company lenders will be interested in any related insurance business and this may be a factor in the availability of funds.

Sales and Leaseback

Institutions who invest in property and provide mortgage loans may also offer finance by Sale and Leaseback. An owner occupier agrees with the institution to sell the property to it at an agreed price, provided the institution enters into a suitable lease agreement with the former owner.

This technique has been used, for example, by rapidly expanding multiple retailers to release finance for company acquisitions.

Domestic Capital Market

Larger companies have traditionally been able to raise fixed interest rate debt in a form which is quoted on the London Stock Exchange. The investors buying these stock are again insurance companies and pension funds, together with investment and unit trusts who regard them as a high yielding alternative to gilts.

The principal form of quoted fixed interest instrument is Debenture Stock. Debentures are formally secured on the assets of the undertaking, either by floating charge or by fixed and floating charges. The security is administered by Trustees and the stock is constituted by a Trust Deed. In addition to the terms relating to the amount of the issue and the interest provisions, a Debenture Stock Trust Deed contains a number of limitations on, for example, the maximum amount of secured debt or a minimum level of interest cover.

Companies of very high standing possessing a sound Balance Sheet and a good earnings record may also issue Unsecured Loan Stocks. In the absence of the security available to investors in Debenture Stock, the Loan Stock Deed will contain restrictions on the granting of security to other lenders, a 'negative pledge'.

In recent years high interest rates have inhibited companies from raising conventional fixed rate finance on the domestic capital markets. The rising stock market has, however, stimulated the issue by companies of Convertible Loan Stocks. These are Loan Stocks issued at a relatively low interest rate, for example 8 per cent compared to a gilt yield of 11 per cent. The investor is compensated by the right to convert his stock into Ordinary Shares of the issuing company at a date perhaps five years in the future; during those five years the holder of the Convertible stock benefits from a yield higher than that on the issuing company's Ordinary Shares but retains some of the potential future capital gain.

Eurosterling Bond Market

The eurosterling bond market and the London capital market cater for a different group of investors. The eurosterling bond market does, however, represent an alternative source of fixed interest rate sterling for large companies. Funds are made available by private investors in the eurocurrency bond market as an alternative to investing in domestic bonds or deposits. Term is normally seven years although recently a couple of issues have been done for longer periods.

International companies can also raise variable rate finance from this eurobond market, again for periods of five to seven years, by issuing Floating Rate Notes. There is an increasing demand for these instruments, on which the interest rate is fixed every six months, as an alternative to deposits.

EXPORT FINANCE

The payment terms in export markets are normally longer than trade between two UK companies. Accordingly an exporter will require finance for the additional period of credit granted to his customer. In the case of exports of capital goods such as machinery, ships or complete plants engineered on a turnkey basis, the buyer will often ask the exporter to provide or arrange the provision of finance with the sale.

Export Credits Guarantee Department

In recognition of these additional financing burdens on exporters, ECGD provides both credit insurance and guarantees to banks in support of export finance. The ECGD credit insurance policy provides cover against non-payment from insolvency or default by the overseas buyer or from transfer problems in the buyer's country. ECGD insures on the comprehensive principle and requires the exporter to offer a broad spread of export turnover in a range of markets, both good and bad. Premium rates are charged on the basis of this spread but also with regard to the past claims experience of that exporter.

Banks will often be prepared to provide increased overdraft facilities if the exporter benefits from an ECGD comprehensive insurance policy (confusingly referred to by ECGD as a Guarantee). To finance sales to particular countries the bank can take an assignment of the debt either formally or informally through the shipping documents and then benefit from an assignment of the exporter's ECGD policy. From the bank's point of view this assignment provides an assurance of the quality of the debt which the bank has taken as security. Banks will therefore advance up to 90 per cent of exports on this basis, a significantly higher proportion than they might otherwise do.

From the lender's point of view, assignment of the exporter's ECGD insurance has the weakness that the exporter may void his ECGD policy, for example, by not declaring to ECGD all his export turnover for calculations of premium; or allowing his customer extra time to pay without seeking ECGD's consent. To overcome this and to facilitate access to cheap finance, ECGD runs two schemes: the Bills and Notes scheme and the Open Account Bank Guarantee scheme. For small- and medium-sized companies these schemes provide finance at competitive rates, even after paying ECGD's guarantee fee of ½ per cent. However, having incurred substantial losses under these schemes, ECGD is withdrawing them with effect from October 1987. A number of banks have introduced schemes under a new insurance policy, the EFST, which enables companies to join in an insurance policy in the banks' name as co-insured; this fulfils some of the requirements which the banks were looking for in the Bank Guarantee scheme.

Short-term support finance is available from a number of sources other than banks.

The small exporter can contact an export merchant experienced in trade with his buyer's country. Instead of selling overseas, the exporter sells to the export merchant who then on-sells to the foreign buyer at his own cost and risk.

Finance can also be arranged through a Confirming House. The Confirming House, based in the exporter's country acts at the request of the overseas buyer, confirming his buyer's order to the exporter with a guarantee of payment. The Confirming House establishes a separate finance agreement with the buyer so that, unlike the export merchant, responsibility for meeting the other terms of the supply contract remains with the exporter.

The technique of factoring is commonly used to provide short-term finance for exports, especially within Europe and North America. Export factors have joined together with companies in other countries to provide their services across national borders, in groupings such as Credit Factors International. This is a very convenient way for small companies, especially those using a factoring company in the UK, to invoice and finance their sales overseas.

Medium-Term Export Finance

Although ECGD is withdrawing its guarantees to banks for short-term export finance, the Department continues to provide Bank Guarantees in respect of export finance for periods of longer than two years. These guarantees are made available on two bases, Supplier Credit and Buyer Credit.

Supplier Credit is used for the support of manufactured goods. The exporter can obtain a Bank Guarantee from ECGD either for a specific contract or, on a comprehensive basis, to cover a series of contracts with different buyers and countries. With this Guarantee, the exporter can readily obtain medium-term finance from his bank, enabling him to grant extended credit terms to his buyer. The exporter need not be concerned that his own bank borrowing facilities will be reduced. The guarantee is available in either Sterling or foreign currency up to 85 per cent of the sales contract price and repayment is normally made in equal instalments every six months. Should the overseas buyer fail to pay an instalment, then the exporter's bank can recover the sum from ECGD.

ECGD Buyer Credit Guarantees are available for larger, specific projects and engineering contracts. They differ from Supplier Credits in that the underlying supply contract is negotiated on cash payment terms but is closely linked to a separate finance agreement between the supplier's bank and his customer. The bank receives a payment guarantee from ECGD. From the exporter's point of view, Buyer Credits have the advantage that the finance is kept out of his Balance Sheet. They are complex and lengthy to negotiate, however, since disbursement arrangements for the loan must be carefully integrated with the commercial contract.

The terms and conditions on which export finance can be made available is governed by the 'Consensus', an agreement on minimum interest rates, downpayment amounts and maximum financing term between member states of the Berne Union. The Consensus aims to prevent excessive competition between exporting countries on financing terms. Initially, because of the impact of these rules on trade with the USSR, but also because of the greater flexibility of the ECGD Supplier Credit Guarantee, the short-term Confirming House technique has been adapted to medium-term export finance. Export Finance Houses, owned by the large banks, act as suppliers of deferred payment terms to the overseas buyer and take out an ECGD Supplier Credit Guarantee. The commercial contract responsibilities are left with the exporter who achieves the advantages of Buyer Credit with the flexibility of Supplier Credit.

Other sources of export finance

There are a number of ways in which banks provide finance for exports not insured with ECGD. An exporter may require his overseas customer to arrange for a bank in the buyer's country to open a Letter of Credit in the exporter's favour. The exporter's bank will guarantee or confirm that payment will be made. If the payment terms under the Letter of Credit are on a deferred basis, a bank may discount bills of exchange drawn on it or purchase the future payment claim.

If the exporter despatched his shipping documents on a Documentary Collection basis, including a term Bill of Exchange for acceptance by his buyer, the exporter's bank will discount the accepted bill. It may also be prepared to negotiate it, that is to say, purchase the bill at the time of despatch and prior to acceptance by the buyer. If the negotiated bill is not accepted then the bank has recourse, that is, seeks repayment from the exporter.

The technique of buying bank guaranteed export bills of from six months to five years term, without any recourse to the exporter, has developed rapidly in the last few years. Known as forfaiting, it developed in Switzerland initially to finance German exports to Eastern Europe. Most British banks have a forfait section in their International Division which will quote for the purchase of such bills and advise their exporting clients on the documentation requirements. Forfait rates are quoted on a straight discount basis, that is, without interest compounding, and for longer term transactions companies should enquire what the interest rate is, expressed on a true yield basis.

SPECIAL TYPES OF FINANCE

Sales aid finance

Sellers of capital equipment, such as agricultural plant and machinery, often need to provide finance for their customers. This finance is frequently made available by finance companies on a conventional instalment credit or lease basis. In exchange for this attractive business, the finance house may be prepared to finance the dealer's showroom stocks. Alternatively, a dealer may decide to establish its own sales aid finance company, obtaining refinance from a larger finance house by block discounting instalment credit agreements.

Property development finance

Builders and developers can obtain finance from banks for up to two thirds of the cost of land and development expenditure. The bank will require to be satisfied by independent valuation that the project is viable: it will also wish to be satisfied with the credentials of the builder and the pricing basis of the contract. The developer will contribute his share of the finance first and the bank will be repaid from sales proceeds of housing units. Interest and professional fees may sometimes be financed.

If the development is commercial, office or retail, the bank will provide more favourable financing terms if the development is prelet or presold to an institution.

Ship finance

In spite of difficulties in the industry, finance is available from banks for ships secured on a ship mortgage. If appropriate, the lending bank will take an assignment of charter hire.

Instalment credit companies

Finance companies can borrow from banks or from other finance companies by the block discount of agreements entered into with customers. Provided the lending institution is satisfied with the quality of credit assessment and underwriting of the company, it will be permitted to borrow several times its capital.

Off balance sheet finance

There is a continuing demand from large companies for off balance sheet finance, that is, debt which does not appear on the borrower's balance sheet. The motive is principally enhancement of return on published capital. In the case of energy projects, where many off balance sheet financings have been structured, repayment, and hence some of the risk, is linked to the volume and price of the resource extracted.

TREASURY ASPECTS

Foreign currency

As explained above, foreign currency loans are freely available from banks. Although interest rates in foreign currencies appear attractive, any company considering such borrowing must analyse its own foreign currency position. If the company does not invoice export sales in currency nor own an overseas subsidiary, then it should avoid incurring the foreign exchange risk of raising currency debt. A company borrowing Deutschmarks leaves itself with the risk that, if the Deutschmark has further appreciated against sterling, the additional sterling amount needed to repay the loan will outweigh any interest saving.

Financial futures and swaps

New instruments have been developed over the past two or three years as a result of two worldwide trends: the deregulation of financial markets and the improvement in computer and information technology. Although these instruments are not widely available to smaller companies, the advantages will in due course be passed down to them.

An example is the Business Loan offered by Lloyds Bank which enables the borrower to switch between fixed and variable interest rates every five years. A second example based on interest rate options, is the interest rate 'collar' which guarantees that the interest rate on a variable rate loan will not rise above a certain level during the life of the loan; this benefit is paid for by the borrower accepting a floor rate below which he foregoes any fall in interest rates.

A further new technique is that of currency and interest rate swaps. If a company has borrowed at a fixed rate but, after the loan has been running some time, decides to switch to variable rate it can do so very simply through an interest rate swap with a bank.

These techniques provide a financial manager with ways to manage all aspects of his debt — whether currency or interest rate — without having to repay or re-arrange the underlying loan.

CONCLUSION

In this section a wide variety of different forms of debt finance have been outlined. They are not all appropriate to every company: unquoted companies do not have ready access to the domestic capital market or to the eurobond market. Nor is there a formula for calculating the perfect debt structure for each company: the gearing of a company subject to a management buy out is not an appropriate or comfortable model for other companies.

The key requirement of a financial manager is that he analyses the state of the company and the effect of future investment plans on profits and cash flow. This enables him to select a sensible balance between short- and long-term debt, alongside his decisions on the equity structure of the company.

13

The UK new issue market

Elroy Dimson

At some stage, most companies need to issue equity to finance new investment. Many firms also wish to be able to issue marketable securities as a means of acquiring other businesses, and the owners of other companies wish to have the option of selling their shares at some future date. By obtaining a Stock Exchange listing, all these objectives can be achieved. Although there are alternative means of attaining these objectives – for example, seeking a partner or selling out to a larger concern – any company of sufficent size is likely to give some thought to a flotation on the Stock Exchange. In this chapter, we therefore describe the UK new issue market and how a company can use it to go public.

We will try to answer six questions. First, what role does the Stock Exchange play in the new issue market? Second, why do companies seek a Stock Exchange listing? Third, what regulations govern companies that are going public? Fourth, what methods of issue can be used to obtain a listing? Fifth, how much does a flotation cost the company? Finally, what are the mechanics of a new issue; who is responsible for each step and when must each event take place?

The new issue market is often confusing to the layman. This is partly because people familiar with it make extensive use of technical terms, some of American origin. In the Appendix, we therefore provide a glossary of the terminology used in relation to the new issue market.

ROLE OF THE STOCK EXCHANGE

The Stock Exchange fulfils two functions. These are the provision of a capital market where investors can be brought together with organizations which require new finance, and of a secondary market for existing financial assets which are already held by investors. This chapter is concerned with the first function. However, the primary capital market is inextricably linked to the existence of a secondary market, as investors are more prepared to acquire new securities if they know their investment will be readily marketable on the Stock Exchange. Thus, although a new issue market could exist in the absence of a stock market, in reality new issues are usually subject to the regulations of the Stock Exchange as well as the relevant statutory rules.

There are three ways in which the Stock Exchange may permit a company's securities to be traded in the stock market. Regular trading is allowed if the securities have an official listing on the Stock Exchange. A company can only acquire listing if, prior to its flotation and subsequently, it meets a series of stringent requirements laid down by the Exchange. At the other extreme, it is possible for unlisted securities to be traded on an occasional basis through the Stock Exchange's Rule 163. This rule permits members of the Exchange to negotiate transactions in such securities as shares in football clubs, certain mineral exploration stocks, and shares in companies which have not been scrutinized by the Stock Exchange. Every transaction in these securities requires prior consent by the Exchange.

Increased use of Rule 163 for trading in unlisted securities (supplemented by worries about the competing over-the-counter market operated by investment bankers M.J.H. Nightingale and the deliberations of the Wilson Committee) led to the creation of the new Unlisted Securities Market (USM) late in 1980. The USM offers a facility to companies that wish to have their shares traded on the stock market without prior approval for each deal, but do not wish to take on the full expense of obtaining listed status. The USM has enabled companies to turn to the stock market to raise sums as small as £100 000. At the time of writing, the typical company coming to the USM has raised about £350 000.

The Stock Exchange stipulates a minimum size for a company which seeks a listing for its shares and a maximum size for a company that wishes to be on the USM. As we mentioned earlier, the Stock Exchange subjects the affairs of the company to detailed scrutiny both before the issue and after it. For example, companies with no earnings history cannot obtain a listing, whereas a company which already has a listing may be suspended by the Stock Exchange if the nature of its business is altered radically.

The stock Exchange exercises control over the procedures followed by the issuing company and the method it uses for offering securities to the public. The basic methods of making an issue have changed only in detail since the periods following the Companies Acts of 1929 and 1948. However the degree of scrutiny applied to a new flotation has increased over the years and the following sections present the situation as it exists in the 1980s.

REASONS FOR OBTAINING A LISTING

There are a number of reasons for obtaining a listing for the shares of a company. However, for the purposes of presenting the general background to a flotation, it is sufficient to classify four reasons for going public. These are

1 Capital requirements of the firm.
2 Financial needs of the owners.
3 Improving the marketability of the shares.
4 Enhancing the prestige of the company.

We will consider each of these in turn.

Capital requirements of the firm

Companies which are unable to generate suffcent capital for expansion from retained earnings or by subscription from their owners must look to outside institutions for new funds. Loan capital is available in many forms and from many institutions. For instance, overdrafts, bill financing, trade credit, factoring, tax delays and deferrals, term loans, hire purchase, leasing, mortgages, sale and leaseback and loan stock all represent different sources, as well as different types, of external finance.

By contrast, external equity is normally obtainable from only two sources. Either the company may establish a link with a venture capital organization, or it may create new shares which are sold to the public by means of obtaining a Stock Exchange listing. The main part of the UK venture capital business is conducted by a single organization, the Industrial and Commercial Finance Corporation (ICFC). This company, and several of its competitors, are 'nursery' organizations and their funds tend to be invested in firms with a prospect of Stock Exchange or USM listing in the future. Both sources of equity therefore involve a firm in giving consideration to a public offering of shares.

The provision of a listing for a company will help it to meet its capital requirements in three ways. First, the firm can raise capital in order to finance current and impending capital expenditures. Secondly, it can reduce its level of gearing, using equity to repay overdrafts or long-term loans which are nearing maturity. Thirdly, the firm will find that future financing is easier and cheaper for a quoted company than it is for a private company. Thus, listing gives strong financial advantages to a firm which is expanded rapidly.

Financial needs of the owners

A company which has been run as a family concern presents a number of financial problems to its owners, which they can overcome by going public. Often, the first motivation for obtaining a listing is the desire to consume some of the capital tied up in the business by selling some of the shares held by the family. A second factor may be a need to diversify the proprietors' investment portfolio out of the family business into a wider spread of assets. Thirdly, the owners may wish to alter their level of gearing, either because they will be able to borrow more against quoted securities than against unquoted securities, or because they wish to reduce their personal debt by selling some of their shares. A fourth reason for desiring a listing is the opportunity for speedy valuation and easy settlement of fiscal debts, such as Capital Transfer Tax. Finally, a listing conveys certain tax advantages to a company which is 'close', under the provisions of the Income and Corporation Taxes Act 1970, provided at least 35 per cent of the voting power is held by the public. This is because a close company is taxed at the relevant rates of income tax, rather than at the present corporation tax rate.

Though the financial requirements of the owners may provide a strong motive for going public, the distribution of a block of existing shares (known as a 'secondary' distribution) does not affect the company financially. However, most new issues are arranged to combine a secondary distribution with raising new capital for the company itself. Furthermore, some 'no new money' issues are made by companies that wish to raise fresh capital by means of a rights issue at some later date, once the share is listed. The distinction between 'new money' or 'primary' issues, which raise funds for the company, and 'no new money' or 'secondary' issues, which are sales of existing shares, is therefore blurred. Since the methods are the same for secondary and primary issues, we will not draw any further distinction between these two types of issue.

Improving the marketability of the shares

The third category of reasons for obtaining a listing is that of improving the marketability of the shares. From the company's point of view, it is the marketability of its shares that enables it to raise capital by means of a rights issue. Marketability also assists companies that want to undertake acquisitions of other businesses, as consideration can then be paid by means of the shares of the acquiring firm.

From the viewpoint of the proprietors of the new issue, marketability facilitates future consumption decisions. The facility to resolve fiscal problems without selling or liquidating the entire company also depends on the existence of a market in the shares. Finally, and most important, many investors are unwilling, and many institutions are not permitted, to hold unmarketable securities. The existence of a listing may therefore substantially increase the value of a company.

Enhancing the prestige of the company

The prestige of being a listed company is a supplementary, though relatively trivial, motive for going public. It is argued that a listing adds respectability to the business, and that mention in the financial press provides free advertising. Staff recruitment may be aided by this prestige and by the possibility of setting up an attractive share incentive scheme. The approval of the Stock Exchange and the dissemination of information is said to give confidence to the customers and employees of the firm.

There is, of course, another side to publicity, and this can be a potential disadvantage to a firm which goes public. The company may lose its family relationships with employees and may be forced into disclosing sensitive or adverse information to a larger and more critical public. The proprietors of the firm may well lose control of the business, the directors' remuneration will be scrutinized publicly, and the proprietors may not wish to be exposed to the risk of being taken over. Another drawback to a public listing is that the value of the firm will be established for tax purposes at a higher level than if it were unlisted, in which case the worth would generally be based on an asset valuation. Finally, it will be seen that the costs of going public are usually very high. A private company does not decide lightly on obtaining a public listing.

REGULATIONS CONCERNING NEW ISSUES

At present, a company's application for an official listing is not considered by the Stock Exchange unless its expected market value is at least £500 000 and each security for which a listing is sought has an expected value of at least £200 000. From 1966 to 1973 the limits were £250 000 and £100 000, respectively, while there were no such requirements earlier than 1966.

At least 25 per cent of the equity must normally be made available to the public. In the case of the USM, this figure is reduced to 10 per cent. However, these requirements are interpreted with some discretion. For instance, Pilkington Brothers was floated on the Stock Exchange with only 15 per cent (£10 millions worth of shares) being offered to the public.

Unless it is a mineral exploration company or investment trust, the company must have a five year financial history. For the USM, however, this is reduced to three years, or less in certain circumstances. The company seeking an official listing must produce audited results for a financial period ending less than six months prior to prospectus publications, while much less onerous requirements are laid down for USM applicants. The current regulations for an official listing are laid down in the latest update of the so-called Yellow Book and in preliminary publications on the USM.

An application for a listing is required of a company that wants to be listed on the Stock Exchange in four circumstances

1   If it has no previous listing on the Exchange.
2   If its previous listing has lapsed.
3   If it has been involved in 'shell' operations.
4   If the nature of its business has changed significantly.

If the proposed flotation involves the issue of an application form for shares or debentures for cash consideration, the Companies Act 1948 requires that the form be accompanied by a prospectus. However, if an issue is a wholly private placing, or a rights issue with no right of renunciation, the prospectus requirement is waived.

The Companies Act also imposes responsibility on those making an issue to ensure that accurate and sufficient information is published. In addition it regulates certain aspects of the issue procedure, ensuring, for example, that at least three days elapse between the appearance of the advertisement and the time the issue takes place.

The Stock Exchange supplements the statutory regulations in many

257

ways. Even when the issue involves existing securities, if an official listing is desired the Exchange insists on a prospectus in the approved form. It requires a variety of information to be disclosed and documents to be supplied, including many items to a specified format. Finally, by means of the sanction of a withdrawal of the listing or a suspension of dealings, the Exchange ensures that it continues to receive up to date accounting information and company documents after the firm receives its quotation.

The Stock Exchange lays down rules governing the methods by which securities may be brought to the market, and these are described in the following section. It also co-operates with the Bank of England in exercising control over the timing of issues which raise £3 million or more. In such cases, it is necessary for the brokers who are sponsoring the issue to apply for a date known as 'Impact Day', which is the first day on which the size and terms of the issue may be known to the market.

METHODS OF MAKING A NEW ISSUE

A company may obtain a new listing by means of the following methods of issue

1   An issue by prospectus (or public issue).
2   An offer for sale.
3   A placing.
4   An offer for sale by tender.
5   A public issue by tender.
6   A Stock Exchange introduction.
7   A transfer of listing from another stock exchange.

In addition, a company which already has a listing for its shares may obtain a listing for additional shares which are created as a result of

8   An issue to existing shareholders (that is, a rights issue or open offer).
9   The exercise of options, warrants or convertibles.
10 An issue of shares in connection with an acquisition.
11 An exchange or conversion of securities into other classes of security.
12 A capitalization (or bonus or scrip) issue or a share split.
13 A placing or offer for sale (both of which can only be arranged in special circumstances).

Since the second group of issue methods do not enable a firm to go public (except in combination with a Stock Exchange introduction), and are largely described in Chapter 14, only methods 1 – 7 will be discussed here.

Before proceeding to explain the main methods of going public, however, it may be helpful to anticipate the thrust of the description by reference to Figure 13.1. The figure shows the types of companies which go public, their principal objectives in so going and the procedures which they can adopt. It also shows some of the interrelationships between issue methods and some of their distinguishing features. The method by which shares are issued by listed companies is principally the rights offering, though in special circumstances listed companies may occasionally make use of the methods normally reserved for unseasoned issues.

Prospectus issues and offers for sale

The prospectus issue and offer for sale are almost identical methods of issue. In both cases, a fixed number of shares is offered to the public at a stated price. In the case of a prospectus issue (also known as a public issue) the offer is made directly by the company. In an offer for sale, however, the company sells it shares to an issuing house, which in turn offers the shares to the public at a slightly higher price. Thus, the company acts as principal in the case of a prospectus issue, frequently employing an issuing house to act as agent to the transaction. On the other hand, the issuing house is the principal in the case of an offer for sale.

These issues are made by means of a prospectus which includes an application form to subscribe. Except for an offering on the USM (which is unusual), the Stock Exchange requires the prospectus to be advertised in full in at least two London daily newspapers. In the case of a company which is offering its share capital to the public for the very first time, the Companies Act requires the prospectus to state the minimum subscription which will enable the objectives of an issue to be achieved. If the issue fails to raise the minimum subscription, all funds offered by applicants must be returned by the issuer. Furthermore, virtually all unseasoned, primary issues (other than those made by investment trusts and property companies) are made by means of an offer for sale rather than a prospectus issue. Because of the high costs of failure and the statutory requirements, both prospectus issues and offers for sale are underwritten against failure.

Financial structure

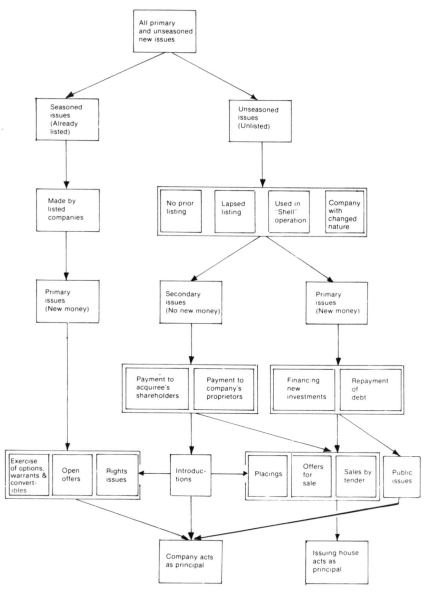

Figure 13.1   The structure of the UK new issue market

The underwriting is arranged by the issue's sponsors, which are usually an issuing house but may be the broking firm which is acting as broker to the issue. The underwriters receive a disclosed commission, which over the recent past has been 1 ½ per cent of the issue proceeds, in return for guaranteeing to purchase any shares not taken up by the public. The sponsor who provides the underwriting does not retain more than a small proportion of the underwriting as it reinsures itself against the failure of the issue. The reinsurance is placed with a range of sub-underwriters who accept a proportion of the underwriting risk in exchange for a slightly smaller commission, normally 1 ¼ per cent. The sub-underwriters concerned are financial institutions, particularly insurance companies, as well as pension funds, investment trusts and charitable funds.

The prospectus specifies the procedure for application, the minimum number of shares which can be applied for, and the opening and closing dates for application, usually several days after prospectus publication. Applicants for equity issues must submit a cheque for the full cost of the shares they require. If the issue is popular, the application lists will be closed immediately after opening, with the offer oversubscribed.

If the issue is oversubscribed, the available securities must be distributed to a sufficiently large number of investors, and in marketable quantities, so that the Council of the Stock Exchange is satisfied that a ready market will develop in the shares when dealings commence, about a week after the offer closes. The basis of allotment usually provides for large applications to be scaled down in line with the degree of oversubscription (to the nearest hundred shares), whereas smaller applications are selected by ballot for allotment in full or on a partly scaled down basis. Usually, the degree of scaling down slightly favours smaller applications in order to spread ownership as widely as possible. Preferential allotments to employees and existing shareholders are limited to 10 per cent of the amount offered.

Placings

In a Stock Exchange placing the issuing house acquires the shares, as in an offer for sale. However, instead of inviting the public to subscribe for the issue the shares are 'placed' with clients of the issuing house and with jobbers. As in the case of an offer for sale, the issuing house is remunerated by the turn between the price it paid and the placing price, and it may also charge a fee.

This method of issue avoids the needs for the payment of underwriting commission and the expenses of administering the application and allotment procedure. The prospectus requirements are less onerous, and the prospectus need be advertised in only one newspaper with abridged details in a second paper. In the case of a USM placing, only an announcement of the placing need be advertised.

The Stock Exchange must give its approval to a placing, which it will not normally do for large companies. At present, a company of more than £4 million or so in value would probably be obliged to resort to an offer for sale, as might smaller issues offered by well-known firms. The USM, in fact, refuses to accept placings of over £3 million. Since the dominant concern of the Exchange is the spread of shareholdings, the guideline for withholding permission for a placing is whether there would be significant demand for the share if issued by means of an offer for sale. With the same motives, the marketing arrangements should provide that at least 25 per cent of an equity placing (or more, if it is a popular issue) is offered to the market through being placed with jobbers, who may not retain more than 10 per cent.

Tender issues

Tender issues utilize a variant of the offer for sale or public issue methods. In a tender issue the offer price is not fixed, potential applicants being invited to tender for shares at the price they see fit, provided it is at or above a stated minimum price. The selling price for the shares is then determined from the bids received.

The tender method has been favoured when an issue is difficult to price. For this reason it has rarely been used by those companies which would otherwise make a public issue, namely investment trusts and property companies. Indeed, since 1962 there have been only a couple of public issues of equity by tender, those of Diners Club in 1964 and City and Gracechurch Investment Trust in 1969. All other tenders were offers for sale by tender, using an issuing house as principal to the issue.

Assuming the issue is not undersubscribed, applications are listed at each price level from the highest tender downwards. Taking each successive application in sequence from the list, there is a market clearing price at which the issue is fully subscribed. In principle all these applications could be accepted in full, but this might not ensure a reasonable spread of shareholdings. The Stock Exchange therefore encourages the issuing house to set a 'striking price' which is below the market clearing price, and to scale down applications accordingly. Regardless of the applicant's tender, applications are invariably (with one exception, Hurst and Sandler in 1963) allotted at the same striking price for all applicants.

The tender method has experienced short bursts of popularity since it was introduced for ordinary shares in June 1961. Though used in the UK in every year throughout the 1960s (especially 1963 – 64 and 1968) and in France until the present time, the tender method was not utilized throughout the 1970s. Its main advantage, namely taking the pricing and (most of) the allotment decision out of the hands of the issuing house, has been its downfall. Although they acknowledge it to have a role in relation to issues which present extreme difficulties of pricing, neither the Stock Exchange nor the issuing houses have lent their support to tenders as a generally acceptable issue procedure. However, water company loan stock issues are required by the Water Act 1945 to be made by means of a tender issue (with discriminatory pricing, in this case). This experience, and the similarity of a tender to a conventional offer for sale, suggests that the tender method could easily be reintroduced to the new issue market. Indeed, two recent issues (Charterhouse Petroleum and Spring Grove in 1980) were offered for sale by the tender method.

Introduction and transfers of listing

Unlike the methods described so far, the primary objective of an introduction or transfer is not the sale of shares to the public. In many cases a reasonable distribution of shares already exists, and a listing is required in order to establish a market in the shares. Transfers of listing from provincial stock exchanges to the Stock Exchange in London were permitted until shortly after those exchanges were unified in 1973. However, a prior flotation was required on the original exchange, and this was only a partial method of gaining a listing.

The introduction method, on the other hand, continues to be available to companies which are going public. Three categories of applications for listing are favoured for this method, namely

1 Securities which are already listed on another exchange.
2 Large unlisted companies which can satisfy the Stock Exchange as to marketability.
3 Shares of a holding company which are issued in exchange for the share of one or more listed companies.

Although the Companies Act does not demand a prospectus for an introduction, as no capital is being offered, the Stock Exchange requires one to be advertised and made available to participants in the introduction. This requirement is, however, waived in the case of a USM introduction of a company previously traded under Rule 163. As in a placing, many expenses, such as advertising the prospectus, are lower than in the case of an offer for sale. Since there is no commitment to sell a pre-specificed number of shares, no underwriting is involved. The sponsors of the issue must be able to lay hands on sufficient shares to meet demand when trading commences, but this is a conventional, non-underwritten transaction.

The Stock Exchange will normally require a firm obtaining an introduction to have at least a hundred or so shareholders before a listing and will expect at least twice this number afterwards,to ensure a free market. As in the case of all other methods, the sponsors must demonstrate that the public will hold at least 25 per cent of the officially listed issue, or 10 per cent if it is seeking an introduction to the USM.

Finally, if a firm is obtaining an introduction but wishes to raise some new money at about the same time, two options are available. First, the shares to be introduced may be made subject to a prior rights issue to existing shareholders, at a price below the expected market price of the shares. Owing to the shares' impending introduction, existing shareholders will be especially likely to take up their rights in full. Alternatively, the introduction may follow a private placing, based on relatively good terms in view of the introduction. The rights issue procedure is more favourable to existing shareholders, who will generally receive a higher price for their shares when they are sold in the market, than if they are placed.

To summarize, the introduction method cannot, in itself, raise new money for a firm. The options explained in the preceding paragraph involve the sale of capital in companies as yet unquoted, and are comparatively unusual. The majority of introductions are of securities which already have a listing: in the past these were principally companies with a provincial listing or ones whose London listing had lapsed. Nowadays most introductions are either reintroductions following a suspension of listing, or involve securities listed on another market. However, a company which was set on an offer for sale is also occasionally permitted to undertake an introduction, if market conditions are especially adverse (for example, Willis Faber in 1976).

Thus, shares which are introduced tend to have two characteristics. They are already listed (that is, they are not really new shares), and they are securities which are already in existence (that is, they do not raise new money). Introductions are therefore excluded from the remainder of our discussion.

ISSUE COSTS

The cost of obtaining a listing may be evaluated under four headings

1 Administrative costs of the company.
2 Cash expenses associated with the issue.
3 Non-cash compensation of issue advisers.
4 Underpricing of the issue.

The first three items form the costs which are usually identified in discussion about the new issue market. The extent to which the shares are underpriced is, however, equally important and we will return to this matter at the end of the present section.

Administrative costs

The adminstrative costs faced by the company span several years, from the time when the directors first begin to contemplate going public. The firm may have formed a liaison with an institution offering private 'nursery' finance, and will certainly have invested considerable time in planning its development into a company with flotation potential. Prior to the issue the company will probably undertake capital reorganizations, company investigations, acquisitions of associated companies, preparation of documentation and negotiation with numerous parties to the issue. The time and effort expended by the issuer probably represent a major cost which, though difficult to quantify, must not be forgotten.

Cash expenses

The cash expenses associated with the issue may be broken down into three parts. First, certain expenses are more or less fixed in magnitude, given the method of issue. Of these, advertising and printing costs are the most important. Secondly, other expenses are paid in the form of a fee which is set as a percentage of the size of the issue. Finally, some expenses will vary with the quantity of work generated by the issue, the relationship between the quantity of work and the size of the issue, being rather tenuous − for instance, small issues may still be heavily oversubscribed.

The work-related expenses consist of the fees due to the two firms of accountants, the two firms of solicitors, the receiving bankers and any other advisers or temporary employees taken on for the issue. The size related expenses consist of the fees payable to the issuing house, brokers and sub-underwriters, the allotment commission, the Stock Exchange listing fee and the capital duty. Some payments are made by the issuing house on behalf of the company, namely those made to the solicitors to the offer, the brokers and the sub-underwriters.

The cash expenses vary not only with the issue size but also with the method of issue. Offers for sale and tender issues are the most expensive methods. Issues by prospectus shift some of the costs onto the company itself, and the cash expenses are therefore marginally lower. Placings are exempt from a number of requirements and are definitely cheaper in terms of cash expenses, whereas introductions are cheaper still.

Non-cash compensation

In calculating the cash expenses, however, it becomes apparent that certain items of non-cash compensation received by the issue advisers are of equal importance. For example, the issuing house will be indifferent between charging a particular percentage fee on the issue and taking an equivalent 'turn' on the shares. If the issuer does not pay a fee, but sells the shares to the issuing house at less than the issue price, this non-cash cost is just as real as a cash expense and must therefore be included in any calculation of cost. This consideration is of particular importance in the Unlisted Securities Market, where the issuing house may be remunerated by means of a buy – sell spread.

The 'conventional' costs (cash and non-cash expenses) associated with the major issue methods are summarized in Figure 13.2. As an indication of their magnitude in the case of an offer for sale, Figure 13.3 shows the average in a year with a large number of issues, 1972. In that year, the 29 offers in the £2.5 million range and the 15 offers over £5 million in size attracted costs of 4.6 per cent and 5.8 per cent, respectively. The remainder of the 118 issues suffered a much higher proportionate burden. These estimates of cost include the non-cash compensation of underwriters, the costs which are paid by the vendors of existing shares rather than by the company, and the cost of sub-underwriting. Since the last of these involves trading in a put option, rather than purely in a service, it is a rather different sort of 'cost' from the others, and it may be more reasonable to consider separately the 1 ¼ per cent fee which is involved. (This point is

Type of expense	Issue by prospectus	Offer for sale	Sale by tender	Placing

Fixed expenses

Advertising	Prospectus in at least two London newspapers. Abbreviated particulars in other paper(s), if desired.			Prospectus in one paper. Abridged particulars in another.
Printing	Prospectus for distribution to public, and letters of acceptance and allotment. Based on number of proofs and complexity of prospectus.			Only a few prospectuses for Extel service.

Work related

Accountants	Based on the complexity of the issue. The auditors to the company and the reporting accountants are usually different firms.
Solicitors	Based on the work to convert a private to a public company. The solicitors to the company and solicitors to the offer are usually different firms.
Bankers	Based on number of applications submitted to the clearing bank's new issue department. — — —
Miscellaneous	Frequently, the company will also utilize the services of management consultants during the period prior to issue, and a firm of public relations consultants near the time of an offer.

Size related

Issuing house	Percentage of the issue proceeds as a fee.	Percentage of the issue proceeds (in form of buy-sell spread) usually plus percentage fee.
Stockbrokers	Percentage of issue proceeds (charged by issuing house, if one is used, and passed on to stockbrokers).	
Subunder-writers	Percentage of issue proceeds (charged by issuing house and passed on to sub-underwriters). — — —	
Allotment commission	Payable to brokers and banks lodging successful applications for their clients. — — —	
Capital duty	Payable at the rate of one per cent on all new money raised. (Prior to the 1973 Finance Act payable at one half per cent on increases in the nominal share capital.)	
Listing fee	Payable to Stock Exchange according to the value of the shares to be listed rather than the size of the issue itself.	

Figure 13.2 Conventional costs of issue

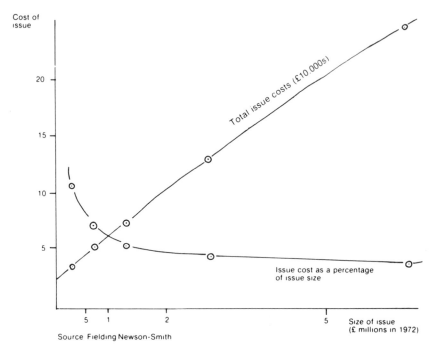

Source Fielding Newson-Smith

Figure 13.3   The costs of an offer for sale in 1972

discussed in Chapter 14.) The costs of issue shown in Figure 13.3 are now out of date. Over recent years, there has been an increase in the extent to which disclosure of information by companies going public is required by the Stock Exchange, by law and by the accounting bodies. This has been accompanied by drastic increases in newsprint costs and capital duty. As a result, the real costs of obtaining a listing have risen substantially. Indeed, this was one of the factors which prompted the creation of the USM.

Table 13.1 shows an estimate of the cost of an offer for sale at the present time, based on discussions with organizations which are active in this area of business. The trend noted by Vaughan, Grinyer and Birley (see Further Reading) who found that 'between 1959 and 1974, costs as a percentage of issue size fell appreciably for offers for sale' has been reversed. Going public is now an expensive business.

Table 13.1
The current costs of an offer for sale

Type of expense	Basis for charging for expense	Typical costs of an offer for sale
Fixed expenses		£'000
Advertising	Prospectus at £10 000 per page in two newspapers; say two pages	40
Printing	Depending on number of proofs, but say...	15
Work related expenses		
Accountants	Reporting accountants' fee of £30–40 000 plus auditors' fees	50
Solicitors	Say £5 000 each	10
Bankers	Priced per sheet of paper handled, but say...	5
Miscellaneous	Other advisers and temporary employees, say...	10
Value added tax	VAT on fixed and work related expenses at the rate of fifteen per cent	20
Size related		*Per cent*
Issuing house	One per cent (less for large issues, more if substantial re-organization required)	1
	One quarter per cent over-riding commission on underwriting	¼
Stockbrokers	One quarter per cent plus extra if special work required	¼
Sub-underwriters	One and a quarter per cent plus one eighth per cent per week for periods in excess of three weeks	1¼
Allotment commission	One eighth per cent on endorsed applications	⅛
Listing fee	According to a scale, but for an average issue, say...	⅛
Value added tax	VAT on size related expenses at the rate of fifteen per cent	½
Capital duty	One per cent of new money raised	1
Total expenses	Fixed cost plus percentage of offer value	£150 thousand + 4½ per cent

Underpricing

If the company which is going public has a free choice of issue method, it might be tempted to choose the one which incurs the lowest conventional costs. However, we have not yet discussed the price at which the shares are sold to the investing public. With all issue methods, it is common for shares to be offered at a discount on the price at which they are expected to trade after the issue. This discount varies with the issue method used.

The tender method provides information to the issuing house on the prices which the public are prepared to pay for various quantities of shares. This makes it possible to issue at a striking price only a few per cent below the ultimate market price of the shares. At the other extreme, placings require the issue advisers to take sole responsibility for estimating the price at which the shares can be sold to clients. The issuing house will lose, both financially and in credibility, if it sets the issue price too high. It is scarcely surprising that placings are offered at a substantial market discount, averaging almost 20 per cent below the value established once stock market trading in the shares commences.

In an offer for sale, the likelihood of severely underpricing an issue is lessened. The company is likely to be larger and less risky and may therefore be easier to value. The pricing decision is more considered, is completed in consultation with the sub-underwriting institutions, and is more in the public eye. Finally, a proportion of the fees are related to the capitalization of the company at the offer price, and hence a higher offer price will generate larger fees for the issue advisers. Thus there is less temptation to underprice the shares. Nevertheless, it is in the general interests of the issuing house and sub-underwriters for the offer to be made at a reasonable discount on the estimated market value of the shares, and in practice the market discount for offers for sale averages some 10 per cent.

Naturally, many factors other than the issue method have a bearing on the extent of underpricing. For example, it is relatively easy to value an investment trust; consequently, prospectus issues (which have been undertaken mainly by investment trusts) show very small market discounts. As a broad generalization, however, we can say that the choice of issue method involves a tradeoff between the conventional costs of issue and the degree of underpricing. For very small issues, placings, which have the lowest conventional costs, are preferable; for large issues, offers for sale, which suffer less underpricing, are preferable; whereas for small- to medium-sized issues, the choice of method will be less clear-cut.

MECHANICS OF A FLOTATION

Although the preparations for becoming a public company may occupy a firm for years, the first formal step occurs when the directors give the go-ahead to a meeting with the issuing house to discuss the strategy and timing of a flotation. This sets off a chain of events which draws a wide range of financial advisers and institutions into contact with the company. These participants in the new issues are

1 Company
   (a) Directors
   (b) Large shareholders
   (c) Management
2 Issuing house
3 Stockbroker
4 Stock Exchange
5 Accountants
   (a) Reporting accountants
   (b) Company auditors
6 Solicitors
   (a) Solicitors to the offer
   (b) Company solicitors
7 Sub-underwriters
8 Bankers
   (a) Receiving bankers
   (b) Registrars
   (c) Clearing bank
9 Public relations consultants
   (a) Public relations consultants
   (b) Advertising agency
10 Press
   (a) News agencies and press
   (b) Extel
11 Printers
12 Investing public

If the issuing house is to lend its name to the new issue, it will require extensive details of the company's performance and prospects. It will therefore request a full financial history of the firm together with information on its business, competitors, management, premises, labour force, expansion plans, and so on. A director of the issuing house will probably visit the company to obtain a closer impression of the business and its senior management, and if all the preliminary enquiries are favourable, the issuing house will instruct an independent firm of accountants to investigate the company. Only after a satisfactory accountants' report will the issuing house make its proposal to the firm.

The issuing house's proposal will outline the capital reorganization required prior to obtaining a listing and will suggest the method and terms of issue. The capital reorganization will involve some or all of the following adjustments to the firm's capital structure

1 Eliminating inappropriate classes of equity (such as non-voting shares, founders' shares, deferred shares, etc.).
2 Repayment of certain loans.
3 Revaluation of fixed assets.
4 Acquisition of existing subsidiary companies.
5 Formation of a holding company.
6 Transfer of proprietor's shares to family trusts.
7 Waiver of dividend rights by large shareholders in high tax brackets.

Over the months leading up to the issue, the company will become committed to such aspects of the terms of issue as the earnings, dividends and asset value per share, and the accounting policies pursued by the company will become obvious from the prospectus. The issuing house will give the company a broad idea of the aggregate value of the shares to be issued, and so the firm's capital structure will have to be reorganized by means of various share splits, scrip issues, and so on, so as to ensure that the price of each share is at a conventional level − probably within the range 50 pence to 150 pence.

Given the number of shares to be issued, the price at which the shares are marketed is the variable of greatest interest to the vendor. By comparing the earnings and dividend yield with firms in comparable industries, and by taking into account the prospects and riskiness of the business, the level of gearing and the prices at which shares have changed hands recently, the issuing house will estimate the market value of the shares. In order to ensure that all the shares are disposed of, the suggested issue price is then set at a discount below the estimated market value. In the case of a tender issue, where the public effectively set the price of the shares, the issuing house is confined to estimating the minimum price at which applications will be accepted.

If the issuing house's proposal is accepted, then a provisional timetable for the issue will be drawn up. Some of the key events of the issue, from initial meeting with the issuing house until well after the issue is complete, are shown in Figure 13.4. The timing of the early events is approximate, and the timetable has been designed to apply to placings as well as offers for sale (provided the application procedure is amended). The listing can be granted on a Friday or, as in this case (day minus 1), on a Wednesday. The impact day (day minus 8) will depend on the place of the issue in the Bank of England's 'queue'.

Much of the ensuing activity centres around meeting the regulations that affect the issue and the development of the prospectus (which is described shortly). The issuing house takes a co-ordinating role through this period until dealings in the shares have commenced. By two weeks before the offer, the prospectus is available in a final proof form, and the price of the shares will be set, subject to amendment before the printers start to produce the prospectuses.

At this stage the underwriting and sub-underwriting agreements are made firm. A week before the offer, the terms of the issue are made known to the market, and the resulting press conference generally prompts some mention of the issue in the financial press. A few days later the prospectus is published, giving investors some three days in which to apply for the issue.

The prospectus provides the information which must be made available to investors under the requirements of the Companies Act 1948 and the regulations of the Stock Exchange. The prospectus presents information under a sequence of headings following a set style; and the application form is also included in the case of an offer for sale, prospectus issue, or issue by tender. The main contents of the prospectus are

1 Background
   (a) Statements of compliance with regulations.
   (b) Application instructions.*
   (c) Company's name and background.
   (d) Capital structure and voting rights.
   (e) Name and address of directors, professional advisers, etc.
2 History and nature of business
3 Management
4 Employees
5 Plant and premises
6 Working capital

Day relative to offer	Key events
−110	Directors and issuing house discuss strategy and timing.
−100	Issuing house instructs reporting accountants and brokers.
−70	Consider accountant's report
−60	First draft of prospectus to printers
−50	Second proof to stock exchange
−40	Discuss Stock Exchange Comments
−30	Prepare application form and letters of allotment, acceptance and underwriting
−20	Meetings to discuss further proofs of documents
−14 (Thur)	FIX PRICE (subject to amendment) and prepare underwriting proofs
−10 (Mon)	Finalize price and send proofs to printers
−9 (Tues)	Post underwriting proofs and letter to sub-underwriters
−8 (Wed)	IMPACT DAY. Press conference
−7 (Thurs)	Completion meeting of directors and all advisers
−3 (Mon)	PROSPECTUS IN PAPERS. Final documents to Stock Exchange
−1 (Wed)	Listing granted by Stock Exchange
0 (Thurs)	APPLICATION LISTS OPEN (10 a.m.) and close
+1 (Fri)	CHEQUES BANKED. Press announcement on basis of allotment
+6 (Wed)	Allotment or acceptance letters posted
+7 (Thurs)	DEALINGS BEGIN
+28 (Thurs)	Last day for splitting
+32 (Mon)	Last day for renunciation
+60 (Mon)	Share certificates ready

The events from −70 to −20 are bracketed together with the note: Meetings of directors, issuing house, brokers, accountants, auditors and solicitors

Figure 13.4 Typical offer timetable

7 Accountants' report
   (a) Profits record (five years).
   (b) Balance sheet.
   (c) Intended acquisitions.
   (d) Dividends record (five years).
8 Profits, prospects and dividends
9 General information
   (a) Articles of association.
   (b) Contracts.
   (c) Recent capital changes and acquisitions.
   (d) Ownership and directors' interests.
   (e) Other statutory statements.
10 Application form*
   (a) Time, date and place for applying.
   (b) Statutory declarations and letter of acquisition.
   (c) Conditions of application
   (d) Space for applicant's signature, name and address.

*Omitted if issue is a placing.

A more detailed description can be found in Stock Exchange's Yellow Book. In conjunction with press comment and other information available to them, investors use the contents of the prospectus to decide whether to apply for the issue, and for how many shares.

A week after the application lists open and close, the shares have normally been allotted and dealings begin. The company has obtained its listing, and only a few details regarding the issue itself are left to be done. So far as investors are concerned these include the periods during which 'splitting' and 'renunciation' are permitted. These are procedures for dividing an allotment of shares into several parts (if necessary), and selling them by renouncing title to the shares in favour of the buyer.

From the point of view of the financial participants (rather than professional advisers) involved in the issue, some key events should be noted from Figure 13.4. These financial events are shown in capital letters in the figure and the most important are:

1 Fixing the price (roughly two weeks before the offer).
2 Publicizing the terms of the offer (one week before).
3 Closing of the application lists.
4 Commencement of dealings (one week after the offer).

The company's financial interests largely terminate at event 1, whereas the underwriters are at risk principally from event 1 to event 3. The applicants to the issue are involved with the company on a regular basis. They can look forward to news about the company's progress, about acquisitions and the financing of new investments, and hopefully to a consistently rising share price.

SUMMARY AND CONCLUSIONS

In this chapter, we have described the current structure of the UK new issue market. First, we looked at the role of the Stock Exchange in relation to new issues. We compared obtaining a Stock Exchange listing with alternatives such as flotation on the Unlisted Securities Market and reviewed the controls imposed by the Stock Exchange. We then went on to appraise four classes of reasons which might motivate a company to obtain a stock market listing. We stressed two groups of motives, those relating to the capital requirements of the firm and those reflecting the financial needs of the proprietors of the business. We also discussed the motives of improving the marketability of the shares and of enhancing the prestige of the company.

In the third section, we looked at the regulatory framework within which companies may seek a flotation. In the next section, we described the methods which are available for making a new issue. These are the offer for sale (and the related prospectus issue) method, the placing method, the tender issue, and the introduction. Each of these issue methods has it advantages and disadvantages, and each imposes different costs on the company which is going public.

The costs of issue were described in the fifth section. We identified four items of cost: the often overlooked administrative costs of issue, the cash expenses associated with the issue, non-cash compensation such as warrants to subscribe for further shares, and the important cost which is imposed through underpricing the new issue. Underpricing was found to be most severe for placings of shares in small companies. Finally, we turned to the mechanics of a flotation. We identified the tasks of the main participants in the issue, we examined a typical new issue timetable and we summarized the contents of the prospectus.

The UK new issue market has responded to the needs of the corporate sector over a long period of time. Especially with the advent of the Unlisted Securities Market, the Stock Exchange now provides a wide range of companies with ready access to the capital market. An understanding of how to use the new issue market is therefore likely to be important to an increasing number of businesses.

FURTHER READING

The steps which are involved in obtaining a stock exchange listing are described in M. Richardson's *Going Public*, published by Business Books in 1976. So far as the regulations of the stock market are concerned, however, it is better to consult an updated copy of the Yellow Book, or *Admission of Securities to Listing*, published by the Stock Exchange in 1979.

There have been a large number of academic studies of the new issue market in Britain and overseas. In *The Efficiency of the British New Issue Market for Ordinary Shares* (Xerox Publishing Group, 1981), the author provides an extensive survey of this research, examines the question of how fairly the issue price is set and elaborates on other matters discussed in this chapter.

A useful study of the UK market is the one by C.D. Vaughan, P.H. Grinyer and S.J. Birley entitled *From Private to Public*. It was published by Woodhead Faulkner in 1977.

The most recent book on the subject is *Marketing Company Shares*, by David Fanning (Gower, 1982). This describes the principles and procedures involved in 'going public' and contains detailed analyses of nine cases.

APPENDIX: NEW ISSUE GLOSSARY

Advisory pricing Pricing of a new issue by the issue advisors (underwriters, brokers, etc.) Refers to the pricing method used in offers for sale and placings. See *Tender issues*.

Aftermarket The market in which new issues are subsequently traded, that is, the *secondary market*.

All-or-none (USA) Agreement for the underwriter to attempt to sell all the issue at the offer price, subject to the issue being withdrawn if all the shares are not distributed. Thus, as in the case of a best efforts agreement, the underwriter is not at risk.

Allotment   The allocation of shares in a new issue to applicants. If the issue is *oversubscribed* large applications are usually scaled down, whereas a certain number of small applications, selected by ballot, are accepted in full. The allotment is notified in an allotment letter.

Application   An application on the official application form, which accompanies the *prospectus* for an issue, to buy a certain number of shares at the offer price. A cheque for the full cost of the shares must accompany the application.

Best efforts   (USA) Agreement by the underwriter to sell only as much of the new issue at the offer price as he is able to, providing no *fixed commitment* to sell all the shares. Small or risky issues may be offered on this basis or on an all-or-one basis.

Close company   A company which has a tax status such that its income is taxed at the rate of its directors or members. Exemption is granted if shares carrying at least 35 per cent of voting power are held by the public and are dealt on the Stock Exchange.

Combination offering   See *Mixed offering*

Discount   (as in 'trading at a discount') The amount by which the market price of a share is below its issue price. See *Premium.*

Firm commitment, fixed commitment   (USA) Agreement by the issue's underwriters to buy all the shares on offer from the vendor at a price below the offering price, accepting the risk of being unable to re-sell the shares (that is, accepting the 'sub-underwriting' risk, in the UK sense). The *market discount* includes the underwriting commission though there may be additional *non-cash compensation*. See *Best efforts and All-or-none.*

Flotation   New issue of previously unlisted shares.

Going public   Literally, becoming a *public company*. Generally used to describe gaining a stock exchange listing by means of a *flotation*, regardless of whether the company was previously public.

Impact day   The first day on which the size and terms of a new issue may be made known to the underwriters, places and the market.

Introduction   A method of obtaining a listing for a share which is already of such an amount and so widely held that an adequate market will develop in the share once it is listed.

Introductory discount   The minimum *market discount* which is required to float an issue successfully.

Issue by tender   An invitation to the public to submit a tender for shares which are offered by the issuing company. See *Tender issue.*

Issuing house   A specialist financial organization which provides advice, *underwriting* and administrative services in connection with obtaining a *new listing.*

Market discount   The difference between issue price and market value at the issue date, expressed as a percentage of the issue price or of the *net receipts* per share. Market value at the issue date is estimated from the price at which the issue is traded, corrected for market movements since the issue date.

Mixed offering   Offering of shares, some of which are newly created and some of which are already in existence. The new issue is a mixture of a *primary offering* and *secondary offering.*

Net receipts   The value of the issue at the issue price, minus administrative and other expenses.

New company   A company which is issuing shares to the public for the first time. A 'new company' might also be one whose previous quotation has lapsed, one which has been used for 'shell' operations, or one whose nature has been completely changed as a result of the issue. See *Unseasoned issue.*

New Issue market   The market for issuing financial securities to the public. The new issue market has no physical location, and consists of the institutions and investors involved in issuing the securities. The new issues may subsequently be traded in a *secondary market.* See *Primary market.*

New listing   Provision of a stock exchange listing for shares which have not previously been quoted on that exchange. The shares may have been listed previously on another exchange.

New money   Money received by the company making a new issue, that is, proceeds of the issue which arise from newly created shares. This figure can be calculated gross (that is, number of new shares multiplied by price per share), net of all administrative expenses and/or redemptions of the company's existing securities, or net of purchases of any existing securities (for example, Midland Bank Statistics, Bank of England Statistics). See *Primary offering.*

Non-cash compensation   (USA) Additional compensation for the underwriters of an issue, provided in the form of warrants to purchase shares after the issue is completed, etc.

Offer for sale   An offer to the public of securities already subscribed by an issuing house or broker.

Offer for sale by tender   An invitation to the public to submit a tender for shares which are offered by an issuing house or broker. See *Tender issue.*

Old company   A company which already has a stock exchange quotation. See *Seasoned issue.*

Overriding commission   A fee payable to the placing agents of the underwriting (including brokers and the issuing house's own investment department).

Oversubscription   An oversubscribed issue is one in which the number of shares applied for exceeds the number offered in an offer for sale, prospectus issue or issue by tender.

Over-the-counter (OTC) market   Organized market in unlisted securities. In the UK, this term usually refers to investment bankers M.J.H. Nightingale's OTC market rather than the Unlisted Securities Market or dealings under the Stock Exchange's Rule 163.

Placing   Method of issue where the bulk of the shares are offered to the sponsor's own clients.

Premium   The amount by which the price at which a share is traded is above its issue price. See *Discount*.

Primary market   The market for issuing financial securities to the public, that is, the new issue market. Frequently used to denote the market for issuing previously ordinary shares to the public.

Primary offering   Offering of newly created shares. A new money offering.

Promotional offering   An offering by a company with no (or virtually no) certified earnings history.

Prospectus   Document setting out the offer price and other particulars of an issue and fulfilling the requirements of the Stock Exchange and of the Companies Act 1948.

Provincial exchange   One of the UK stock exchanges which provided listings for companies, prior to the unification of the stock market in the UK in 1974. At this date, they became trading floors for the UK Stock Exchange.

Public company   A company, whose shares may be listed or unlisted, which has 50 or more shareholders other than employees.

Public issue or prospectus issue   An offer to the public by the issuing company itself of securities which are sold at the price stipulated in the prospectus.

Quotations department   The arm of the Stock Exchange responsible, among other things, for granting listings. This it does through the regular Wednesday and Friday meetings of the Committee on Quotations.

Registered offerings   (USA) Public, interstate offerings over $500 000 (before 1971, $300 000) in value must be registered under the Securities Act 1933. Smaller issues fall under *Regulation A*, whereas interstate offerings come solely under state jurisdiction.

Regulation A offerings   (USA) Interstate public offerings of shares which are exempt from the normal process required of registered offerings. Regulation A issues have a market value of under $500 000 (before 1971, $300 000).

Renunciation   Until a definitive share certificate is issued, (that is until one to two months after trading in a new issue starts), the holder of an allotment letter may sell his shares by renouncing his entitlement in favour of the buyer. All such dealings are free of stamp duty and registration fee.

Rights issue.   An issue of shares to existing shareholders in proportion to their holdings, at an issue price which is generally below the current market price.

Rule 163   A special provision under the Regulations of the Stock Exchange, whereby dealings may take place in any security which has an official listing on another exchange, and also through Rule 163(2) in unlisted securities. In the case of the latter, prior approval is required for each transaction.

Scaling down   Large applications to an *oversubscribed* new issue are usually allotted in part only. They are usually scaled down by a factor which is slightly larger than the *times subscribed* and rounded to the nearest hundred shares, so as to facilitate a wide spread of shareholdings.

Seasoned issue   Issue of shares which already have a stock exchange quotation. Issue of shares by an *old company.*

Secondary market   The market for the purchase and sale of existing securities. The most important secondary is the Stock Exchange.

Secondary offering   Offering of shares already in existence, (that is, sale of shares owned by proprietors of the company). A no new money offering.

Sponsor (of an issue)   Issuing house or stockbrokers who act as principal or as agent in the issue of shares to the public.

Stag   An individual who subscribes to a new issue, not with the intention of holding the shares he receives but anticipating that he will sell his allotment at a profit when dealings start.

Standby fee (USA) The *sub-underwriting* commission paid to financial institutions, in return for their agreement to *take up* a specified proportion of any shares remaing as a result of *undersubscription*.

Striking price The price at which shares are sold in a tender issue. It can be the minimum price (if there are insufficient applications in total), or the market clearance price (which will just clear the offering), or below the market clearance price (which will entail some scaling down of applications).

Subscription See *Times subscribed.*

Sub-underwriting The agreement by various financial institutions not directly associated with a new issue, to accept the risks taken on by the *underwriters* in return for a commission which is usually ¼ per cent below the underwriting fee of 1 ½ per cent.

Take-up fee (USA) Fee payable (in addition to standby fee) on the proportion of an issue which is taken up by sub-underwriting institutions.

Tender issue Issue in which shares are offered to the public at a minimum price, and tenders are invited at or above the stipulated minimum. The share are issued at a striking price which is set so as to enable the issuer to sell all the shares. Tender issues can be by means of the *offer for sale by tender* or *issue by tender*.

Times subscribed The number of shares applied for in an *offer for sale, prospectus issue* or *issue by tender* divided by the number on offer. (In the case of tenders, it is necessary to state the price at which the times subscribed has been calculated).

Turn Percentage difference between the price per share at which the issuing house sells an issue and the price per share which is paid to the company which is going public.

Undersubscription An undersubscribed issue is one in which the number of shares applied for is less than the number offered in an *offer for sale, prospectus issue* or *issue by tender*.

Underwriting (UK) Agreement by the sponsors of an issue to take a specified proportion of any part of an offer which is not subscribed by the public. In return they receive an underwriting commission which is generally 1 ½ per cent of the issue price. Most of the risk is laid off to *sub-underwriters*. (USA) The complete process of marketing shares in a new company to investors, including all the functions of the *sponsors* of the issue.

Unlisted Securities Market (USM) The Stock Exchange's organized market in unlisted securities.

Unseasoned issue Issue of shares which have no previous listing on a stock exchange. Issue of share by a *new company*.

Yellow book Nickname for the Stock Exchange book of listing regulations, entitled 'Admission of Securities to Listing'.

14

Equity rights issues

Paul Marsh

Rights issues are the method by which companies quoted on the Stock Exchange in the UK raise virtually all their new equity finance. An equity rights issue is an offer of shares for cash to existing shareholders (and possibly holders of other securities in the company) in proportion to their existing holdings. This chapter describes the principal problems encountered by a company making a rights issue.

The topics covered are

1 Issue methods for quoted companies raising money on the Stock Exchange
2 Rights issue method
3 Timing of external funding and rights issues
4 Rights issue procedures and timetable
5 Rights issue costs
6 Setting the terms and the underwriting decision
7 Market reaction to rights issues
8 Raising money at existing market prices
9 Summary and conclusions

ISSUE METHODS FOR QUOTED COMPANIES RAISING MONEY ON THE STOCK EXCHANGE

Essentially, four basic issue methods are open to quoted companies raising money on the Stock Exchange. They are

1 *Rights issues* – offers of new securities for cash to existing shareholders (and possibly holders of other securities in the company) in proportion to their existing holdings.
2 *Open offers* – offers of new securities for cash to existing shareholders (and possibly holders of other securities in the company) other than in proportion to their existing holdings.
3 *Public issues* – offers of new securities for cash, made to the general public either by the issuing company or by an issuing house or broker which has either subscribed for, or agreed to subscribe for, the securities of the company in question. Normally, the offer will be made at a fixed price, but occasionally it may be carried out by the tender method. The normal procedure in the case of tenders is that applicants are invited to submit a tender stating a price together with the number of shares they would accept at that price.

With public issues, it is fairly common for preference in allotment to be extended to applications from existing security holders, particularly ordinary shareholders, although typically this applies to only a proportion of the total issue.
4 *Placings* – issues of new securities for cash whereby the new securities are 'placed' with both private and institutional clients of the issuing house and with jobbers, rather than being offered to existing holders or to the public. It is a Stock Exchange regulation that at least 20 per cent of any placing must be available for purchase by the clients of other brokers through the medium of the market, that is, through the jobbers. However, since January 1975, the Stock Exchange has been prepared to dispense with the latter requirement in the case of placings of additional shares of an existing class.

The choice between these four methods is largely dictated by the type of security being issued. For example, virtually all cash issues of equity or securities convertible into equity including options, warrants and convertible loan stocks are made via the rights issue method. Indeed it is a Stock Exchange regulation that 'in the absence of circumstances which have been agreed by the Council to be exceptional', the rights issue method is the only one permissible for the issue of such securities unless shareholders' prior approval has been obtained in general meeting. Even with such approval, prior to January 1975, the Stock Exchange would not allow equity issues of more than £1 million or convertible stock issues for more than £5 million with an overriding limit that no issue could exceed 5 per cent of the existing listed equity capital.

In January 1975, the Council of the Stock Exchange announced that they had 'temporarily relaxed the current requirements governing issues of equity capital' because of 'existing market conditions', and would henceforth consider applications 'from existing listed companies for placings of additional shares or securities convertible into equity without limit as to the size of the issue'. During 1975, however, there were only ten new equity placings, raising a total of only some £10 million. The only other non-rights equity issue made by a quoted company was a public offer for sale by the Rank Organization to raise some £28 million. In

Type of Security \ Issue Method	Rights Issue	Open Issue	Public Issue	Placing
Equity	Virtually all issues	Very infrequent	Very infrequent	Infrequent (very infrequent prior to January 1975)
Warrants		— — —	— — —	
Convertible loan stocks and convertible preference		Very infrequent	Very infrequent	
Loan stock and debentures	Very infrequent	Fairly common	Large issues only	Majority of issues – virtually all small issues
Preference	Very infrequent	Fairly common	Very infrequent – large issues only	Majority of small issues
Combined units	All issues	— — —	— — —	— — —

▭ requires shareholders' approval. Prior to January 1975 only equity issues less than £1m and convertible issues less than £5m permitted.

Figure 14.1 Issue methods for quoted companies raising money on the Stock Exchange

contrast, over the same period, there were more than 150 rights issues which raised a total of more than £1.2 billion. Figure 14.1 summarizes the frequency of the various issue methods by the type of security involved.

The main reason for favouring the rights issue method is that it avoids any possibility of unfairness to existing shareholders. By giving all holders the opportunity to subscribe for new securities in proportion to their existing holdings, wealth transfers are prevented both between shareholders and also from existing to new shareholders, since shareholders can either take up their rights, or sell them at their market price. The same is not true for placings or offers since the securities are nearly always issued at a discount, thereby giving rise to a transfer of wealth from existing holders to the placee.

As we saw in Chapter 13, public issues (including offers for sale) and placings are also the principal methods used by previously unquoted companies when they go public (that is, obtain a Stock Exchange listing).

RIGHTS ISSUE METHOD

This is best illustrated with a simple example. Consider a company that wants to raise £1 million via a rights issue. Suppose that there are

Table 14.1
Rights issue terms

	Terms	
Details	1 for 1 at 50p	2 for 3 at 75p
Prior to issue		
Number of shares	2m	2m
Share price	£1	£1
Value of company	£2m	£2m
After ex-rights date		
Number of new shares	2m	1⅓m
New money raised	2m × 50p = £1m	1⅓m × 75p = £1m
Value of company	£2m + £1m = £3m	£2m + £1m = £3m
Total number of shares	4m	3⅓m
Share price	£3m/4m = 75p	£3m/3⅓m = 90p
Price of the rights	75p − 50p = 25p	90p − 75p = 15p

2 000 000 shares already in issue with a market price of £1 each, so that the company is valued at £2 million. The first column of Table 14.1 shows the effect of making a one for one issue (one new share offered for each share currently held) at 50 pence and the second column shows that the £1 million could equally well be raised by a two for three issue at 75 pence.

A rights issue can be viewed as an issue of shares at the current market price combined with a scrip issue. Looked at this way, the terms above differ only in the size of the scrip issue involved. Although the two different sets of terms lead to different share prices after the issue, this will not affect shareholders, since the value of the company will be the same in each case, as will be the fraction of the company which each shareholder owns.

Nevertheless, many finance directors, merchant bankers, brokers and press commentators still discuss the 'attractiveness' of rights issue terms, although very few of them would dream of applying the same terminology to scrip issues. Furthermore, they frequently argue that the larger the scrip element involved, the greater the dilution of earnings and dividends. One even sees the view put forward that the cost of the rights issue is the dividend yield calculated on the issue price, so that the lower the issue price is set, the higher the cost of the issue. This argument would presumably imply that scrip issues are infinitely expensive! This is clearly nonsense. Underwriting considerations apart, and excepting the fact that shares cannot be issued below a value, the terms of rights issue and the level at which the issue price is set are irrelevant.

Finally, it is often argued that rights issues are unfair to shareholders who are unable to take up their rights, since this allows other shareholders or underwriters to 'get in' at a 'cheap' price. Again this view is misguided. Shareholders who are unable to take up their rights can sell them at a fair market price − 25p or 15p, respectively, in the examples given in Table 14.1. Even if such shareholders do not sell their rights, they seldom suffer financial loss, since in the majority of issues the rights will be sold on their behalf.

TIMING OF EXTERNAL FUNDING AND RIGHTS ISSUES

Stated simply, companies should raise external funds when the amount of money they require to finance profitable ventures (that is, those with positive NPV's, see Chapter 2) exceeds the amount available from internal sources. For the corporate sector taken in aggregate, this has been the overall situation for at least the past 25 years.

Contrary to what one might at first suspect, there has been a clear general tendency, both in the USA and the UK, for companies to raise new external finance during, or shortly after, periods of buoyant sales. The usual explanation for this phenomenon is as follows:

After a company has been operating at a low level of capacity, any increase in sales is likely to result in a sharp improvement in profitability and therefore in retained earnings. Such an improvement will not generally be matched by an immediate increase in expenditure. Major investment in fixed plant is unlikely to be authorised as long as the company still has significant spare capacity and, even if it were authorised, there would be some delay before any payments were made. Furthermore, the initial effect of the pick-up in sales could lead to some involuntary temporary reduction in inventories. Thus, the net effect of the more buoyant conditions is an improvement in company liquidity, and it is only after the boom has persisted for a year or two that the pressure on funds is likely to be felt. In just the same way the initial result of any decline in sales will usually be a fall in retained earnings and a continued high level of investment in fixed plant and inventories. A more prolonged decline in sales will induce a reduction in investment expenditure to boost company liquidity. The net effect is that changes in company activity tend to precede changes in the raising of external funds.

Since both the total volume of external financing, and the level of the stock market are affected by economic prospects, it is not surprising to see an association between the two. After a rise in the market, companies are more prone to issue equity. Furthermore, there is also a tendency for equity issues to be made by companies whose shares have performed abnormally well in the period prior to the issue. A study of 997 UK rights issues between 1962-75,[1] revealed that over the year leading up to the issue, the shares of companies making rights issues experienced abnormal gains of over 30 per cent after adjusting for risk and market movements (see Table 14.2).

However, there is no corresponding tendency in the UK for increases in debt issues to follow rises in bond prices (i.e. falls in interest rates), though several studies indicate a contrary experience in the USA.

This tendency for equity issues to follow share price rises is rather puzzling. Increases in share prices, after all, will have increased the equity base and should, if anything, encourage new debt issues. Why then do companies choose such times to reduce their gearing even further?

One possible explanation is that management's choice between debt

Table 14.2
Summary of rights issue studies

Author	Country	Date of sample	Sample size	Type of returns	Pre issue	Announce-ment	XR date	Post issue
Weller	USA	1956–7	81	Market adjusted capital gains	—	–3%	—	—
Boden-hammer	USA	1962–5	61	→	—	–3%	—	—
Scholes	USA	1926–66	696	Abnormal returns	Unusual gains	—	–0.3%	Zero
Merrett/ Howe/ Newbould	UK	1963	110/ 95	Market adjusted capital gains	—	—	+1%	+3% (1 year)
Smith	USA	1926–75	853	Abnormal returns	+9%	—	–1.4%	1.4%
Marsh	UK	1962–75	997	→	+33%	–½%	–¼%	+4% (2 year)

and equity partly reflects its assessment of future share price movements. Such behaviour would be open to a number of criticisms. First, given the large body of evidence on stock market efficiency, it seems extremely unlikely that corporate management or their financial advisers will have any superior forecasting ability with regard to the future movement of share prices. This argument is borne out by the fact that there is absolutely no tendency for increases in the level of equity issues to be followed by any abnormal movements in share prices. Secondly, given the use of the rights issue method for virtually all equity issues by UK quoted companies, it is not obvious that existing shareholders would always benefit even if management could forecast future share prices. For example, if management's forecasting ability were limited to the residual movement in the price of their company's shares, existing holders would gain only if they failed to take up their entitlement and the shares were overvalued at the time of the issue. Similarly, if management's forecasting ability were limited to market movements, existing holders would gain if management correctly forecast a rise in share prices relative to other assets and if, as a result of the issue, their existing shareholders increase the proportion of their wealth held in equities (see Figures 14.2 to 14.4).

Shareholder action	Share values relative to other asset values	
	Fall	Rise
Takes up rights by (a) selling other shares (b) selling other assets (c) reducing consumption	— Loss Loss	— Gain Gain
Sells rights and (a) reinvests proceeds in other shares (b) reinvests proceeds in other assets (c) increases consumption	— Gain Gain	— Loss Loss

Figure 14.2   Timing of rights issues

Existing shareholders	Loss or gain to existing shareholders if shares are:		
	Undervalued	Correctly valued	Overvalued
Take up rights	—	—	—
Don't take up	Loss	—	Gain

Figure 14.3   Timing of rights issues and overall market movements

The second alternative explanation is that management's choice between debt and equity is based on incorrect notions of the cost of equity capital. It is still fairly widely believed, for example, that the cost of equity is either:

(a)   the dividend yield, or
(b)   the earnings yield.

In both cases, increases in the company's share price will lead to an apparent fall in the cost of equity, and for management who subscribe to this notion, equity appears much cheaper when the share price is high. Again, while belief in these views may help to explain the observed financing behaviour, these concepts of the cost of equity are extremely misleading.

Neither of these alternative explanations of the strange 'cycles' in the choice of financing method are very impressive in terms of modern financial thinking. Nevertheless, discussions with both corporate management and their financial advisers indicate that a great deal of attention is paid to the careful timing of issues with respect to market conditions, and that considerations such as those above do play an important role in explaining management's behaviour. It is difficult to escape from the conclusion, however, that much of this effort is misplaced, and that there is still a great deal of misunderstanding.

Date relative to XR date	Companies not requiring EGM	Companies requiring EGM	Dealings CR	Dealings XR	Dealings R	Dealings FP new
1 year	Management/Advisors review financing plans, possibly some hint or advance warning of issue	Management/Advisors review financing plans, possibly some hint or advance warning of issue				
9 to 12 weeks						
−6 to 8 weeks	Decision taken to go ahead with issue	Decision taken to go ahead with issue				
	Company/issuing house/brokers discuss various drafts of circular/terms/forecasts/timetable	Company/issuing house/brokers discuss various drafts of circular/terms/forecasts/timetable				
−3 weeks	Holders registered date	Issue price/terms finalized; underwriting; sub-underwriting; issue announcement				
−1 to 2 weeks	Issue price/terms finalized underwriting; sub-underwriting; issue announcement	Holders registered date; Notice of EGM and circular letter sent to shareholders				
	Circular letter and provisional allotment letter sent to shareholders					
−1 to 2 days		EGM; provisional allotment letters posted				
XR date	Latest date on which PALs received; shares marked 'ex'					
+3 weeks	Last acceptance date: payment in full (or part)					
+3 weeks	Shares not taken up either sold (placed) for benefit, or allotted to applicants for excess shares.					
1–2 days	Cheques or allotment letter sent out					
+7 weeks	Last splitting date					
+7 weeks	Share certificates sent out					
2 days						

Figure 14.4 Rights issue procedures and timetable

294

RIGHTS ISSUE COSTS

The following costs are incurred in the course of making a rights issue

1   Administrative costs
   (a)   Printing and postage of circulars and provisional allotment letters.
   (b)   Costs of arranging Extraordinary General Meeting if necessary.
   (c)   Costs of postage and printing of notices and proxy forms.
   (d)   Fee to receiving bankers.
   (e)   Stock Exchange listing fee.
2   Tax
   Capital duty (1 per cent).
3   Professional fees
   (a)   Fee to broker.
   (b)   Fee to solicitors.
   (c)   Commission to advisers (½ per cent).
   (d)   Fee to receiving bankers, (see above).
4   Underwriting costs
   Sub-underwriting fee (1¼ per cent) – not a true 'cost' (see below).

With the exception of the underwriting fee and capital duty, all the other costs decrease as a percentage of the money raised as the size of the issue increases. As a rough rule of thumb, the cost of a rights issue (excluding underwriting) has been about 2.4 + (0.7) — (issue size in £million) per cent of the money raised.

SETTING THE TERMS AND THE UNDERWRITING DECISION

Purpose of underwriting

When companies make rights issues, the timing of events provides a period of approximately three weeks during which shareholders can decide whether to subscribe.

   If the share price is above the issue price on the last acceptable date, the issue will be successful. However, if the share price falls below the issue price, the new shares will not be taken up since they could be bought more cheaply in the market, and the issue will fail unless it has been underwritten.

Underwriters therefore perform a useful service by taking on risk. Whether or not a company should underwrite will depend on the fee charged and the probability of the market price falling below the issue price. This, in turn, depends upon the terms of the issue, and the company could set the issue price low enough virtually to assure success. If this were done, the company should be prepared to pay only a trivial sum for underwriting and could effectively dispense with it altogether.

In recent years, however, over 90 per cent of rights issues have been underwritten. Normally, the merchant bank or broker advising the company on the issue acts as principal underwriter but passes on the major part of the risk of a failed issue to sub-underwriters, who almost invariably charge a fixed fee of 1¼ per cent per week or part thereof. Note that while this fee is fixed, underwriters can still effectively vary the price they charge through the advice they give on the issue terms. The lower they advise the company to set the issue price, the higher the price the company will effectively pay for any underwriting.

Underwriting is thus the major single item of 'cost' in making rights issues, and for large issues, underwriters' fees can be substantial. ICI, for example, paid £2.8 million to the underwriters of its 1976 issue, and BP's massive 1981 rights issue cost not less than £12 million in underwriting fees.

Profitability of underwriting

A study of 671 underwritten UK rights issues between 1962 and 1975 showed that underwriters made an average return of 1.1 per cent per issue.[1] In only 35 cases (about 5 per cent) was any part of the issue left with the underwriters. The average loss in these 35 cases was 4 per cent, and the maximum loss over the whole period was only 13 per cent.

Valuing the worth of underwriting

Although the figures above suggest that underwriters have done very well on average, at the expense of the issuing companies, this may be unfair to underwriters since the figures take no account of risk. However, it is possible to define a 'fair' return to underwriters, making due allowance for risk, when we recognize that underwriters are selling a put option.

A put option is nothing more than the option to sell shares (or any other assets) at a given price at some specified date or dates in the future.

Figure 14.5 shows how a company underwriting a rights issue is in the same position as a purchaser of a put option. If the market price falls below the issue price by the last acceptance date, the shareholders will 'put' the failed issue onto the underwriters at the issue price. As the diagrams show, the closer the issue price to the market price, the higher the fee for underwriting should be.

Figure 14.5   Underwriting as a put option

A precise value for the underwriting put option can be calculated by using an ingenious option valuation model derived by Black and Scholes.[2] They showed that the value of underwriting increases with the ratio of the issue price to the current share price, the length of the period over which the underwriters are at risk, the variability of the company's share price and the current short term interest rate. No other variables affect the underwriting value.

The precise valuation formula is rather complicated and is not given here. However, the items of information required in order to use this formula to value underwriting are very straightforward and an example is given in Table 14.3.

Historical returns to underwriters

The Black and Scholes valuation formula was applied to 539 under-written UK rights issues between 1962 and 1975 to determine whether

Table 14.3
Calculating the value of underwriting

Information required	Actual values for the Tube Investments rights issue made in April 1975
Share price on data underwriting arranged	236 p(− − 229 ex rights)
Issue price	190 p
Duration of underwriting agreement	22 trading days
Standard deviation of returns on the share	40% per year
Short-term interest rate	9¼ %
(Treasury Bill rate)	
Underwriting value (as % issue price) =	0·11%

underwriters made excess returns; that is, returns over and above the risk adjusted 'fair' value.

The average excess return to sub-underwriting was approximately 0.7 per cent. As can be seen from Figure 14.6, the distribution of the excess returns was very skewed with a median value of 1.11 per cent. In other words, in the majority of cases, underwriting appeared grossly over-priced. Underwriting values were greater than the fee paid in only 14 per cent of cases.

Conclusions on underwriting

It may be unfair to conclude too readily that underwriters overcharge companies for their services. The relationship between company and financial adviser is not limited to underwriting rights issues, and it is possible that merchant bankers undercharge for other services or advice.

However, the evidence strongly suggests that companies should be cautious, and not accept too readily the issue terms suggested by the principal underwriter. The company can use the Black & Scholes formula to assess the value of underwriting at the terms suggested. If the company

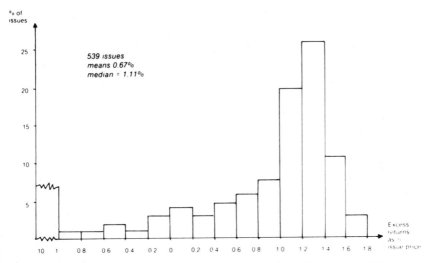

Figure 14.6 Distribution of excess returns to sub-underwriting

cannot get a reasonably 'priced' underwriting arrangement, it should consider whether to set the issue price lower and dispense with underwriting.

MARKET REACTION TO RIGHTS ISSUES

A study of 997 UK rights issues between 1962 and 1975 found that on average, the announcement of a rights issue prompted only a negligible decline of less than ½ per cent in the company's share price (see Table 14.2), suggesting that companies' financing needs cause little surprise or concern to the market. However, the way in which individual companies' share prices react to the news of an issue depends, of course, on the information accompanying and conveyed by the announcement. This information may concern:

1 *The company's existing business.* Rights issues announcements are frequently timed to coincide with the announcement of the annual or interim results, and are often accompanied by other new items on the company's existing business. Even in the absence of explicit announcements, the market may interpret the rights issue as

299

indicating unforeseen problems in the company's existing business, or previous underestimation of financing requirements.

2 *Management's assessment of prospects.* Rights issues are frequently accompanied by earnings forecasts, and almost invariably by forecasts of future dividends. The market's reaction to the news of the issue will therefore depend partly on whether these forecasts come as a pleasant or unpleasant surprise. In fact, the study referred to above found, roughly speaking, a 1 per cent increase in the share price for every 15 per cent increase in the forecast dividend.

3 *Uses of the new money.* If the finance to be raised is for investment in new projects or acquisitions, the market's reaction to the issue will depend upon its assessment of the NPV of the new projects, and this, in turn, will depend upon its view of the quality of the company's management. If the new money is to be used to repay debt, the market's reaction could be unfavourable if this heralded an unanticipated reduction in the company's target debt/equity ratio. These common sense views are again borne out by the empirical evidence which found that the share prices of companies announcing rights issues to finance new investment rose by 2.1 per cent from the day before the announcement to one month later. Companies announcing issues for the purposes of reducing gearing, however, experienced an average fall of ½ per cent in share price. Similarly, companies with a good track record, both in terms of share price and accounting measures of performance experienced share price rises of 1.8 per cent over the month of the announcement, whereas companies with a relatively poor or indifferent record experienced an average decline of 0.6 per cent.

4 *Capital structure.* If an equity issue is announced when an issue of debt was expected, the market may take this to imply a downward revision in the target debt/equity ratio, and this may lead to a fall in the share price. This is again borne out by the evidence in that there is a difference of approximately 2 per cent in the market's reaction to the rights issue announcement, depending on whether or not the market was expecting an equity or a debt issue.

Thus while there is, on average, little share price movement on the announcements of rights issues, the market's reaction can differ quite widely from one company to another. Furthermore, it is difficult to disentangle price movements due to the rights issue from those due to the accompanying announcements of other information.

RAISING EQUITY AT EXISTING MARKET PRICES

A view widely held by both professional investors and by finance directors is that, because it increases the supply of a company's shares, a rights issue will have a depressing effect upon the company's share price. This effect is usually referred to as 'price pressure', and belief in its existence is implicitly based on the assumption that the demand curve for a company's shares is not perfectly elastic but slopes downward.

Price pressure implies temporary price depression and cheap buying opportunities, and hence is inconsistent with stock market efficiency. The alternative view consistent with market efficiency is that the demand for a particular company's shares is perfectly elastic so that increases in the supply of its shares alone will not lead to a decline in the share price.

According to this view, the company selling shares is in a position precisely analogous to that of the wheat farmer in the standard economics textbook example who is able to sell large additional quantities of wheat at existing market prices and, in so doing, has essentially no effect on the world price of grain.

In both cases, the high elasticity of demand stems from the existence of very close substitutes, in one case this being the produce of other farms, and in the other, the existence of alternative risky assets. Since shares are valued purely on the basis of their risk and expected return, one share will prove a very close substitute for another.

Unless the additional supply of wheat or shares is large relative to the total supply of grain or risky assets, respectively, its effect on market prices should be negligible. The largest rights issue ever made on the London Stock Exchange was by BP who raised £624 million in June 1981. At the time of this issue, the new money raised was less than 0.2 per cent of the total value of London quoted equities, and thus was very small in relation to the total supply of risky assets, especially if the definition of the latter is extended to include fixed interest securities, property, commodities, works of art and so on.

Which of these two views is correct can be determined by examining the evidence. If price pressure exists, companies making rights issues should experience an abnormal price decline on the ex rights date, and this price decline should be greater the larger the issue. As can be seen from Table 14.2, the mean abnormal return for the one-week period over the Xr date for 997 UK rights issues made between 1962 and 1975 was between -½ per cent and -¾ per cent. Although this could be taken as weak evidence of price pressure, the effect is very small and could, of course, be explained by other factors.

However, further investigation showed that there is no relationship between the abnormal price movements at the time of the issue and the issue size, regardless of whether the latter was taken as the absolute size of the issue or the size of the issue expressed as a percentage of the issuing company's market capitalization. Figure 14.7 shows the scatter diagram

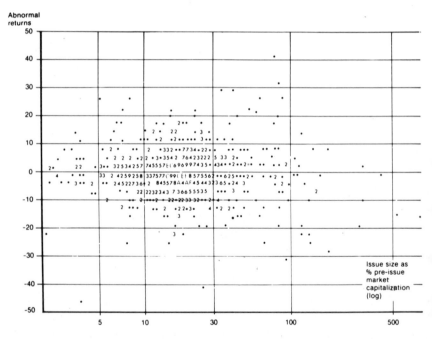

Figure 14.7   Abnormal returns and relative issue size

of abnormal returns against issue size for the relative size case. It is worth noting that the estimated elasticities of demand, although not remotely significant statistically, were approximately + 650 and -300 for the absolute and relative size cases, respectively. Thus, contrary to the predictions of the price pressure hypothesis, the demand curves are almost horizontal in both cases, and in the case of absolute issue size, the slope of the demand curve is not even in the predicted direction. To put these figures in perspective, the estimated relationship for the relative size case implies that a company increasing the size of its rights issue from 10 per cent to 20 per cent of the value of its existing equity will induce a price fall of less than 0.2 per cent, while a further increase from 20 per cent to 100 per cent will result in an additional fall of only ½ per cent. On the basis of this evidence, the price pressure hypothesis can be firmly rejected. Companies can raise money at existing market prices.

SUMMARY AND CONCLUSIONS

Rights issues are a fair and equitable method of raising equity. The cost of equity is the return shareholders require for the risk involved and is not the dividend yield or the reciprocal of the P/E ratio. The Government tax subsidy on interest payments is the only factor which might make debt preferable to equity.

Companies should raise equity when they have profitable uses for the money; except in this sense, the timing of rights issues appears very much less relevant than some city traditions suggest.

The issue terms are irrelevant except from the point of view of underwriting. The apparent earnings and dividend 'dilution' resulting from setting a lower issue price does not matter.

Underwriters appear to earn large excess returns at companies' expense, and finance directors need not accept too readily the issue terms suggested by the underwriter.

The news of rights issues produces, on average, only a slight price fall, and appears to cause neither surprise nor concern. The market reacts efficiently to the new information contained in the rights issue announcement, and the incidence of a rights issue does not provide investors any opportunity to make abnormal gains. The evidence indicates that price pressure does not exist and that the stock market is a highly liquid market in which companies can raise equity at existing market prices.

REFERENCES

1   Marsh, Paul, 'An Analysis of Equity Rights issues on the London

Stock Exchange', Unpublished doctoral dissertation, London Business School, 1977

2 Black, F. and Scholes, M., 'The Pricing of Options and Corporate Liabilities' *Journal of Political Economy* 81, pp. 637–54, May–June 1973

Part IV
EXTERNAL ENVIRONMENT

OVERVIEW

A company must be aware of the financial environment in which it operates. The environment is complex and dynamic: it reflects the legislative, economic, commercial and political systems of a country in the simplest case and the global interaction of domestic systems in the most complex case. For smaller companies, shareholders and bankers providing funds are probably known personally: the idea of acquisition is unthought of: international considerations are classed as exogenous and matters of taxation are 'dealt with by the accountant'. In larger companies, shareholders and servicing bankers need not be individually known: the idea of acquisition or merger can represent a real opportunity or threat: international events can have major repercussions on domestic performance and taxation advice is an expensive service. Irrespective of company size, it is of paramount importance that every trading business fully appreciates the implications of its financial behaviour in the external environment. Ramifications can be unwanted and severe if not analysed and taken into account.

Shareholders and bankers supply capital and the company needs to maintain good relationships with them to ensure an adequate flow of investment funds. Maintaining these relationships entails publishing relevant up-to-date information so that investors can value their company, decide whether to subscribe new funds and monitor the use of assets.

The ultimate sanction that the capital market can apply is a company takeover and the replacement of senior management. Thus, mergers and acquisitions form important aspects of the financial environment, both for companies seeking to grow by this method and for those wishing to avoid being taken over.

Multinationals and companies trading internationally are obliged to conduct transactions over numerous technical barriers. A major change in the nature of a firm's financial management problem usually occurs when trading results are determined by operations overseas. Thus international monetary management becomes crucial to a company generating profit outwith its national border.

Finally, the tax regime under which the company operates has a large impact on the cash flows resulting from financial decisions. Effective use of tax laws to minimise the cash drain on the company requires that the tax impact of all decisions be understood and incorporated into the decision making process.

These four aspects of the financial environment: presentation of external accounts, acquisitions and mergers, international monetary management and taxation are covered by this section. Chapter 15, by George Thomson, explains the regulations concerning disclosure in company accounts. These requirements form the basis for external financial reporting, but there may be good reason to disclose more than the minimum required. The kinds of extra information that are likely to prove most helpful and the agreements for providing such details are explored and explained. So is the recent requirement to present inflation-adjusted accounting information, which is the major change in this area in recent years.

As investors use company accounts for three main purposes, valuation, portfolio decisions, and monitoring asset use, the information provided must be appropriate to these ends. Valuation and portfolio decisions require more than just raw accounting information. Somehow, information on the company's position in its product markets, strategic plans and operation performance has to be communicated, in addition to the dry numerical data.

This additional requirement is achieved by a mixture of formal and informal contacts with the investment community, of which the published accounts are merely the tip of the iceberg. Given the high cost of raising funds when relationships with investors are poor, and the threat of takeover if the situation deteriorates too much, effort spent on keeping investors informed is an important part of good financial management.

Although investors can refuse to provide companies with new funds when asked, many concerns manage to operate for long periods of time by using retained earnings rather than making rights issues. Such companies are not immune to external financial markets, however, since their share prices may fall to such a level that it becomes attractive for another company to purchase a majority of the shares and gain control of the assets. The other side of this coin is that a company with a very high share rating resulting from able management can gain control of more assets by merger or acquisition.

In Chapter 16 Julian Franks analyses in detail the various motivations that are put forward for mergers and acquisitions: managerial skills, economies of scale, new product opportunities and valuation differences. In addition to these operational motivations, several purely financial incentives are sometimes suggested. Dr Franks shows that some of these may not be such powerful reasons for merging as is often stated. In particular, diversification through merger is not likely to benefit shareholders much, since they can diversify their own portfolios.

Even when there is a legitimate reason for merging, care must be taken that the premium paid does not exceed the synergistic benefits of the merger. Dr Franks describes the various techniques that are applied in analysing acquisition opportunities. Finally, he examines the profitability record of past mergers, to indicate whether they have achieved the expected gains, and, if so, how these gains have been split between acquirors and acquirees.

Chapter 17 addresses the important area of International Money Management; Andreas Prindl demonstrates the basis for effective cash management in a domestic context. He then generalises this approach to international management of the corporate cash resources. Special instruments of international financing are discussed, as well as the effective use of the institutional framework available for effective international money management.

In the final chapter of Part IV, Robert Scott covers the taxation of corporations in the UK. Almost all financial decisions have an impact on the amount of tax paid, and this must be included in the financial evaluation of any decisions: as previously discussed, the tax deductability of interest payments for example means that the value of projects financed partially by debt is increased by the value of the tax saving. Clearly, an understanding of the way that corporations are taxed is essential to good financial management. Mr Scott describes the way that the tax system operates with respect to corporations. Many corporations do not pay corporation tax, and it might be argued that such companies can ignore the tax impact of their decisions. This is fallacious, since companies which have unused tax losses are wasting opportunities to save money. Common ways of taking advantage of unused tax losses include merging with or acquiring a profit-making company, sale and leaseback of assets from profit-making companies, or reduction of interest payments through retiring debt.

In these and other ways, understanding the financial environment is crucial to good financial decision making. Mismanagement in the four areas covered in particular can be hazardous to the separate existence of a company, but good external relations and management ensure a continued flow of capital to support the growth and development of a soundly based and progressive organization.

15

Presentation of external financial reports

George R. Thomson*

This chapter is concerned with the requirements to be met by UK limited companies in corporate external financial reporting, that is, publication of financial information for use by people outside the business. These requirements are discharged by the inclusion of accounts and related information in the company's published annual report. This information is subject to audit, and it is the task of the auditors to report on whether or not the requirements have been met.

Financial reporting requirements for companies stem from three sources

1   The law, principally the Companies Acts 1948, 1967, 1980 and 1981, together with the Directives of the European Economic Community as and when these are reflected in UK law.
2   Financial accounting standards laid down by the accounting Standards Committee of the UK accountancy bodies as Statements of Standard Accounting Practices (SSAPs).
3   For companies whose securities are listed in the UK Stock Exchanges, the rules of the Stock Exchange.

Requirements may fall into either or both of the following categories

1   Disclosure requirements: that is, what information elements should be provided.

*This chapter was comprehensively revised by Simon Archer.

2   Measurement standards: that is, the methods whereby the amounts reported under particular headings should be determined.

The law and the Stock Exchange rules are concerned with disclosure, with the proviso that the amounts reported should provide a 'true and fair view' of the company's financial position and results. Specification of measurement standards is left to the Accounting Standards Committee. In addition to its concern for accounting measurement, however, the Accounting Standards Committee also includes further disclosure requirements in its SSAPs.

Financial reports of 'accounts' required for external users include two financial statements and accompanying notes, a balance sheet and a profit and loss account, plus a third statement required under SSAP No. 10, namely, a statement of sources and application of funds, or funds statement. In addition, the Stock Exchange rules for listed companies require

1   A statement giving reasons for any departures from prescribed SSAPs.
2   A geographical analysis of sales turnover.
3   Details of shareholdings of more than 5 per cent in other companies.
4   A statement giving details of directors' shareholdings in the company.
5   A similar statement of directors' interests in company contracts.
6   Details of dividends waived by directors or other shareholders.

The role and implications of the SSAPs call for particular comment. In the first place they do not have the force of law. Neither is compliance mandatory for listed companies under the Stock Exchange rules; however, as already noted, if a listed company fails to comply with an SSAP, it is required to publish a statement giving the reasons for non-compliance. Finally, it is up to the company's auditors to decide whether the failure to comply with one or more SSAPs means that the accounts fail to provide a 'true and fair view' of the financial position and results; for if so, it is their duty to word their audit opinion accordingly.

Naturally, the view of the Accounting Standards Committee and of the UK accountancy bodies is that, with very rare exceptions, failure to comply with either a disclosure requirement or a measurement standard laid down in an SSAP means that a 'true and fair view' has not been published. This would seem to imply that failure to comply with an

SSAP is tantamount to failure to comply with the law which requires that a 'true and fair view' be provided. However, this proposition has not been established by the courts.

Nor do SSAPs cover all aspects of financial reporting, although coverage is increasing as new SSAPs are added. In fact, companies have considerable discretion as to how they report their financial position and results. The requirement to provide a 'true and fair view' is inherently subjective. We return to these issues later in this chapter.

A further point which must be made regarding SSAPs concerns current cost accounting. The existing law considers financial reporting requirements in terms of the hitherto generallly accepted 'historical cost' accounting conventions. In 1980, however, the Accounting Standards Committee laid down SSAP No. 16 which requires all companies, excluding smaller firms and a few designated kinds of business, to produce financial reports – a balance sheet, a profit and loss account and accompanying notes – based on a set of 'current cost' conventions, in addition to those produced on the 'historical cost' basis. No 'current cost' funds statement is required. More will be said about these requirements later in this chapter.

OBJECTIVES

In deciding its presentation of existing financial reports, management has to consider appropriate objectives. The minimum objective is to show proprietors how their funds have been used and what profits have been made. This can be said to have been achieved by presenting a balance sheet, profit and loss account and funds statement, which show, 'a true and fair view' of the state of the company's affairs. 'The true and fair view' implies an appropriate classification and grouping of the various items involved and the consistent application of generally accepted accounting principles. The law also requires that annual accounts show figures for the preceding year as well as the most recent year. Consistency is insisted upon by a further legal requirement for disclosure of any material changes in the accounting treatment and a statement of how such changes have affected the latest and the previous years' figures.

A manager who is also a controlling shareholder, with only a few unsophisticated relatives as minority holders, may be right in judging that presentation should end at this point. Before doing so he should take other considerations into account. Is the business likely to need outside cash, either through borrowing or through an extension of the shareholding? Is it likely to acquire another business or be acquired by one? Will death duties or other reasons make it desirable to sell existing shares, either privately or through a stock market flotation?

In any of these (and in numbers of other) cases, the accounts will be scrutinized by sophisticated outsiders. They will want to know the answer to a number of points which are not covered by minimum statutory requirements. They will almost certainly wish to see accounts for some years previously. Indeed, it is a legal prospectus requirement that at least five years' figures must be produced by a company seeking to raise money in the market. Application for a stock market quotation normally has to be supported by ten years' figures.

Bearing these factors in mind, it is obvious that the objectives of a presentation of annual accounts should take note of many things beyond the immediate objective of producing a single year's figures economically and with the least fuss possible. Financial management should regard presentation as an important element in promoting the general image of a company. Presentation is concerned with good public relations. Properly done it confers many benefits.

The main benefits can be listed as follows: first, against any given economic background, to make it easier and cheaper to borrow money or to attract new capital either from existing or new investors; secondly, to make it cheaper and easier to expand by acquisitions or to get better terms from a merger; thirdly, to make it easier to resist an unwanted takeover bid. Many other, less tangible, benefits accrue even down to helping individual salesmen to sell a company's product.

Financial managers of the majority of big stock market quoted companies are aware of these factors and would regard it as failure on their part not to carry the point with any higher managerial executive.

Technically, the accounts are only being presented to shareholders, as in the case of the indivdual controlling head of a family business mentioned above. The latter may only have to publish for circulation to one or two people. The big public company will have many thousands of shareholders all of whom have to be circulated. The essential objectives of presentation are the same.

In the nature of things the big publicly quoted company will be more complex than the small family business. Statutory requirements insist on a greater degree of disclosure, and other organizations, such as a stock exchange, require further disclosures.

What is scarcely germane in modern circumstances is the number of shareholders. For weal or woe it is simply a fact that a greater proportion of thousands of shareholders in a quoted company is no more likely to be sufficiently interested, or knowledgeable, in the study of accounts than the one or two members of a family business.

And because it requires a vastly greater effort to communicate with and herd together a multitude than a taxi-cab load, the theoretical concept that a business is owned by a democracy of proprietors (shareholders) seldom has any relevance in practice.

Only short-sighted managers would take the view that, because this is so, shareholders should not be told more than is necessary. Institutional investors (the insurance companies, investment trusts, unit trusts, pension funds, etc.) are invariably large shareholders who can exercise considerable influence. The financial press is a powerful force in guiding investment thinking and is very much the champion of the private investor.

Both of these forces will be highly critical if they suspect that relevant information is being withheld unnecessarily and their criticisms will be echoed throughout the investment world.

Degree of disclosure

Obviously, a prime objective of presentation should be for accounts not to lay themselves open to suspicions and criticisms which can blight a company's financial standing for years after the original causes have been put to rights. It follows that careful attention should be given to the degree of disclosure. The general principle should be that disclosure of significant information should not be avoided unless it can be shown that it would damage a company's interests. The most thorny aspect of this is non-disclosure on the grounds that the information would be of value to competitors.

In a few cases, usually concerning consolidation of overseas subsidiaries' accounts, Board of Trade absolution from full disclosure can be given. In others, permission can be obtained from the Council of the Stock Exchange not to give such items as a full breakdown of turnover. Exemptions like these confer the highest guarantee that the case for disclosure is unarguable. Where such exemptions have been given the fact should be stated clearly.

In all other cases the best criterion to be followed is for a financial manager to ask himself: 'Could I justify non-disclosure to an intelligent third party such as an investment manager of an institution or a city editor?'

The majority of companies recognize today that the tide of political, trade union and investment opinion in favour of the fullest reasonable disclosure continues to flood ever more strongly. It is almost a quaint thought that, until the 1967 Companies Act insisted upon it, many companies refused to disclose their total sales on the plea that this would be damaging. Obscurantism on this scale, or even the suspicion of it to a far lesser degree, wins no marks. Today it merely arouses suspicion, which is the mortal enemy of confidence. Moreover, following the 1981 Companies Act the profit and loss account must now provide an analysis of expenses.

Only one degree less dangerous to a company's image is when non-disclosure continues to flood ever more strongly. It is almost a quaint editor (for the sake of convenience this character will serve as an archetype for any influential person whose opinions count in deciding a company's financial rating) who states disclosure of a certain figure would be giving aid and succour to a main competitor if the city editor can pick up a telephone and discover that the competition is well aware of the figure concerned.

Even if such tales, and there are many, do not get into print, they are enjoyed as jokes among the financial coterie.

In all this it should be remembered that the normal professional inquisitor of accounts is a reasonable chap who has a wide experience of the problems involved in their presentation. He will understand, for instance, a reluctance to split an overall figure on research and development down to a level at which the precise spending on development of a potential product, which cannot be marketable for several years, will give valuable information to the competition.

What he will want to know is how, overall, research and development has been treated in the accounts. If it is being written off profits as it is incurred, published profits will be conservative. If it is being capitalized (in other words, being put into the balance sheet as an asset), there will be a day of reckoning if the project fails to become commercial.

The majority of larger companies today have interests in different areas of a single industry and, in many cases, in totally different industries. In the case of quoted companies, the accounts are expected to give a clear indication of the division of profits and turnover between these different interests.

Even when such treatment is not mandatory it is often desirable. A financial analyst tends to use comparative statistics as measures of managerial efficiency. Where he is not fully in the picture his judgements may be quite unfair but, none the less, damaging.

Example

Two companies are both in the food supply industry. Company A shows a profit of £1 million from sales of £25 million. Company B shows the same profit from sales of only £14 million. The analyst may jump to the hasty conclusion that Company B is more efficient.

Company B, however, gets all of its sales from retailing. Company A sells only £5 million retail on which it earns £500 000. The remaining £20 million of sales comes from wholesaling, which involves big turnover and small margins. A profit of £500 000, or 2 ½ per cent, from this source is quite acceptable.

Given the additional information, the analyst will realize that he is not comparing like with like and will revise his first judgement. Of course, it can be argued that he would have revised his first judgement anyway through other statistics such as the return on capital employed. But there is no virture in letting him puzzle out the position for himself when a simple line of explanation makes everything clear.

Explanatory notes

Disclosure usually involves a short explanatory text to elaborate the bare figures. To attempt to do this directly against every item would call for elaboration in the profit and loss account, the balance sheet and funds flow statement and would give a muddled and unpleasing result.

The presentation of accounts, like the presentation of goods, should aim at aesthetic appeal. The typographical layout deserves as much consideration as that bestowed by a newspaper editor on the appearance of a front page. Maximum simplicity and clarity are the keynotes. For this reason it is normally desirable to confine each account to a single page.

Further disclosure should take the form of notes which should be numbered clearly against each relevant item. For the reader's convenience, notes appertaining to profits should be on the page or pages immediately following the profit and loss account. Similarly, notes dealing with assets and liabilities should follow immediately after the balance sheet.

Because of the complexity of legislation, accountancy procedures, stock market requirements, international complications and the differing nature of businesses, it is impracticable in a chapter of this scope to give an example of every accountancy figure which may call for an explanatory note. The items which most frequently do so are listed under their appropriate headings in the following text. The Companies Act 1981 specifies standard formats and line items for the profit and loss account and the balance sheet, as well as the information which, if not disclosed on the face of these statements, must appear in the accompanying notes. The example given in Tables 15.1 and 15.2 reflect the requirements of the Act.

PROFIT AND LOSS ACCOUNT

It is assumed that the reader is familiar with the way in which the profit and loss account classifies items. An example is shown in Table 15.1. Certain items which call for additional disclosure in the form of notes are as follows.

Table 15.1
Profit and loss account, following Format 1 of the Companies Act, 1981

GENERAL TRADING LTD
Profit and loss account for the year ending 31 March 1982

	Notes	1982 £000	1981 £000
Turnover	1	2400	provide
Cost of sales		1900	compara-
			tive figures
Gross profit		500	
Distribution and administrative costs	2	330	
Operating profit		170	
Interest payable	3	10	
Profit on ordinary activities, before taxation	1	160	
Taxation	4	70	
Profit for year		90	
Dividends	5	50	
Retained profit for year		40	

NB. An alternative format (Format 2) is allowed under the Companies Act 1981, reflecting Continental European disclosure practice. It is expected that most British companies will prefer Format 1, which resembles US disclosure practice.

Turnover and profit

Note 1. Turnover should be analysed into different business categories such as printing, engineering, leisure activities, etc., with disclosure of proportionate profits before taxation in each subdivision.

Another subdivision required is a geographical analysis of sales turnover and profits before taxation.

Distribution and administrative costs

Note 2. The split between distribution and administration must be given.

Note 3. Interest payable. This should be analysed according to the type and term of indebtedness, for example, bank loans and overdrafts repayable in total within 5 years, other loans repayable in total within 5 years, other loans not repayable in total within 5 years.

Taxation

Note 4. The note should show the basis of corporation tax on profit from ordinary activities, so that the relationship of the two figures can be understood.

A high tax figure can result from a number of factors. A company may derive considerable income from trading overseas in areas of high taxation. Depreciation may have been applied in excess of that allowed by the Inland Revenue. The Revenue may have caught up on tax undercharged in previous years.

A low tax figure can result from the opposite of any of the factors in the last paragraph, or it may result from losses made in previous years. In the latter case it is desirable to indicate the extent of the remaining relief to be expected from this source.

Note 5. Dividends. These should be analysed into preference and ordinary, interim and final, the amounts per share being shown.

BALANCE SHEET

There are two methods of presenting a balance sheet which are acceptable under the 1981 Companies Act.

Net asset format (Format 1)

The method which has been gaining ground in recent years is the net asset format.

In this case the same figures are shown in a single column vertical tabular form. First come fixed assets and net current assets. The latter figure is derived from an inset table listing current assets and liabilities with the latter being deducted from the former to show net current assets. Below appear non-current liabilities followed by capital and reserves, these figures being totalled to produce a figure of total long-term funds employed.

Although the same figures are used in both presentations the resulting balance sheet total in the account format is lower to the extent of the current liabilities figure.

In the net asset method it is becoming increasingly common to use a form of presentation which shows no details in the face of the statement. All detail is supplied in the form of notes.

An example of Format 1 is shown in Table 15.2, with detail indicated in note form.

Account format (Format 2)

The older account format consists of opposing columns. On the left is itemized the share capital followed by reserves (which together comprise shareholders funds). Then come long-term liabilities, followed by current liabilities.

The right-hand column details fixed assets followed by current assets.

Fixed Assets

Note 6. Fixed assets as defined in the Companies Act 1981 include intangible assets (for example, goodwill, patents) and long-term investments as well as tangible fixed assets. The Act specifies the minimum breakdown to be given either on the face of the balance sheet or in the notes (see the Appendix). In the case of General Trading Ltd. all the fixed assets are tangible. The note should show, for each subdivision: gross cost or valuation and accumulated depreciation at the beginning of the year, and at the end of the year; and the total amounts of additions, disposals, revaluations, depreciation charges and any other items needed to explain the change during the year.

Notes, 7, 8, 9 and 10. Current assets, current liabilities and non-current liabilities. The Companies Act 1981 specifies the minimum breakdown to be given of the various components, either on the face of the balance sheet or in the notes (see Appendix).

Table 15.2
Balance sheet, following Format 1 of the Companies Act, 1981

GENERAL TRADING LTD

Balance sheet, 31 March 1982

	Notes	£000	1982 £000	£000	1981 £000
Fixed assets	6		800	provide	
Current assets				compa-	
Stocks	7	400		rative	
Debtors	8	350		figures	
Cash at bank and in hand		150			
		900			
Current liabilities – creditors due within one year					
Trade creditors		180			
Sundry creditors	9	120			
		300			
Net current assets			600		
Total assets less current liabilities (net assets employed)			1400		
Non-current liabilities – creditors due after more than one year	10		200		
Capital and reserves					
Called-up share capital	11	1000			
Profit and loss account	12	200	1200		
			1400		

Notes 11 and 12. Called-up share capital and reserves.   The notes should show

1   The number of shares authorised and their nominal value
2   The number of shares issued and paid up, and their nominal value
3   The reserves, divided into revaluation reserve, other reserves, and profit and loss account (retained profits). A breakdown of other reserves is required (see the Appendix).

Notes on accounts generally

Where the affairs of a company are complicated, which is invariably the case with large holding companies, there is a danger that the notes to accounts will be so numerous and so lengthy that sheer mass will defeat the object of illuminating the figures.

This problem can be minimized by devoting a page immediately preceding the accounts to a description of the accounting policies being pursued. The disclosure of accounting policies on significant items is required by SSAP No. 2 and hence by the Stock Exchange rules.

It is important to remember that notes on the accounts form part of the accounts themselves and, like the balance sheet and profit and loss account, are subject to the reports of independent auditors.

FUNDS STATEMENT

The purpose of a funds statement, or statement of sources and applications of funds, is 'to identify the movements in assets, liabilities and capital which have taken place during the year and the resultant effect on net liquid funds', (SSAP No. 10, para 1). Since publication of such a statement is required under the SSAP in question, it is also a normal requirement under the Stock Exchange rules.

The form of the funds statement and, to a lesser extent, its content are matters about which there is less general agreement than in the case of the balance sheet and profit and loss account. Nor is any minimum content laid down by law. SSAP No. 10 does not prescribe a particular format, but provides an Appendix giving an example which is reproduced in Table 15.3. (Other alternative presentations are also given in the Appendix to SSAP No. 10.)

Table 15.3
Sources and application of funds

GROUPS LIMITED: Statement of source and application of funds
(based on the accounts of the group and showing the acquisition of a subsidiary as a separate item)

	This year				Last year	
	£'000	£'000	£'000	£'000	£'000	£'000
Source of funds						
Profit before tax and extraordinary items, less minority interests		2,025			2,610	
Extraordinary items		450			(170)	
		2,476			2,440	
Adjustments for items not involving the movement of funds:						
Minority interest in the retained profits of the year		25			30	
Depreciation		345			295	
Profits retained in associated companies		(40)			—	
Total generated from operations		2,805			2,765	
Funds from other sources						
Shares issued in part consideration of the acquisition of subsidiary*		290			—	
Capital raised under executive option scheme		100			80	
		3,195			2,845	
Application of funds						
Dividends paid	(650)			(650)		
Tax paid	(770)			(970)		
Purchase of fixed assets	(370)			(736)		
Purchase of Subsidiary Ltd*	(351)			—		
Debentures redeemed	(890)			—		
		(3,030)			(2,356)	
		165			489	
Increase/decrease in working capital						
Increase in stocks	80			166		
Increase in debtors	70			122		
Decrease in creditors – excluding taxation and proposed dividends	115			17		
Movement in net liquid funds:						
Increase (decrease) in cash balance	(35)		10			
Increase (decrease) in short-term investments	(65)		174			
		(100)		184		
			165			489

Analysis of the acquisition of Subsidiary Limited

Net assets acquired		Discharged by	
Fixed assets	290	Shares issued	290
Goodwill	30	Cash paid	60
Stocks	40		
Debtors	30		
Creditors	(40)		
	350		350

DIRECTORS' REPORT

This does not, strictly speaking, form part of the accounts of a company, but it is an important element in presentation. Indeed, the report and the accompanying chairman's statement, which most companies issue each year, are likely to be more widely read than the accounts themselves.

Contents

Because of this it is usual to give a brief summary, in the simplest form, of results for the year. Any major changes in the company's structure should be listed, such as acquisitions or disposals of assets, and it is desirable to give reasons for these.

Unless covered separately in the chairman's statement, the report is expected to review operations during the year, give an indication of trading to date in the current year and some comments about future prospects.

The report offers great scope for presentation. The growth of a company can be shown by simple charts and graphs of such items as sales and pre-tax profits over a number of years. Many reports shows a ten-year record of important extracts from the accounts. Where these include earnings and dividends per share it is important that adjustments should be made for scrip issues and rights issues.

Well presented graphs, diagrams and statistical surveys are undoubtedly a desirable feature of a report. The sophisticated analyst is grateful to them for the toil which they save him. The unsophisticated small shareholder finds them meaningful in a way in which the actual accounts never could be; they help to make him feel more truly a real member of the company.

The bulk of a directors' report normally consists of volunteered information. In addition, certain information, not all of it of an accounting nature, must be shown if not shown elsewhere. For instance, the report must show the directors' individual shareholdings at the beginning and the end of the accounting year. It may be that a substantial reduction is shown in the holding of a director. He may have given shares to his children, or he may have sold them in order to make safer provisions for death duties or for some compelling business reason.

In such a case it is obviously desirable that an explanation should be given. Equally, it is undesirable that the fact should appear to be tucked away in some obscure corner or in unduly small type. Such treatment would be sure to arouse suspicion.

CURRENT COST ACCOUNTS

The 'current cost' set of accounting conventions, contained in SSAP No. 16, differs from the hitherto generally accepted 'historical cost' set of conventions in two main respects

1 Assets are stated at their value to the business, on a current cost basis. This is generally the current replacement cost of equivalent service (or operating) capability, except in the relatively rare case where both the net realizable value and the expected value in use are lower, in which case the greater of the two latter will be used.
2 Profit is calculated as the surplus out of revenue after making provision for maintaining the operating capability of the business, as represented by the value to the business of its net assets at the time the revenue is recognized.

This second point identifies the main motivation for the efforts which led to the introduction of SSAP No. 16 – the feeling that a profit which was not a surplus after making provision for maintenance of operating capability was not a 'real' profit. These issues are further discussed in the Accounting Standards Committee's Guidance Notes to SSAP No. 16.

The following categories of company are not required to comply with SSAP No. 16

1 Those which do not have any class or share or loan capital listed on the Stock Exchange and satisfy at least two of the following three criteria
  (a) They have a turnover of less than £5 million per annum.
  (b) Their balance sheet total on an historical cost basis at the beginning of the relevant accounting period was less than £2.5 million, the balance sheet total being calculated as follows
    Fixed assets (net book value) other than investment
    Investment
    Current assets including prepayments and accrued income (before deduction of current liabilities).
  (c) Their average number of UK employees (UK companies) or Irish employees (Republic of Ireland companies) is less than 250.
2 Wholly owned subsidiaries of companies where the parent is registered in the UK or the Republic of Ireland except where the parent is excepted under (3) below.

325

3 (a) Authorized insurers.

   (b) Property investment and dealing companies, with the exception of companies which hold the properties of another company within the group which is not excepted from SSAP No. 16.

   (c) Investment trust companies, unit trust and other similar long-term investment businesses.

The information required to be disclosed under SSAP No. 16 is

1 A current cost profit and loss account.
2 A current cost balance sheet.
3 Notes which describe the bases and methods adopted particularly in relation to:

   (a) The value to the business of fixed assets and the depreciation thereon.

   (b) The value to the business of stock and work in progress and the cost of sales adjustment (difference between historical and current cost of goods sold).

   (c) The monetary working capital adjustment (see below).

   (d) The gearing adjustment (see below).

   (e) The bases of translating foreign currencies and dealing with translation differences arising.

   (f) Other material adjustments to the historical cost information.

   (g) The corresponding amounts (SSAP No. 16 para. 58).

The monetary working capital adjustment is a measure of the effect of specific price changes on the monetary amount of trade credit given less trade credit received (trade debtors less trade creditors and, where applicable, short-term bank borrowings). Under SSAP 16, this amount is required to be deducted (or where trade creditors, etc., exceed trade debtors, added) in arriving at current cost profit.

The gearing adjustment is that fraction of the cost of sales and monetary working capital adjustments and the depreciation adjustment (difference between historical and current cost depreciation) which corresponds to the proportion of net operating assets financed by borrowings. According to SSAP No. 16, this amount is not part of the provision which needs to be made for maintaining the operating capability of the shareholders' interest in the business. It should therefore be added back to the current cost profit from operations in arriving at the current cost profit attributable to shareholders.

Examples of a current cost profit and loss account and balance sheet, as provided in the Appendix to SSAP No. 16, are given in Tables 15.4 and 15.5.

Table 15.4
Example of current cost profit and loss account

Y LIMITED AND SUBSIDIARIES
Group current cost profit and loss account
for the year ended 31 December 1981

1980 £000		1981 £000
18 000	Turnover	20 000
2 420	Profit before and taxation on the historical cost basis	2 900
1 320	Less: Current cost operating adjustments (Note 2)	1 510
1 100	*Current cost operating profit*	1 390
180	Interest payable less receivable	200
920		1 190
610	Taxation	730
310	Current cost profit after interest and taxation	460
170	Gearing adjustment	166
480	*Current cost profit attributable to shareholders*	626
400	Dividends	430
80	Retained current cost profit of the year	196
16.0p	Current cost earnings per share	20.9p
5.2%	Operating profit return on the average of the net operating assets	6.0%

Statement of retained profits/reserves

£000		£000
80	Retained current cost profit of the year	196
1 850	Movements on current cost reserve (Note 4)	2 054
NIL	Movements on other reserves	NIL
1 930		2 250
14 150	Retained profits/reserves at the beginning of the year	16 080
16 080	Retained profits/reserves at the end of the year	18 330

It follows from what was said earlier that, to comply with the Stock Exchange requirements, a company which does not fall into one of the categories exempt from SSAP No. 16 must either comply with that Standard or publish a statement giving its reasons for non-compliance.

Table 15.5
Example of current cost balance sheet

Y LIMITED AND SUBSIDIARIES
Summarized group current cost balance sheet
as at 31 December 1981

1980			1981	
£000	£000		£000	£000
		Assets employed:		
	18 130	Fixed assets (Note 3)		19 530
		Net current assets:		
3 200		Stock	4 000	
700		Monetary working capital	800	
3 900		Total working capital	4 800	
(400)		Proposed dividends	(430)	
(600)		Other current liabilities (net)	(570)	
	2 900			3 800
	21 030			22 330
		Financed by:		
		Share capital and reserves:		
3 000		Share capital	3 000	
12 350		Current cost reserve (Note 4)	14 404	
3 730		Other reserves and retained profit	3 926	
	19 080			21 330
	1 950	Loan capital		2 000
	21 030			23 330

CONCLUSIONS

The presentation of accounts should take into consideration the various categories of people who will be reading them, the diverse interest of these categories and their relative importance. The broad categories are shareholders, small and large, the financial press, employees, potential investors, creditors, customers and the government.

The wider the potential readership, the more desirable it is to make disclosures well in excess of statutory or stock market requirements.

The result should be a successful financial public relations operation which enhances the company's image in commercial and investment circles.

REFERENCE

1   Reid, W. and Myddelton, D.R. *The Meaning of Company Accounts,* Gower (Aldershot 1982)

APPENDIX: REPORTING REQUIREMENTS OF THE 1981 COMPANIES ACT

Profit and loss account – Format 1

1   Turnover
2   Cost of sales
3   Gross profit or loss
4   Distribution costs
5   Administrative expenses
6   Other operating income
7   Income from shares in group companies
8   Income from shares in related companies
9   Income from other fixed asset investment
10   Other interest receivable and similar income
11   Amounts written off investments
12   Interest payable and similar charges
13   Tax on profit or loss on ordinary activities
14   Profit or loss on ordinary activities after taxation
15   Extraordinary income
16   Extraordinary charges
17   Extraordinary profit or loss
18   Tax on extraordinary profit or loss
19   Other taxes not shown under the above items
20   Profit or loss for the financial year

Balance sheet – Format 1

A   Called up share capital not paid
B   Fixed assets

I   Intangible assets
         1   Development costs
         2   Concessions, patents, licences, trade marks and similar
             rights and assets

         3   Goodwill

         4   Payments on account

II   Tangible assets

         1   Land and buildings

         2   Plant and machinery

         3   Fixtures, fittings, tools and equipment

         4   Payments on account and assets in course of construction

III   Investments

         1   Shares in group companies

         2   Loans to group companies

         3   Shares in related companies

         4   Loans to related companies

         5   Other investments other than loans

         6   Other loans

         7   Own shares

C   Current assets

I   Stocks

         1   Raw materials and consumables

         2   Work in progress

         3   Finished goods and goods for resale

         4   Payments on account

II   Debtors

         1   Trade debtors

         2   Amounts owed by group companies

         3   Amounts owed by related companies

         4   Other debtors

         5   Called up share capital not paid

         6   Prepayments and accrued income

III   Investments

         1   Shares in group companies

         2   Own shares

         3   Other investment

IV   Cash at bank and in hand

D   Prepayments and accrued income

E   Creditors: amounts falling due within one year

1   Debenture loans
2   Bank loans and overdrafts
3   Payments received on account
4   Trade creditors
5   Bills of exchange payable
6   Amounts owed to group companies
7   Amounts owed to related companies
8   Other creditors including taxation and social security
9   Accruals and deferred income

F   Net current assets (liabilities)

G   Total assets less current liabilities

H   Creditors: amounts falling due after more than one year

1   Debenture loans
2   Bank loans and overdrafts
3   Payments received on account
4   Trade creditors
5   Bills of exchange payable
6   Amounts owed to group companies
7   Amounts owed to related companies
8   Other creditors including taxation and social security
9   Accruals and deferred income

I   Provisions for liabilities and charges

1   Pensions and similar obligations
2   Taxation, including deferred taxation
3   Other provisions

J   Accruals and deferred income

K   Capital and reserves

I   Called up share capital
II   Share premium account
III   Revaluation reserve
IV   Other reserves

1   Capital redemption reserve
2   Reserve for own shares
3   Reserves provided for by the articles of association
4   Other reserves

V   Profit and loss account

16

Acquisitions and mergers

Julian R. Franks

Every year larger numbers of companies combine into new corporate organizations. A formal combination is called a merger when it results from a friendly arrangement between the managements of two or more companies of roughly equal size or strength. A holding company may be set up and stockholders advised to exchange their existing stocks for those of the holding company. Alternatively, one of the two merging companies may play the role of the holding company and offer an exchange of ordinary shares, cash or some combination of securities and cash as payment for the other company. This latter arrangement is often called an acquistion or a takeover, especially when the merger has not been agreed between the two managements. Why, one may ask, should companies merge in a competitive economy? Why should it be worth one company paying a bid premium in excess of otherwise normal market prices to acquire the assets of another company? In this chapter we examine the economic and financial rationale for merging. We also provide a framework for valuing a company for acquisition purposes and point out the problems arising from the use of alternative valuation methods.

LEVEL OF MERGER ACTIVITY IN THE UK

In Table 16.1 we have reproduced data on merger activity from the Department of Trade and Industry which shows how the rate of merger activity has changed over time. Both in number and value, there have been substantial fluctuations with peaks occurring in 1968, 1972 and 1985. Furthermore, by the end of the first six months of 1986 the value of merger activity was set to exceed the previous record £11.14 billions in 1968.

Table 16.1
Acquisitions and mergers 1963 to 1985

Year	Number acquired	Value £m (historic prices)	Value £m (1985 prices)	Year	Number acquired	Value £m (historic prices)	Value £m (1985 prices)
1963	888	352	2429	1975	315	291	806
1964	940	505	3371	1976	353	448	1064
1965	1000	517	3295	1977	481	824	1690
1966	807	500	3077	1978	567	1140	2159
1967	763	822	4928	1979	534	1656	2763
1968	946	1946	11 145	1980	469	1475	2067
1969	846	1069	5794	1981	452	1144	1447
1970	793	1122	5730	1982	463	2206	2569
1971	884	911	4255	1983	447	2343	2608
1972	1210	2532	11 023	1984	568	5474	5806
1973	1205	1304	5197	1985	474	7090	7090
1974	504	508	1749				

This peak of activity can be put in some perspective by comparing the peaks of merger activity with the percentage of investment. In both 1968 and 1972 the value of merger activity equalled about 75% of all investment in industrial and commerical activities.

In subsequent sections we describe a variety of economic and financial reasons for a merger. However, each of these reasons explains why an individual merger may take place; none of those reasons satisfactorily explains the large fluctuation in aggregate merger activity. The latter remains a puzzle although some academics have suggested that aggregate merger activity may be related to the changing level of stock market prices. Why mergers should be correlated with (say) rising stock markets has not been well explained, but it has become popular folklore.

ECONOMIC BENEFITS

One should be clear about the difference between a merger and a capital investment. A merger does not increase productive capacity but simply records the transfer of title or ownership over a set of assets from one party to another, whereas a capital investment actually adds to the real assets of the firm. The former is, on its own, simply a financial transaction, and it is this aspect that should lead managers to be careful when valuing a potential acquisition. After all, if you are paying a substantial bid premium, the only way to justify the premium is to increase the profitability of the assets over and above that expected under existing management. As a result, it is difficult to see how a merger can be successful unless the acquiring firm has some plan for adding value to the acquired or acquiring firm as a result of the merger.

Purchase of managerial and technical skills

Acquirers often make a bid because they wish to acquire unique managerial and technical skills in the acquired company and use these skills to improve their own profitability. Before undertaking an expensive takeover bid for this purpose, management first must consider alternative means to the same end. A less costly alternative may be to make handsome job offers to key individuals either in the potential takeover company or in other companies. The premium paid to individuals with unique skills might be less than the premium which must be paid in the market for a company which includes these skills within its ranks.

The alternative of hiring indivudals may not always be practicable, however, when the unique managerial and technical skills are embodied within a large team or organization. Also, the acquiring company may have no way of determining from the outside what subtle combination of elements within the team may make it effective. Hiring sufficient numbers of the team to be assured of the 'critical mass' may not be possible. Although a friendly merger could provide a rapid means of obtaining an excellent managerial and technical team intact, one should be sceptical in the case of a contested takeover as to whether a management team will maintain its effectiveness if it is hostile to the acquiring management at the outset.

Changes in economies of scale

One of the more obvious incentives to merge is the economies of scale which might arise from the merger. For example, let us assume a new plant has been developed that will reduce the unit costs of making a barrel of beer by 20 per cent: the first question is: 'should we replace existing plant with the new plant?' That change will only be worthwhile if the reduction in the operating costs, discounted to present value, is greater than the capital investment required for the new plant.

Even if it is profitable to scrap the existing plant, the present market share of the firm may be less than the minimum capacity of the new plant. Thus a merger may be necessary to capture the extra market share required to obtain the new economies of scale. Mergers of small breweries in the UK and Germany in the 1960s were justified on this basis. When it is not economic to scrap existing facilities, market growth will seldom be sufficient to justify immediate investment in large new plant if the market is divided between many firms. Companies with the larger market shares can often obtain the benefits of scale more rapidly by installing additional new plant.

In Figure 16.1 we have a simple diagram that illustrates how this incentive to merge may arise. There are three firms, A, B and C. For historical reasons firm A has the much larger share of the market with sales totalling 50 units. A new plant with much lower operating costs is available, but it is not profitable to replace the existing plant with the new plant in the near future. An increase in market demand from 100 units to 140 units is allocated to each firm on the basis of past market shares. The increase in demand for firm A is large enough to justify an investment in the new plant; however, this is not so for the other two concerns. Firms B

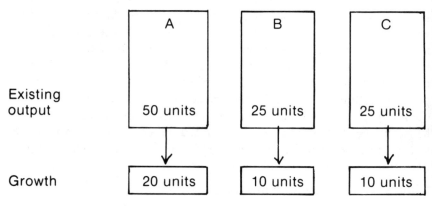

Figure 16.1   Growth and incentive to merge

and C must either build on outdated plant (with higher unit costs) to cope with the new demand or lose the opportunities for growth and a maintained market share. An alternative is for B and C to enter a joint venture to exploit their combined growth or agree to a full scale merger. The third possibility is for B and C to persuade firm A to acquire them.

Exploiting a new product

A firm may wish to produce a new product but may require additional facilities (production, marketing, etc.) to make it in quantity. Construction of new facilities takes time, and it may be more profitable to acquire the existing facilities of another company. If these existing facilities are unused, then they should cost no more than the depreciated cost of similar new facilities. If the existing facilities are being used, it may still be profitable to buy them and switch their production to the new product.

Time may be as important a reason as cost for acquiring another company's facilities. Since a product's comparative advantage over similar products does not last long, it is often essential to exploit a new product as quickly as possible. Delays involved in building new facilities may be too costly in strategic terms. Competition may erode the advantage of the new product, reduce its potential market share and thereby reduce its prospective revenues and net present value. Similarly, a firm with a new product may not have an established brand name in the market place. Frequently, products which lack established brand names sell at a lower price than well-known products. The reason is that consumers are either unaware of the new product or require a lower price to change their purchasing habits. The lower price must compensate the consumer for the possibility that the product will not live up to its claims or that the guarantees (or warranties) may prove costly for the purchaser to exercise. The costs of establishing a brand name and the resulting delay in exploiting the new product may make it worthwhile to buy another company's brand name.

Market power

Monopoly is one of the reasons frequently given for merging. The reason is that competition inevitably leads to lower prices and lower profits. Although it is undeniable that maintaining or increasing a company's market share can justify a merger, there are still some qualifications to be made. The first is that the merger may be contested by the Monopolies Commission. A challenge by the Commission can prevent a merger or, at the very least, delay its consummation. Secondly, high profits will attract new entrants into the industry and encourage the development of close substitutes; thus, the market protection afforded by a merger may only be temporary.

By the beginning of 1986, 86 takeovers had been referred to the Commission. Of this total, 15 of the mergers were rejected and did not proceed, and 34 were accepted (some of which did not proceed). The remaining 27 were laid aside, which means that for one reason or another the acquiring company decided not to proceed with the bid before the Commission completed its report.

Valuation differences

Some mergers have been justified because the acquiring management believes the assets of the acquirer are undervalued in the stock market. Such an undervaluation may be due to one of three reasons

1   The assumption that the stock market is generally 'undervalued' and that the acquirer knows better than everybody else. Such an attitude does not provide a convincing justification since shareholders are just as capable of perceiving an undervalued market as managers.

2   The acquired company's stock is really a 'good buy' at the current price. Again, we do not find this argument convincing because managers can always buy some shares in the 'undervalued' firm without trying to obtain control and without paying the large bid premium that is usually required for control.

3   The assets of the firm are priced below their replacement cost. This argument is clearly justified if and only if the acquiring firm can exploit the assets and obtain a net present value from their use. In 1978 the second-hand value of ships was substantially below their replacement cost; however, the reason was that the prices merely reflected the low profitability of operating the ships. Only if a firm could operate the ships more profitably than other companies would it be profitable to buy other company's ships. Clearly, as more and more companies find it profitable to buy ships in the second-hand market, so prices will rise. Until prices exceed replacement cost, few new ships will be built.

The stock market may not always reflect the value of a firm's assets. Since it costs money to obtain information, neither the market nor the management of the acquisition may be aware of a profitable alternative use of assets envisioned by the management of an acquiring company. A merger may not be the best way of improving this situation, however. The acquiring company could merely make speculative purchases of a company's shares and then provide the vital information lacking to existing management and to the stock market. If it is unlikely that the existing management will be willing or able to take economic decisions on the basis of the new information, then a takeover could be justified.

FINANCIAL BENEFITS

Merging and diversification

Theory suggests that diversification for the purposes of risk reduction can only be justified from a shareholder's viewpoint if default or bankruptcy would entail substantial costs. In the absence of such costs, the argument is that shareholders can always achieve such risk reduction for themselves by investing in a diversified portfolio of equities on their own account, or by investing in unit trusts. However, there are a number of reasons why managers of the firm may take a different view.

From a shareholder's view the costs of bankruptcy lie primarily in the legal costs of reorganization. There are, however, costs to other parties; for example, to managers. A bankruptcy may not only deprive a manager of his salaried job but also undermine his value in the job market when he seeks alternative employment. Since information is imperfectly disemminated, the bankruptcy may reflect unfairly on the perceived competence of individual managers involved. The risk is not easily diversified by managers whose main wealth is human capital: that is, in their ability to earn a high salary. In these circumstances a wise manager may reject some takeover projects which would be profitable to diversified shareholders. An alternative strategy would be to diversify the assets of the firm.

One should not imagine that the self interest of managers in this regard is wholly at odds with the interests of shareholders. Managers and other employees in risky, undiversified companies will tend to demand higher salaries or other benefits to compensate for the risks entailed in working for such concerns. The resulting additional labour costs must be borne by the owners or the shareholders. Furthermore, managers who are exposed to unnecessary risks to their job security are more likely to bias investment decisions towards lower risk situations. This bias is seldom in the interest of diversified shareholders. If it is not too costly, both share-holders' and employees' interests may be served by some degree of company diversification. Diversification also provides a means of preserving goodwill.

Only if the company stays in existence can it seize future opportunities to make profitable investments. Diversification helps to remove the risk of losing the value of such growth. Furthermore, as argued elsewhere in the chapter, diversification may actually increase the portfolio of growth opportunities available to the merger partners.

Once managers and employees are protected in these ways, manage-ment can identify more closely with the interests of diversified shareholders when making investment decisions. When company diversi-fication is too costly, shareholders often grant options to managers to purchase the company's shares at a fixed price. This provides a financial incentive for management to take decisions which favourably affect shareholders' wealth. The effectiveness of this method is limited by the fact that it does not eliminate the manager's vulnerability to the unique risks of capital projects. Share options in the company of employment increase an already large stake which managers have in the fortunes of that one enterprise. There is some obvious scope here for devising imaginative compensation schemes to bring executive incentives more closely into line with the interests of diversified shareholders.

Risk reduction and lower borrowing costs

When two firms merge the risk of the combined earnings stream may be reduced as a result of the diversification effect. In Table 16.2 we show a simple example of the way in which diversifying mergers can reduce the risk of the merged companies' earnings stream compared with their pre-merger state. The example is unrealistic because we assume the earnings of the two companies move in opposite directions (that is, the earnings of the two are perfectly *negatively* correlated). At the end of the year there are only two possible outcomes for earnings (called outcomes 1 and 2). In outcome 1 the operating earnings of company A will be £150 while the operating earnings of B will fall to -£30. In outcome 2 the earnings of A will be -£50 and the earnings of B will rise to £120. Obviously, the expected earnings of each company are risky and move in different directions. However, if the two companies merged, the operating earnings of the combined firms are £120 for each outcome, and therefore

Table 16.2
Earnings of two companies before and after merging

	Earnings at the end of the year
Company A	
Outcome 1	150
Outcome 2	− 50
Company B	
Outcome 1	− 30
Outcome 2	170
Company A + B	
Outcome 1	120
Outcome 2	120

the merged firm is riskless. Of course, the assumption that earnings of two firms are perfectly negatively correlated is unrealistic, but the variability of earnings (or their range) would always be reduced unless the earnings moved in lockstep. Thus, provided earnings of the two firms are not perfectly positively correlated some risk reduction, as a result of the merger, will always take place. But, even when this is so, the question remains whether the value of the two merged firms is greater than the sum of their individual parts. It might be argued that if the merged firm's earnings are less risky, borrowing becomes cheaper; the lower borrowing costs provide an incentive to merge. In our analysis, we must distinguish carefully between the effect of a merger upon outstanding debt and the effect of a merger on the terms for raising additional debt. We shall discuss raising additional debt first.

A merger of two companies reduces the risk of the combined earnings stream below the risk of the individual companies pre-merger, if the two earnings streams are imperfectly correlated. As a consequence, the merged firms are able to borrow at a lower interest rate than before the merger. The reason that the risk has been reduced is that when one of the firms would otherwise have defaulted, the surplus of the other firm is applied to the deficiencies of the first (this is known as the 'coinsurance effect'). Thus, the merger of the two firms reduces the risk of default only because the shareholders give up some of the protection of limited liability; for without the merger the surplus of one firm would not be applied to the debts of the other when it defaulted.

It is easier to understand this problem when one considers an individual who controls a business which has the protection of limited liability. Currently his firm is borrowing from a bank at 3 per cent over the bank's base interest rate. The owner is wealthy, owning a large house and some stocks and bonds besides the stock in his company. The bank suggests to the owner that if he would only guarantee the loans of his company, the bank would gladly reduce the interest rate on the outstanding loans. Is the bank being generous? The answer is No! It is asking the owner to permit his personal assets to be applied to any deficiences of the company, should default occur. It is asking the owner to give up the protection of limited liability. Put another way, it is asking for a merger of his personal assets and the assets of the firm. Consequently, a merger may reduce the risk of the earnings stream and the cost of borrowing, but this will not increase the value of the firm since the lower interest rate charged by the bank merely reflects the less risky claim it now holds. However, if there are default costs, (such as legal costs attendant on liquidation) then a merger will reduce the probability of default and therefore reduce the expected value of the default costs. The reduction in expected default costs would provide an incentive to merge. This said, the probability of default is usually small and the costs of default are also small (about one per cent of the value of the assets according to Warner, 1977). Thus the expected benefits to merging from this source may not be significant.

Now consider the effect of a merger on the value of the equity when there is existing debt outstanding in the two firms. If the earnings of the two firms are imperfectly correlated, the coinsurance effect of the merger will reduce the probability of default to the combined debtholders. Debtholders will gain since previously agreed interest payments were based upon a higher probability of default. The shareholders suffer a corresponding loss equal to the gain of the debtholders. If the firms had not merged, a default by one firm would not have affected the other firm's shareholders. Thus, shareholders must lose as a result of the coinsurance of debt. After the merger the value of limited liability, as an option to default, is reduced by virtue of a lower probability of default.

Unused debt capacity

It is often claimed that if a firm does not utilize its debt capacity, it will prove a valuable asset to any would-be bidder. However, Franks and Broyles (1979) have shown that the advantages to debt financing are probably not very large and certainly not sufficient to justify bid premiums of 15 per cent to 20 per cent plus the costs of transacting the bid. Secondly, the acquiring firm does not need to acquire control over the assets to obtain some advantage from the unused debt capacity. The acquiring firm needs only to buy the shares of the inadequately geared company and borrow, using the purchase shares as collateral for the loan. Thus, unused debt capacity does not provide very much incentive for a merger. [See Franks and Pringle (1982) for a more detailed review of these points.]

Tax losses and unused capital allowances

A company that has made losses in the past is able to carry such losses forward and offset them against future taxable profits in order to reduce tax liabilities. For example, the (American) Anaconda Company made losses totalling hundreds of millions of dollars in 1971 as a result of the nationalization of its assets in Chile. Such losses could be offset against future profits in order to reduce tax liabilities. However, Anaconda might have tried to seek a merger with another company which had sufficiently large taxable profits to absorb the tax losses immediately. The benefit would derive from obtaining the reduction in tax liabilities much earlier than the company could hope to do without the merger.

A second tax reason for merging arises if a company is investing large sums in capital equipment and so qualifies for capital allowances that cannot be absorbed by taxable profits when they occur. A merger with a profitable company can absorb the unused tax allowances at an earlier date than would otherwise be possible, as in the case of accumulated tax losses. When a company is investing heavily on its capital account, leasing can provide an alternative method to merging for the purpose of accelerating the benefit of tax shields.

EVIDENCE OF THE PROFITABILITY OF MERGERS TO SHAREHOLDERS

Evidence in the US on the profitability of mergers, as measured by the stock market, is fairly unambiguous: the shareholders of acquired firms gain substantially whereas the shareholders of acquiring firms either gain or do not lose. For example, Mandelker examined 241 mergers in the USA and measured the effect of the merger on the stock market prices of the merging firms. He calculated the incremental returns to the merger by subtracting from the returns of each company that proportion estimated to be attributable to movements in the market. As shown in Table 16.3 Mandelker found that bid premiums of about 14 per cent were obtained in the bid month. In fact, this understates the true bid premium, since there was evidence that the market anticipated the merger prior to the month of the bid (and therefore part of the bid premium). The acquiring companies were also found to have gained but the gains were small at 3 per cent and were not statistically significant. The evidence in the UK is rather mixed. Firth examined a sample of UK mergers for the period 1969 through to 1975 and found that although acquired firms gain substantially (28 per cent), acquiring firms suffered significant abnormal losses. After adjusting for differences in size, Firth found that the gains to acquired firms were virtually entirely offset by losses to acquiring firms. This contrasts with the evidence of Franks, Broyles and Hecht who examined a sample of 71 mergers in the Breweries and Distilleries Industry and found that bid premiums average 26 per cent and acquiring companies earned around 3 per cent. These latter results would suggest that stockholders gained from mergers; they are supported by a much larger sample of 1814 mergers by Franks and Harris who found that acquired companies gained and acquiring companies either gained or did not lose.

Table 16.3
Evidence on the profitability of mergers to shareholders

Author	Period	Sample size	Gains to acquiree (%)	Gains to acquiror (%)
Halpern (USA)	1950–65	78	30.4	6.2
Mandelker (USA)	1948–67	241	14†	3.0*
Asquith (USA)	1946–71	320	9.7	0.6
Firth (UK)	1969–75	434	28.00‡	−6.3
Franks, Broyles Hecht (UK)	1955–72	71	26	3*
Franks, Harris (UK)	1955–85	1814	23.3	1

* Not statistically significant
† Estimated over 60 days straddling merger announcement, most of gain (34%) occurred in 30 days prior
‡ Loss over 60 days, all occurring in 20 days after bid. If significant, and solely due to bid, it is large in PV terms (since average acquiror much bigger than acquiree)

The results of some of those share price studies contrast rather sharply with those of accounting based studies (for example, those of Singh and Meeks) which show declines in accounting measures of profitability subsequent to merger.

ACQUISITIONAL VALUATION – FOUR QUESTIONS

In any acquisition valuation four important questions must be answered

1 What is the value of the company as it is presently constituted? In answering this question we shall look first at the market value of the company's securities and make some adjustment for any 'bid prospects' already impounded in the share price. For companies whose securities are not traded we shall look for the market values of individual assets. When markets in the assets do not exist, we must estimate values by alternative means.

2 What is the source and value of the merger benefits? In the previous section we have outlined some of the benefits to merging, both economic and financial. The present value of the expected merger benefits establishes the maximum premium that can be paid in excess of the value of the acquisition as it is currently constituted. It is important to deduct from these merger benefits the professional and administrative costs of acquiring the company, including a charge for managerial time.

3 What are the alternatives to merging? The potential acquirer should establish the other methods (if any) of capturing the benefits of the merger. For example, a new capital investment may prove a viable alternative. The difference between the net present values of the merger benefits and of the best alternative provides the maximum bid premium which can be given to the acquiree's shareholders.

4 What price will be adequate to gain control of the acquiree? The answers to the first three questions must provide a price that management and its advisors consider is acceptable to the acquiree's shareholders. It is important to establish this framework prior to the bid, since an aborted bid is expensive both in management time and in direct costs such as legal fees and advertising.

Valuing a quoted company

In a competitive stock market the price of a security reflects the underlying worth of the assets plus the present value of expected growth opportunities. If we can accept this proposition, then the maximum price that should be paid for a company is its existing market value plus the present value of any benefits that may accrue from merging which have already been anticipated by the market.

If the merger is to be profitable to the acquirer, the maximum premium that can be paid above the current market price must be no more than the difference between the value of the merger benefits expected by the acquirer and the value of the merger benefits already anticipated by the market. Of course, if there are alternatives to the merger, then the maximum ɒid premium should also be reduced by the net present vaiue of the most attractive alternative.

The valuation of the premium is easier and provides a more interesting exercise than the attempt to value the entire company. There are, however, some difficulties attached. The current market price may already reflect part of the benefits of this particular merger or of another possible merger. The evidence strongly suggests that the market anticipates a merger prior to its announcement. Thus if one finds that the share price of the acquiree has risen more than the market (or has fallen less than the market) after adjusting for risk, then one should suspect that the current market price reflects some of the bid prospects.

An easy method of computing the price 'ex bid prospects' is to subtract any abnormal returns over the period when a merger rumour may have been circulating. This computation is accomplished by estimating the returns that would have been realized if the security had moved with the market. Roughly speaking, this means that if the market has risen by, for example, 5 per cent over the 3 months prior to the merger announcement and if the security were twice as risky as the market, then we would expect the security to rise by 10 per cent.

If the actual increase were 15 per cent, then we would say that there are abnormal returns of 5 per cent. We would assume that the abnormal returns of 5 per cent were related to the merger and subtract these returns from the current share price to obtain the value of the company 'ex bid prospects'. Let us examine an example.

A company is about to announce a bid for another company. The share price of potential acquisition (Table 16.4) is currently 97 pence.

The management has estimated the present value of the merger benefits at 25 pence per share. What is the maximum price the acquirer should pay? If the market expects the bid, and the share price reflects part of the premium to be paid the premium must be taken into account in deciding the maximum bid terms.

Over the six months prior to the announcement date, the share price of the acquisition has risen 20 per cent, after adjustment for changes in the total number of shares, whereas the market has risen only 5 per cent. We would have expected the security to rise twice as fast as the market, or 10 per cent, because the estimate of its beta value is 2.0. The difference between what we would expect, given the movements in the market, and the actual returns constitutes the abnormal gain. Thus, since the security has risen by 17 pence against the 8 pence we would have expected, the abnormal gain is 9 pence (Table 16.4).

Table 16.4
Estimate of abnormal gains from share price movements

	Dates relative to announcement date		
	− 6 months	− 3 months	0 months
Financial Times index	500	512	525
Expected price of acquisition (pence)	80	85	89
Price of potential acquisition (pence)	80	88	97
Abnormal return (pence)	0	4	9

Risk, beta, of acquisition = 2.0.

Beta is a coefficient of systematic risk which measures the tendency of price changes for a share to move with changes in the market index. Thus the value of beta for the average equity is 1.00. Beta values are obtainable for quoted companies from the London Business School's Risk Measurement Service

If the merger is expected to be profitable for the acquirer's shareholders, the bid price must not exceed the current price plus the difference between the expected merger benefits per share and the past abnormal return per share. The maximum bid price is therefore 113p [97p + (25 − 9)p]. Of course such abnormal returns may reflect circumstances other than bid rumours: for example, unexpectedly good earnings results. Judgement must therefore be exercised in adjusting market prices to their ex bid prospect value.

Traditional methods of asset valuation

In the past there has been a great deal of confusion regarding acquisition valuation methods. In this section, we shall review the more familiar methods. Initially, let us confine ourselves to quoted companies.

Earnings per share

The most familiar valuation method is based on an analysis of the earnings per share of the acquirer with and without the acquistion. Let us consider the following example taken from Franks and Broyles (1979). Table 16.5 shows the financial details of two companies: company A is the acquirer and Z is the potential acquisition. Table 16.6 shows the earnings and the earnings per share expected by the market for each company. We assume that A purchases Z on the basis of two shares of A (valued at £5) for every three shares of Z held (valued at £3.90). Thus A is paying a bid premium of 28 per cent.

Table 16.5
Financial data

	Company A	Company Z
Current earnings after tax (£)	1.0 million	2.41 million
Number of shares outstanding	10 million	18.5 million
Earnings per share	0.10	0.13
Market per share (£)	2.50	1.30
P/E ratio	25	10
Expected annual growth rate in earnings in the absence of a merger (%)	15	0

If we now calculate the earnings per share of the combined company (AZ) over a period of years and compare them with the earnings per share of A, what do we find? Initially the combined EPS exceeds the EPS of A alone by an amount totalling 5.3 pence. Is this good news? The answer is, 'not necessarily', and for two reasons. First, the growth expectations for AZ are lower than for A alone. The effect of growth differences can be seen by following the EPS forecasts. In the fifth year, the EPS of A is expected

Table 16.6
Earnings of A and Z before and after the merger

Years	0	1	2	3	4	5	6
(a) Earnings (£m)							
A at 15%	1.0	1.15	1.32	1.52	1.75	2.01	2.31
Z at 0%	2.41	2.41	2.41	2.41	2.41	2.41	2.41
AZ	3.41	3.56	3.73	3.93	4.16	4.42	4.72
(b) Earnings per share (pence)							
A at 15%	10	11.5	13.2	15.2	17.5	20.1	23.1
Z at 0%	13	13	13	13	13	13	13
AZ	15.3	16.0	16.7	17.6	18.7	19.8	21.2

Number of shares outstanding: A, pre-merger, 10 million; Z, pre-merger, 18.5 million; AZ, 22.3 million.

to be 20.1 pence and that of AZ only 19.8 pence. In the sixth year, the EPS of A is expected to be almost 2 pence greater than that of AZ.

This example suggests that focusing attention on current earnings per share is misleading. Shares are valued for their growth opportunities. Putting it another way, why are shareholders prepared to pay on 10 times the EPS of company Z but 25 times the EPS of company A? It can only be because A's earnings are in some sense more valuable. We have already provided one reason, that of future growth prospects. Another possibility could be that the earnings of A are less risky compared with those of Z. Risk will be perceived in terms of the variability of future earnings. It has been suggested that the incremental loss or gain in EPS of the combined company compared with that of the acquirer on his own should be discounted at an appropriate rate. If the present value of the earnings addition is greater than the present value of earnings dilution, then the acquisition at that price might be considered acceptable.

There are a number of objections to this analysis. First, there is evidence that share prices reflect cash flows rather than reported earnings. Second, the value of a quoted company is measured by the price traded on the Stock Exchange. If the company's analysts try to value the combined company, they are in danger of using different forecasts from those used by other market analysts. The previous analysis does not separate the value of the company without the bid prospects from the value of the merger benefits. In valuing a quoted company the important question is, what value should be placed on the acquirer's ability to extract benefits from the acquisition which are not already impounded in the present market price? The answer can only be obtained from a detailed analysis of what the acquirer is intending to do after the merger.

The valuation of shares of traded companies is relatively straight-forward because we assume that the price of the share represents the value of the company's assets and existing growth opportunities. We do not have such data for unquoted companies and consequently we would propose a variety of methods of arriving at the value for their assets.

Written-down replacement values

The written-down replacement cost (WDRC) method has been increasingly discussed as an alternative to valuations based upon historic cost accounting. It is based upon the following formula

$$\text{WDRC} = \text{Cost of current asset} \times \left\{ 1 - \frac{\text{Age of existing asset}}{\text{Economic life of asset}} \right\}$$

where 'current cost' represents the price of an equivalent asset if it were purchased now. Replacement cost accounting is an improvement on historic cost accounting for two reasons. First, in an inflationary period asset values are constantly rising; replacement cost accounting captures this increase in price. Secondly, if specific assets are being used in a highly profitable way, the primary producers of the assets will probably be able to charge higher prices in consequence. Similarly, if the industry using the capital assets is finding business difficult and profits are low, asset values are likely to be weak, otherwise asset replacement will not take place. Thus replacement cost accounting can capture some of the changes in both positive and negative economic values which accrue with changing business conditions.

However, there are still a number of limitations to this method. First, somewhat arbitrary depreciation methods must be used for existing assets and their economic lives must still be estimated. Secondly, current prices of new assets charged by primary producers will still be below their economic values if firms are replacing assets (at positive net present values); or replacement may not even take place if replacement costs are above economic values. Finally, it may be difficult to obtain the prices of new assets which are similar to existing ones; for instance, where there is rapid technological change, prices of new (replacement) assets will reflect different levels of operating efficiency compared with similar assets in existing use.

In summary, replacement costs should be expected to provide superior estimates of asset values compared with historic cost accounting. Such numbers provide useful estimates of value for firms which are comparing the cost of acquiring a company with the alternative of buying new assets from primary producers. However, the analyst should be aware of the pitfalls in order to know how valuable his data really is.

Market value of the assets

If the individual assets of the company are traded in a second-hand market, recent prices may provide a good estimate of their value. However, the second-hand market may be relatively inactive. Also the price of the asset may reflect a use value other than that currently applicable. For example, a building may be worth far more as an office block than as a factory.

If the firm is using the asset as a factory the question is: 'What is the cost of converting it to the alternative use?' Other assets, such as patents or specialized machinery, may only have a value in one particular use. Also, even if approximate values can be obtained for all the assets of the firm, some price may still have to be paid for growth potential.

Present value of future cash flow

One obvious valuation method is to forecast the future net cash flows of an asset and discount them at some risk-adjusted rate of return. The rate chosen should reflect the prevailing risk free rate of interest plus some premium for the risk associated with post-merger activity (see Chapter 2 for a method of arriving at a discount rate). This may be an essential step even if a company's shares are traded on a stock exchange, because, in order to find the value of the merger benefits, the difference between the pre-merger and post-merger value of the assets must also be determined, and that difference may often only be found by forecasting and discounting future cash flows.

CONCLUSIONS

In this chapter, we have stressed the need to justify mergers in terms of potential economic benefits. In examining these benefits it is important to compare them with alternatives to mergers. A merger is frequently costly in terms of legal costs, management time and the bid premium which is paid by the acquirer to the acquiree. The benefits might be obtained at a lower cost by, for example, direct investment in real assets. We have also described in some detail the financial advantages shareholders may expect from a merger. Although some can be significant, others seem minor if not worthless, for example, unused debt capacity and the coinsurance effect. Finally, we have briefly described methods of valuing quoted and unquoted companies and the bid premium.

FURTHER READING

Asquith, P. 'Merger Bids, Uncertainty, and Stockholder Returns', *Journal of Financial Economics*, 1983, 11.

Firth,M. 'Takeovers, Shareholder Returns and the Theory of the Firm', *Quarterly Journal of Economics*, 1980, 94, No 2, March pp 235 – 260.

Franks, J. R. 'An investigation into the Distribution of Gains from Merging', PhD Thesis 1979, London Business School.

Franks, J. R. and Broyles, J. E. *Modern Managerial Finance*, Chichester: Wiley 1979.

Franks, J. R., Broyles, J. E. and Hecht, M. J. 'An Industry Study of the Profitability of Mergers in the UK', *Journal of Finance*, 32, No 5, December 1977, pp 1513 – 25.

Franks, J. R. and Harris, R. 'Shareholder Wealth Effects of Corporate Takeovers; The UK Experience', *London Business School Working Paper*, 1986.

Franks, J. R. and Pringle, J. J. 'Debt Financing, Corporate Financial Intermediaries and Firm Valuation', *Journal of Finance*, June 1982.

Mandelker, G. 'Risk and return: The case of merging firms', *Journal of Financial Economics I*, pp 303 – 335.

Meeks, G. 'Disappointing Marriage: A Study of the Gains from Mergers', Cambridge University Press, *London Occasional Paper 51*, 1977.

Singh, A. *Takeovers: Their Relevance to the Stock Market and the Theory of the Firm*, London Cambridge University Press, 1971.

Stapleton, R. C. 'Merger Bargaining and Financing Strategy', *The Manchester School*, June 1971, pp 131 – 144.

Stapleton, R. C. 'The Acquisition Decision as a Capital Budgeting Problem', *Journal of Business Finance and Accounting*, No 2, 1975.

17

International money management

Andreas R. Prindl

International Money Management (IMM) deals with the problem of collecting, utilizing and protecting the financial assets of internationally involved companies. The term 'IMM' is used to designate both the operating responsibility of the treasury of a multinational corporation and the array of techniques and tools available to co-ordinate that task. This problem is difficult enough in domestic firms; greater structural and environmental impediments for the multinational company place its treasury's responsibilities on a different level of complexity.

Despite the size and power of many multinational companies, they can be characterized as fragmented, rather than monolithic. Multinational companies are divided into a number of local units, separated by distance, exchange control, and tax and legal systems. Such technical barriers to treating a company's finance as a whole are structural ones. They include the obvious problems of being far away from parent or subsidiaries, speaking in different languages, relying on inefficient communications systems, accounting for worldwide operations under various principles, following diverse legal practices, paying differing rates of tax and being restricted by exchange control systems.

These elements have always been found in international companies which have set up operations abroad. A quantum change in financial management problems, however, has come from the chaotic environment since exchange rates began to float in the late 1960s. Thus, added to structural impediments are today's unpredictable and fast moving exchange rates, as well as large interest and inflation differentials, all of which are environmental factors. Not only must assets be correctly collected and maintained, they must be protected against depreciation caused by outside economic changes which have taken on a magnitude not seen since Depression years.

The field of IMM attempts to give an ordered approach to these various problems. Much of it is based on correct reporting systems and optimal use of banks, whereas the remainder is anticipatory, attempting to forecast the liquidity and foreign exchange risks of the firm, in order to position the company's assets and liabilities properly. The field is divided into two important parts: International Cash Management, which deals with the more mechanical areas of cash collection, holding and disbursement, and International Financial Management, which involves utilization of liquidity and foreign exchange risk management.

DOMESTIC CASH MANAGEMENT

Collection process

Domestic cash management has three distinct stages: collection, treasury management and disbursement. Although the outer stages are mechanical and semi-automatic, they are used to maximize the amounts of funds for treasury management, which should then concentrate on optimal deployment of available resources and reducing external borrowing to a minimum.

It is instructive to analyse these activities in more detail. Collections, for example, are broken down into distinct stages, as shown in Figure 17.1.

Order received	Shipment date	Invoice date	Payment due	Payment initiated	Goods/funds received	Advice received
Order processing	Invoicing delay	Credit terms	Customer delay	Bank/Mail delay	Advice delay	

Figure 17.1   The collection process in cash management

Besides credit terms extended to customers, other possible delays before sales proceeds can be utilized include invoicing delays within the company, customer non-adherence to credit terms, and delays within the banking/mail system. The last are designated as 'float', and each type deserves careful study.

Order and invoice systems

The first step of cash management is internal: to check whether the billing procedure involves unnecessary delays or inadvertent credit extension. For example, if credit terms are stated to be x days from date of invoice, and invoice creation is delayed after shipment, extra credit is given to customers; this can be particularly costly if a weekend is involved. Even if month-end terms are used, late invoicing can dip over a month-end, and allow greater credit to buyers. It is a simple matter, particularly with computers, to ensure that statements are created simultaneously with shipment, or back-dated to coincide with shipment dates.

Customer payment methods

More important is the way in which local customers are asked to pay, as many methods are generally available, for example: paying cash, using bank transfers, sending cheques, accepting direct debiting by the supplier.

The treasury should analyse customer payment habits to determine what delay, if any, derives from non-adherence to maturity dates. The competitive situation will determine which pressures can be put on customers to pay promptly, or whether different credit instruments can be used to ensure payment at maturity. Discount practices need to be studied as well; discounts offered to customers may have become inconsistent with market rates of interest.

Bank delays can benefit either the payer, if he sends his own cheques, or the banks making the transfers. Proper utilization of bank systems forms a major portion of account receivable management: it requires analysis of customers' locations, how they pay or instruct their banks, which banks are used, and to which accounts funds are paid.

An excellent collection instrument, now available in a number of European countries, is direct debiting. This can reduce customer delay to zero (the payment is tapped by the supplier at maturity) and cut bank delay to minimal levels, as the payment request can be put into the system in advance. In effect, the supplier takes cash from its customers with good value at maturity — an optimal system from both delay and forecasting standpoints.

Guidelines for accounts receivable management

If arranged correctly, a company's collections can be set up in a virtually automatic way and any float can be reduced to a minimum. The following questions should be studied

1   Is inadvertent credit given to customers by slow billing?
2   Do discounts offered reflect the true value of funds invested or costs saved from reduced overdrafts?
3   Are clear instructions given to customers as to payment method?
4   Can a single nationwide bank's network be used to collect, and then concentrate, inflows?
5   Are salemen or messengers, who pick up cheques, depositing them in the most efficient manner?
6   Is the best use being made of computerized bank transfer possibilities?
7   Are inflows being directed to banks where overdraft lines are maintained, so that net borrowing is reduced?
8   Is direct debiting possible?

Local treasury management

In a one-country setting, the treasury management function is that of identifying cash surpluses and cash needs at the various domestic locations during the production/sales cycle. The chief task is to do so in advance, so that appropriate funding or borrowing procedures can be undertaken, eliminating the chances that funds will lie idle somewhere in the system. Given a single tax, legal and currency system, this relies primarily on good cash forecasting, portfolio management and banking relationships. Banking ties must be examined; commonly there are too many accounts and too many banks. A subsidiary in one part of the country may have surplus cash whereas another may have to borrow. Pooling of local subsidiaries' funds can be achieved in a number of ways, through negotiation with a nationwide bank or daily adjustment of positions. Where possible, payments should be made into accounts where overdrafts are held, to reduce them on a daily basis.

Disbursements

Disbursement control is the converse of account receivable management. Although the firm tries to reduce its customers' payment delays, its suppliers will act similarly. Disbursement analysis ascertains that discounts offered are properly evaluated, that all but small local payments are properly evaluated, that all but small local payments are centralized and reported and that payments are not made before maturity.

INTERNATIONAL CASH MANAGEMENT

International transfer of funds

International cash management involves longer distances, exchange controls, different currency units and unrelated banks. The sequence of the international collection process, however, is the same as that of local account management, and delays are analysed in the same fashion.

A variety of instruments exist for the international transfer of funds. Lodged in and flowing between banks, they can be simple payment instructions in written form or evolve from documentary sales incorporating some form of credit. The standard method of transferring funds internationally is by mail payment order. In it, the remitter of funds asks its bank to make a transfer to the recipient in its own or another currency. The remitter's local currency account will be debited on the day the remitter presents the payment order to its bank (in some countries with back value).

Mail transfer is a lengthy process, despite the routine use of airmail. The remitter's local bank may not maintain foreign currency accounts abroad as they are chiefly held by the head offices of the large indigenous banks. It must then send the payment instructions through its main office, central savings bank organization or domestic bank correspondent. Allowing for mailing time and processing at each bank, a mail transfer which involves several banks in two countries can take eight to ten business days or more.

Cable transfers reduce remittance time appreciably. By instructing its local bank to inaugurate payments by cable, the remitter ensures that the recipient of funds is paid as soon as the foreign bank receives the cable order from its correspondent. A cable transfer results in a debit to the paying bank's foreign account more quickly than mail transfer does, and involves a higher cost or less favourable rate of exchange when a conversion is involved. In addition, a nominal charge is made, usually $5 to $10 equivalent per cable, depending upon the length of the text.

Other international payment instruments include bank drafts, cheques and trade bills. A subsidiary may purchase a bank draft from its house bank to send directly to the payee. Bank drafts are payable to order upon presentation and are drawn by a bank upon itself or another branch of the same bank.

Sight and time drafts, acceptances and letters of credit fall into the area of documentary credit. A sight draft is an international financial instrument in which the importer's (drawee's) obligation to pay a certain amount at sight to the drawer is formally confirmed in writing. Time drafts add a credit element as the payment is designated as due at a certain future date and the obligation is accepted by the drawee. Acceptances (time drafts drawn on a foreign buyer whose obligation is accepted by its bank) and letters of credit are extensions of payment orders that take into account the credit risk of dealing with distant customers. These instruments are well known and are generally processed by international banks in a structured manner that has long proven to be efficient. Thus cash management concentrates on payments arising from open account sales.

The underlying principle of international payments is that currencies are ultimately transformed on the books of banks in the country whose currency is involved. Dollars sent from Tokyo to Zurich become entries in the books of a US bank in which the working accounts of international banks are held in dollars. Acceleration or interception of international dollar payments thus lies in the US banking system. Deutschmark transactions are made over the books of German banks, pounds over those of British Banks, and similarly with other currencies. This structure determines the way in which export proceeds can be intercepted and accelerated.

Acceleration of export proceeds

A foreign customer has no reason to accelerate payments abroad after its own account is debited, and banks have no incentive to expedite the transfer of funds to a foreign entity. Many banks traditionally depend more on float and commissions than on compensating balances, which accounts for part of the slowness of mail transfers. By using cable transfers increased yields can accrue to the recipient even if it absorbs the cable charges of its customers. A minimum break even amount (where interest gained on funds available earlier exceeds the cable cost) should be set and instructions given to customers to make all payments above that minimum by cable net of its cost.

Smaller export payments can often be intercepted in the country whose currency is involved. For USA dollars, this involves directing payments to a USA bank, rather than using the lengthy procedure that characterizes international transfers. When export receipts are in large numbers but in amounts that do not warrant cable transfers, the standard procedure is to use a dollar lockbox system, incorporating a post office box in a major USA money centre.

A USA bank has the authority to open and empty daily a postal box held in the name of the exporter, which instructs its customers to have dollar-denominated cheques or drafts sent directly to the specific postal box rather than to the exporter or its bank for the account of the exporter. The cheque, drawn on a USA bank, is airmailed to the postal box, whereupon the responsible bank will process and present it immediately to the Federal Reserve clearing system. Delays are reduced to the mailing time plus one day for clearance and credit to the exporter's USA dollar account. Usually, the standard delay in receiving export mail payments is reduced by three to five days or more.

Dollar interception of non-USA exporters

Since the underlying principle is that USA dollars are transferred by banks in the United States of America, an identical procedure can be followed even if the exporter is not a USA company. An exporting company located in France and invoicing in dollars, can also use a dollar lockbox in New York to accelerate dollar collections. Ideally, it will maintain one account in America and another with the Paris branch by cable of the amounts received; it will give details of each remittance to comply with French exchange control regulations. Larger amounts can be received by cable and credited in the same manner. Similarly, dollar amounts received in favour of a British exporter can be intercepted and credited to a retained dollar account in the United Kingdom.

Interception in other currencies

In most European countries, IMM systems can be set up to allow interception of a currency in its home country. The principle remains to intercept the funds from abroad at a point close to the account to which the funds are directed. Belgian franc payments, for example, can be requested from an importer or foreign dealer in the form of a Belgian franc cheque sent directly to the bank holding export documents. The Belgian bank will present the cheque directly to the clearing system after matching payments and documents and immediately credit the proceeds to the exporter's account. Both acceleration of receipts and compliance with exchange control regulations are assimilated in such a system. Similar mechanisms can be inaugurated for British exporters invoicing in pounds sterling, Dutch exporters invoicing in guilders and so forth.

Retained foreign currency accounts

The use of retained foreign currency or 'hold' accounts complements control over international cash flows. Exchange control commonly recognizes that a trading or exporting company, which receives foreign currencies for its exports, may have foreign currency obligations against which such proceeds can be applied. In most countries, domestic exporting companies are permitted to hold foreign currency receipts in local accounts set up for that purpose. Upon presentation of the proper documents, foreign currency export proceeds can be credited to such accounts held at local banks or abroad and held in suspense until they are needed for authorized payments in that currency. There should be a reciprocal, although not necessarily identical, flow; in general, funds may not be held in such accounts for an indefinite period.

Foreign currency accounts give an exporter a two fold advantage. They avoid exchange conversion costs, which would normally be borne twice if proceeds were converted and reconverted, and they maintain a neutral exposure position in the currency for those transactions. In fact, such foreign currency holdings may constitute a short-term hedge against the exporter's local currency. Conversion costs of transferring dividends in foreign currency to a parent company can also be avoided.

Accumulation accounts

In certain countries, currency accounts can earn interest at Euro-currency rates, which transforms them into an accumulation account, maintained over longer periods. Exchange control authorities may require that they be converted into local currency, because investment in foreign currency is not their underlying justification. The same advantages of and rationale for foreign currency accounts exist for exporters in countries where there are no restrictions on international transfers or foreign exchange holdings.

Intercompany transfers

Intercompany transfers arise from sales between affiliates and from such financial transactions as royalties and dividends. Since the time lost in transferring funds from one affiliate to another represents a loss of availability of funds to the group, it is important to rationalize intercompany transactions.

Intercompany transfers of sizeable amounts should be made by cable as of routine. A simple comparison of cable cost and interest saved by reduction of overdrafts or gained by short-term investment of accelerated payments shows the advantage of making even relatively small payments by cable. If overseas subsidiaries are reluctant to absorb recurring cable costs, they should be instructed to make payments net of cable charge.

Value compensations

To reduce the transit time of intercompany transfers further when foreign exchange conversion is necessary, value compensations should be negotiated. Under standard foreign exchange procedures, the remitter's account is often debited two days before the foreign currency counterpart is actually provided. Assuming two-day notice is given, the remitting bank should agree to debit the local currency account on the actual day of transfer and thus save two interest days for the remitter.

International bank branches that make payments between two subsidiaries, both of which are customers, offer value-compensated cable transfers, as a routine matter. They look at their relationship with a multinational company globally and make concessions at one paying branch in the light of activity or relationships at another. They may even waive cable charges for intercompany, intrabank payments.

Netting

The systems discussed so far are rather mechanical and can be designed to operate virtually automatically by using careful instructions and agreement with banks. The area of intercompany transfers leads to more managerial decisions, such as the use of payment dates to keep liquidity in a subsidiary, or to accelerate it to another — moves which have both liquidity and exchange exposure implications. Manipulation of intercompany transfers ties together the field of cash management and that of international financial management (IFM).

A first step towards IFM is to institute netting systems where applicable. Even though value compensation and cables may reduce most intercompany float, there are still conversion and payment costs to bear; these are often estimated around one eighth per cent flat on average. One should analyse whether intercompany payments can be offset bilaterally or multilaterally on the books of subsidiaries, thus saving the potential costs of converting and moving gross payable amounts by paying only the net balance. A group of subsidiaries selling to each other multilaterally will report their gross intercompany payable/receivable position to a central point, which then works out mathematically the net payments to be made at precise dates and so informs the participants. Exchange controls in most countries permit this system. Export and import documentation continues as before and needs to be centralized in the banks making the net payment. Such systems nearly always go through the branch network of a single multinational bank to ensure efficiency. Once the reporting and central control systems are set up, changing the matrix of the payments can give rise to more sophisticated use of group funds.

INTERNATIONAL LIQUIDITY MANAGEMENT

The management of liquidity held in the international firm is limited by exchange control and other barriers, which usually prohibit the flow of funds in desired directions. Funds held by individual subsidiaries in different countries cannot be considered fungible and there is little or no chance of international pooling of funds. Even intracountry liquidity management can be impeded by weak capital markets which offer few investment media or banking systems which Expropriation or funds blockage are continual possibilities in certain parts of the world.

The area is also affected by mechanical impediments in banking and mail systems. As shown above, an appreciable portion of a company's apparent liquidity may be delayed or in transit due to the slowness of customers in paying and the tardiness of banks in transferring funds in settlement of international transactions. These inefficiencies and delays diminish liquidity, impair credit control and add to the general difficulties of financial management. Good IFM is thus based on good cash management systems both at the local and the international level.

International liquidity management cannot be divorced from exchange factors. Almost every borrowing/investment decision made is implicitly exchange related. To leave funds in one country, to convert and deposit them covered or uncovered, or to lend them internationally, involves an acceptance or a transmittal of exchange risks. Uncertainty about future rates shapes the policy of the international treasurer's liquidity decisions as it does his attempt to optimize exchange risk management.

Thus, liquidity management directly embodies the fragmentation which characterizes the multinational firm. Government monetary or financial policies, specifically those designed to influence balance of payments flows, can limit the deployment of the firm's working capital. Most government measures constructed on macro-economic grounds can be seen as hampering the international company's micro-economic liquidity policies.

Need for centralization

Given these parameters, liquidity management must be centrally co-ordinated and directed by a control point which has full knowledge of resources and needs. Normally, this function will be based at the parent level, although it may be partially delegated to regional centres. Local implementation of policy may be carried out with appropriate guidelines.

Liquidity management needs to be based on a detailed, treasury orientated reporting system which goes beyond that necessary for accounting purposes. It must be anticipatory, fostering proper determination of liquidity implications of all financial transactions in advance. It should allow proper response by forecasting liquidity shortages or uninvested surpluses.

Such centralization has implications for profit centre accounting. Interest income/costs beyond purely local levels, where directed from above, may be eliminated from the internal operating reports of subsidiaries. This correction eliminates group considerations from local operating statements without eliminating subsidiaries' responsibility to keep asset levels down.

Centralization assists in reducing the total amount of liquidity needed by the corporation. Total assets held abroad and their related financing costs will be minimized. The specialized knowledge needed to place and optimize the use of liquidity can more easily be built up in one central location, which has ready access to tax and accounting assistance which the local locations may not enjoy. As in multilateral netting, only a central point is in a position to see liquidity shortfalls and surpluses, to appraise different markets and evaluate interest arbitrage opportunities.

Utilization of funds internationally

There are a number of ways in which liquidity can be utilized internationally

1 Leading/lagging, that is, extending longer, or shorter credit terms to importing affiliates, or paying before maturity.
2 Pre-paying import payables to third parties.
3 Intercompany lending.
4 Covered arbitrage abroad (that is, investing in a foreign currency asset while covering the exchange risk by forward sale of that currency).
5 Uncovered arbitrage abroad.
6 Parallel loans with companies in a second country, in which each side makes its local currency available to a subsidiary of the other for a fixed period of time.
7 Repayment of international borrowings.

Liquidity decisions have an effect on exposure by definition, unless totally covered, and it is a moot point whether the corporate treasurer, grappling with an array of assets and risks should turn first to the liquidity problem or the exchange risk aspects. Since the risk of parity change is the common denominator, prior assessment of that risk should form the initiative to analysing opportunities.

Vehicle companies

The use of vehicle companies can optimise liquidity management. Such intermediary companies are usually located in a country with nominal exchange control and low rates of taxation, such as Switzerland or Bermuda. They are incorporated resident companies with a local board and set of accounts. Typically, their major role is to buy the export products of the group, and to reinvoice these for sale to the ultimate customers. The credit terms, currency of invoicing and price to third party borrowers remain unchanged.

Reinvoicing takes place either manually or by computer and the actual goods are shipped as before; thus the tariff/customs framework is unaffected. This is particularly important in multinational groupings with advantageous internal tariff regulations such as the EEC.

The intermediary company may also buy from each exporting affiliate in its local currency, and purchase their imports for them, reinvoicing back in local currency. If carried out rigorously, this puts all the trading exposure of the group into a central entity and creates a linkage of intercompany receivables.

Such centralization of funds is as close to international pooling as is now possible; by using intercompany trade and other transactions, adjustment of credit terms can change, augment or reduce liquidity as desired. A vehicle company creates more ties between the subsidiaries, even where there is no direct trade between them, and materially increases the flexibility and range of liquidity management. The network of inter-company linkages thereby created is among the more powerful tools open to the large, sophisticated company which has the initiative to create such an enterprise, and the understanding to operate it successfully.

Foreign exchange exposure

Definition of exposure

The term 'exchange exposure' has several meanings. **Accounting exposure** relates to the necessity to value (translate) disparate financial items in terms of a single currency. The publicly stated value in local currency of the company's assets, equity and income may be affected adversely by the movement of currencies in which it has dealings. Translation losses in terms of the base currency can reduce its reported profits and nominal net worth. A corporation's image may be endangered, its stock market appeal diminished, or its ability to raise loans or equity put into question after reporting such losses.

Transaction exposure is a second commonly used term. It refers to the actual receipt or payment in foreign currency of funds which result from trade or financial transactions. Payments larger, or receipts smaller, than originally booked (because rates have changed) have an actual operating effect on the company.

Some companies regard the risk of adverse accounting changes as ephemeral, depending on their own stockholder make-up and perception of risk. Translation losses are seen more as an embarrassment, or as an unavoidable cost of doing business abroad. The firm may be regarded as a permanent ongoing concern where realized profits and remitted dividends are more material factors. Long-range implications of rate movements on investments or profit streams will be of more concern than short-term bookkeeping effects. This approach to foreign exchange risk concentrates on **economic exposure**; the long-term operating effects of parity changes.

Foreign exchange risk management is an integral part of the overall financial management of the firm. The international monetary system remains highly volatile and relationships among currencies are impossible to predict in the short run. Multinational companies must weigh the foreign exchange risk element in each major decision area: management of liquidity and borrowing, reporting financial results, declaration or payment of dividends, and long-term investment decisions.

Financing decisions are affected directly by the appreciation or depreciation of the borrower's currency or that which is borrowed; nominal interest rates alone are only part of the decision making analysis. The timing of dividends requires an exchange rate judgement and falls into the overall strategy of dealing with exchange risk. Foreign investment decisions, normally based on productivity, competition, market and economic factors, must include a perception of long-term exchange risk. Equivalent investments in different countries, otherwise offering the same apparent advantages, can be differentiated, and thus graded, by the long-term outlook for currencies involved.

Main components of exchange risk management

After defining the nature of the risks borne by the company, a series of reporting and analytical stages follows: identification of exposed positions, analysis of the potential impact of future rate changes on present and forecast positions, strategy setting to deal with these risks, and carrying out appropriate tactics, all within a larger framework integrating with liquidity and tax management (see Figure 17.2).

Identification of exposed positions

Actual transactions in foreign currency on a realized basis present different operating effects at all levels of the company. These may or may not be anticipated in traditional accounting statements. Additional definition and reporting elements are necessary to quantify changes in the company's positions over time and to identify the exchange risks engendered.

Reporting systems are at the heart of the identification and analysis systems, which also identify the external constraints on company response. Only after the projection of all types of exposure is achieved can the potential impact on a firm and its constituent parts be quantified. Only then can a company develop a strategy to eliminate, reduce or accept its perceived risks. The company will review its position individually by currency and by location.

I	II	III
Definition of exposure	Identification of present and projected exposed positions	Analysis of potential impact
(a) That based on accounting rules (b) Risks of actual transactions (c) Economic exposure	(a) Reporting systems: — internal positions — external data (b) Forecasting systems	Effect of forecast exchange rate movements on corporate positions
IV Strategy setting	V Tactics for implementing strategy	VI Integration
(a) Cost/risk analysis (b) Use of mathematical tools	(a) Selection of hedging techniques — internal — external (b) Regulatory limitations	(a) Co-ordination with liquidity management (b) Tax considerations (c) Personnel implications

Figure 17.2   Components of exchange exposure management

Projection of possible losses

Assessing the potential impact of exchange exposure on any company is the next stage. Once adequate reporting and forecasting are achieved, the determination of impact on the firm becomes a process of comparing future expected rate changes to the positions maintained — and expected to be maintained — by the group on a currency-by-currency basis. Determining that impact involves an assessment of market trends which can be graded in terms of probability.

Setting strategy

The previous stages are analytical, a strategy of accepting or covering individual risks. Creating a strategy is again a function of the individual firm's attitude to risk, the degree to which any bad results must be reported publicly and the actual after-tax effects if the worst possible set of events happens. A policy of maximizing earnings might foster a different strategy from one directed towards preservation of assets or maintenance of sales volumes. If a firm's policy is simply to protect reported income, it might consider covering all risks; this would be appropriate for a simple exporting or importing firm. A more sophisticated firm might decide which potential risks are unacceptable from the point of view of potential realized losses or reduced liquidity.

The firm should perform cost/risk analysis based on the above criteria, its own particular risk structure and flexibility in hedging risks. The logic in covering only certain exchange hazards derives from the calculation of individual risks in each currency, deciding which are acceptable and which are not, and selecting one, or an array of, methods to cover the latter at the lowest cost.

Decision responsibility

The way in which a firm goes about this task is also importnat. The centralization necessary for ascertaining all types of risks and alternatives can be achieved in more than one way if strict guidelines for co-ordination are developed. The corporation must designate clear responsiblity for exposure management. One way to do so is to make the finance department a profit centre with direct attribution of foreign exchange gains,losses and hedging costs, as well as certain interest costs and yields. It is also necessary to decide how hedging or risk-acceptance decisions are made: whether they are the responsibility of a single designated individual or a committee. The role of regional headquarters can form an effective complement to the whole process, if a structure is created in which the experience of more than one source can be used. Any independent action by subsidiaries should not be undertaken without central approval.

Computer application

Because of the complexity of the area, the amount of data to be assimilated and the element of uncertainty, mathematical/computer application is of major interest. For compilation and permutation of statistical data, computers are increasingly useful, as they are also in simple simulation models. Owing to the unpredictability of short-term rates in the exchange markets and the unknown co-variances between spot rates and interest rates, more ambitious optimization programs have not been very successful to date.

Hedging

The international company has a variety of techniques at its disposal to neutralize, minimize or avoid exchange risks. The application and selection of hedging techniques vary directly and proportionately with the complexity and international penetration of the firm. Thus the exporting/importing company has only certain hedging methods available, while a much fuller range is open to the true multinationals. Both types of company must consider in advance the appropriateness of internal as well as external hedging possibilities, regulatory limitations, tax effects and cost factors. Techniques used to change or reduce risk have a basic cost, although this may fall in marketing areas. All are based on the firm's accounting conventions used to translate foreign currency items, which shape the way in which the corporation will select and apply hedging techniques. All need to be reviewed on an after-tax basis.

Internal techniques affecting outstanding positions

Pre-payment of existing third-party commitments

Exchange risks arising from third-party transactions fall into export, import or financial categories. Outstanding third-party export receivables cannot be changed by internal adjustments. Import commitments, however, normally can be pre-paid if the currency in which they are invoiced is expected to appreciate vis-a-vis that of the importer. Foreign currency loans, where there is a pre-payment option, may be paid down. The cost of such transactions is the domestic financing expense (or the interest foregone) from the time of early payment to the original maturity. The principal restrictions are found in the exchange control regulations of the importer's country, which may rule out pre-payments, or of the exporting/lending country, which may prohibit the premature receipt of funds by explicit decree or financial charges.

Intercompany term adjustment

Greater scope is offered in intercompany positions where original payment dates can be accelerated or delayed to change the basic position of the group in a specific currency. Commonly called leading and lagging, this is a widely used and legitimate technique to shift risk or liquidity.

Exposure netting involves creating or acceptance of open positions in two (or more) currencies, which are considered to balance each other and, therefore, to require no further internal or external hedging.

A short position in such a currency can be considered offset to some degree by a long position in a closely related currency. An exporter with Belgian franc payables and Dutch guilder receivables might decide that these two positions covered each other and that forward contracts were not necessary. A long position in a traditionally hard currency, such as the Deutschmark, might be used to offset eventual depreciation of assets in a softer currency.

Internal techniques affecting future positions

The above techniques — chiefly lagging or leading payments — form a limited and short-term range of hedging techniques related to existing positions. Anticipatory exposure management offers a greater variety of useful risk adjustment possibilities. These fall into two types: changes in pricing/currency billing policy, and changes in balance sheet positions.

Anticipatory local subsidiary price increases are often the only way to protect against the negative effect of depreciation of a local currency. For example, if the local sales price can be raised before devaluation, the reported income stream and ultimate dividends are protected, which will prove doubly valuable if a local price freeze follows currency devaluation. Treasury input can be an important factor in a decision which has more than one justification.

Export price increases depend on marketing factors, since there are often both international and local competitive products. When exports are denominated in a currency likely to depreciate, selective price increases protect revenues just as local price adjustments do. A discount option for more prompt payment has somewhat the same effect.

A more subtle price adjustment strategy is through changing the currency of billing to that of a parent or to a stronger currency. Billing in weaker currencies, when the home currency is inherently strong, can be considered if sales increases are fostered, with sufficient margins to allow external protection methods. Exchange risk enters even if one switches from a supposedly weak currency of billing to a stronger one. No currency trends are so predictable, or so long lived, that one can assume with certainty that a billing switch will remain as attractive in the future. Currencies of billing cannot easily be reversed and cannot be changed often.

The second major area of internal anticipatory changes in exposure management comes in asset or liability adjustment. The goal is to wind up with reduced assets/increased liabilities in currencies likely to depreciate, and increased assets/reduced liabilities in harder currencies.

Either the parent itself, or a subsidiary concerned can build up cash, short-term investments, receivables and/or inventories denominated in currencies expected to revalue. Subsidiaries will be instructed to pay bills as slowly as possible, to convert foreign currency holdings or investments into local ones and to delay intercompany settlements or dividends. They may also delay purchase of, or settlement for, raw materials. All these moves will build up short-term local currency assets, those items both translated/consolidated at spot rates and likely to be realized in the near future. A net increase in short-term asset positions could also be achieved by reducing group members' short-term debt denominated in hard currencies, by pre-payment of hard currency payables, and analogous techniques.

When a devaluation-prone currency is involved, the techniques apply in reverse. Cash and short-term security holdings will be run down, local debt increased, certain payables accelerated, and intercompany payments rescheduled. The goal is to reduce long positions or increase debt and other commitments in a soft currency so as to benefit from, or be protected against, its expected depreciation.

Export financing vehicles

Hedging of foreign commitments is constrained by the restrictions imposed by each exchange control and by exchange market structure. The typical situation is that each local affiliate must cover its own transaction exposures locally under specific external regulations.

A way to rationalize this situation is to create a finance company vehicle which buys the export receivables of the group and assumes the credit risk and covering responsibility. The vehicle company purchases the export receivables of each group member as created or buys outstanding receivables under previous agreement. The finance vehicle's assets consist of export receivables with varying dates and currencies; its liabilities of short-term borrowings. It can cover those risks and maturities exactly, or can leave them uncovered as to timing and amount as part of an overall risk strategy. Centralization in a vehicle operating essentially 'off-shore' in the Euro-markets gives a great deal more flexibility and the ability to put a trained group in charge of all such risks. Such a vehicle can usually be established with moderate capital input and legal costs (the former since its borrowings will be guaranteed by the parent).

Reinvoicing vehicles

A finance house, however, can only react in the receivable portion of risks. Since it holds title solely to the underlying paper involved, legal recourse in the case of customer default is also more problematic. A more useful approach is to use a reinvoicing intermediary company, as already discussed. Advantages for exposure management are

1   Local personnel are left to concentrate on production, marketing or local financing.
2   Identification of exposure and any requisite hedging are facilitated.
3   Exposures may be mutually offsetting.

External hedges

External hedges are more clearly delineated and usually their cost can be precisely determined in advance. They fall into the following categories

1   Forward exchange contracts.
2   Foreign currency loans.
3   Discount/sale of foreign receivables.
4   Retained currency accounts.
5   Borrowing/deposit arrangements in two currencies.
6   Factoring.
7   Leasing.
8   Export risk guarantees.

With forward exchange contracts, future receipts or payments are sold, or bought, for the same date forward as the payment maturity, at a fixed price. In the final analysis, forward rates are a function of the interest rate differentials of the two countries involved. In the major currencies and larger markets, forward exchange contracts can be negotiated not only for periods beginning with the present to some fixed maturity, but also from one future date to another. Similarly, it is possible to have two simultaneous forward sale/purchase contracts, in essence a swap, which cover the company for any time period up to one year (or whatever limits the markets permit). This cover is achieved for instance by buying a currency forward for three months and selling it forward for six months. These contracts give cover for exchange risk exposure between the two dates permitting both a more flexible and directed hedging policy and a reduction of hedging costs, since the cost factors involved will comprise the discount (or premium) only in the exact period covered. A forward contract is not irrevocable, and in normal markets can be closed out during its existence. This would be done if the underlying reason for the hedge had changed or if other exogenous factors had intervened to make the hedge superfluous.

Where an exporter is invoicing in a currency other than its own, and which is expected to weaken, it can consider borrowing the same foreign currency for the tenor of the outstanding receivable and selling the loan proceeds spot at the outset for its own currency and placing them on time deposit. The ensuing interest yield will reduce the gross borrowing expense.

Export bills denominated in foreign currency can usually be discounted in local markets, exchange controls allowing this as an aid to exporters. The bank discounting such currency bills will itself apply a mixture of the domestic rate and the net cost/yield of the swap transaction. This technique is not possible in many exchange control-based countries, where foreign currency borrowings are permitted only under strict limitation, or not at all.

An analogous risk-avoiding possibility for importers owing foreign currency is to borrow their own currency, use the proceeds to buy the foreign currency spot and place the funds on deposit.

Where an exporter is selling on open account and therefore receives no discountable bills, it is sometimes possible to assign the actual receivables as collateral for related bank financing. Both commercial banks and specialized factoring institutions in certain countries offer factoring facilities for this purpose. It is possible to factor receivables denominated in foreign currency, as well as those in local units. The equivalent local value of the receivables is then advanced to the exporter until maturity.

A less used hedging method for the export of capital goods is leasing. For marketing reasons, an exporter of capital goods may not be able to bill in his own currency nor wish to receive an importer's weak currency. It may be possible to sell the goods outright to a leasing company in the country of the importer, which leases them on to the ultimate user. Neither side then has an exchange risk, and the exporter is paid immediately. Although attractive in certain cases, it is not always easy to negotiate a tripartite arrangement covering all the legal and fiscal considerations between seller, leasing company and buyer/lessee.

Even the above wide range of external risk hedging techniques does not cover every eventuality, since exchange and banking markets are neither perfect nor long term in orientation. For this reason, several governments have established exchange risk guarantee (ERG) programmes to add to the flexibility of exporters. These programmes are usually found in hard currency countries where exporters of industrial equipment sell under long-term contracts and where traditional short-term cover is neither available nor appropriate.

Banking policy, market limitations and/or exchange control regulations will constrain or prohibit the use of these techniques in many instances. All methods will seldom be available to any company, nor will all be equally advantageous. The relevance and cost of each method should form part of the normal managerial analysis when setting hedging strategy.

To summarize, the international corporations dealings with exchange risk should

1 Review the definitions used internally to determine exchange risk.

2 Make its exposure management anticipatory, based on perception of future risk as well as present positions.

3 Centralize control over exposure risk as far as possible.

4 Review reporting systems as regards their adequacy and timeliness.

5 Cover economic and transactional exposures generally and translation risk when the maximum potential translation losses are considered to be unacceptable to definitive corporate criteria. This implies a selective coverage policy, not one of complete cover at all times in all currencies. All hedging possibilities — internal and external — should be studied and their cost effectiveness determined.

6 Analyse and make exposure decisions on a post-tax basis.

7 Co-ordinate exchange management closely with liquidity management, as both have common goals and are equally affected by environmental and structural constraints.

8 Be aware of the non-financial implications of exposure strategy, particularly the personnel effects of centralization and the necessity to deal with an array of governmental and institutional contacts.

18

Taxation of corporations in the UK

Robert A. Scott

An understanding of the corporate tax system is a prerequisite to a full understanding and appreciation of those entries in the financial accounts labelled 'taxation', and the impact of taxes on project profitability. The treatment of deferred taxation can dramatically affect such ratios as earnings per share, return on shareholders' funds and 'gearing'. This chapter sets out the main provisions of the UK tax system as it affects companies.

STATUTORY PROVISIONS

The main Taxing Act governing corporations is the 1970 Finance Act plus subsequent Finance Acts which are issued every year after the Budget. In addition, Inland Revenue extra-statutory concessions and fifty-three volumes of case law govern how tax is assessed on corporations and individuals. Despite the volume of law, rules, practice and other factors, the taxing of corporations is usually straightforward.

Direct and indirect taxation

Income tax, corporation tax and capital gains tax are the three main direct taxes on profits or income.

Value added tax (VAT), stamp duties, custom duties and excise taxes are the main indirect taxes based on expenditure. There is a view that employers' national insurance contributions are really an additional indirect tax on businesses.

Schedule within the tax system

The income of corporations and others is divided into various categories or schedules. The main trading schedule is schedule D but the headings are

Schedule A: Income from land, rents and certain leases.
Schedule B: Income from woodlands or timber run on a commercial basis.
Schedule C: Income from gilt edged securities and certain overseas dividends, payable in the UK.
Schedule D: Case I   Trade
              Case II   Professions – not corporations
              Case III Interest received
              Case IV Overseas share income
              Case V   Overseas trade or loan income
              Case VI Miscellaneous 'catch-all' section governing items not covered in Cases I – V.
Schedule E: Wages and salaries from employment. This is split into three cases and is subject to residential qualification.
Schedule F: Dividends paid by companies.

Who pays tax on corporations?

A UK resident company pays tax on income and gains wherever they arise and irrespective of whether or not they are remitted to the UK. A non-UK resident company pays tax only on profits arising from a trade within the UK. Non-trading income of a non-resident UK company, but arising from within the UK, bears income tax at a maximum rate of 30 per cent.

The question of residence has not been defined by statute but, the Inland Revenue statement issued 27 July 1983, indicates that corporate residence will be determined in accordance with well established case law. The main governing approach is to establish where control is exercised. This whole area of corporate residence is a minefield of case law and extreme care is needed. Where a tax avoidance motive can be established, the Revenue will pay particular attention and may overrule a scheme even when the corporation has been properly constituted. There are several recent examples of the Courts attacking such schemes even when all the rules, etc. have been properly observed but where the main purpose was tax avoidance.

Accounting periods

Each corporation must decide on its financial year-end known as the accounting reference date (ARD). This is chosen when the company is incorporated but if no choice is made it will be given an ARD of 31 March. The rate of tax to be applied will be based on the actual rates covering the corporation's financial year based on a time allocation if the rate should be altered – normally at the budget in March each year. However, the Chancellor advised as of the Finance Act 1984 the various rates for each of the financial years to 31 March 1987.

CORPORATION TAX

Tax is chargeable on

1 Trading profits.
2 Investment income (franked).
3 Capital gains.

Various reliefs are available against these income sources.

TAXABLE TRADING PROFITS

The corporation's financial accounts are the basis on which its corporation tax will be calculated, subject to certain adjustments for non-allowable costs and expenses. Capital allowances are given as a deduction in the tax computation replacing depreciation charges which are one of the several disallowed expenses. Likewise, any income already taxed is taken out of the computation and treated separately. The overriding criterion is whether or not the expense is 'wholly and exclusively' for the purposes of the business. There are no lists of agreed costs that are allowed – the costs must fit into the 'wholly and exclusively' category. This can cause problems, for example, business entertaining is normally not allowed and yet it is part and parcel of every day business. In the main, however, the financial profits are the taxable profits subject to a few well-known adjustments, for example, capital allowances instead of depreciation.

CAPITAL ALLOWANCES AND CASH GRANTS

(a) *Cash grants.* Various schemes are in operation in the UK to encourage businesses to set up, expand or invest in new machinery. Grants are available and if these grants are for specified investment in plant, fittings or buildings, then the cost is reduced by the grant received. There are a few exceptions where the grant may be non-deductable (Highlands and Islands of Scotland) but the general rule is that the grant is deducted from the cost of the asset.

(b) *Plant and machinery* is, oddly, not defined but is a statutory phrase. The Courts have taken a fairly lenient view on what is plant and machinery, for example, office equipment, computers, software, telephones, apart from the obvious items of plant. A lessee who incurs expenditure on the fabric of a building, lifts, ventilation, etc, can also obtain relief for these costs. This is a recent decision by the Courts and is incorporated in the Finance Act 1985.

A first year allowance of 50 per cent is given for the financial year 1985 but is nil thereafter. The balance remaining, that is, 50 per cent, or 100 per cent after 1985, is further reduced by 25 per cent from the second year onwards on the reducing balance method. Certain adjustments have to be made when plant is sold. Normally, the sales price is deducted from the 'pool' of unused written down balances forward from the previous year. In exceptional circumstances where the disposal proceeds exceed the value of the pool, a balancing charge is made, that is, a sum can be brought back into profit. This is very unusual except in a break-up or discontinuation of trade.

(c) *Motor cars (not motor vans or lorries).* Vans and lorries are treated as plant. Cars are treated separately and the only allowance due is 25 per cent of original cost and 25 per cent thereafter on a reducing balance. Cars are normally pooled except those costing over £8000. These are each treated separately and the relief is restricted to £2000 per year until the written down value is less than £8000. Leasing of expensive cars, that is, above £8000, are also restricted. The rules are complex but a car costing £15000, leased for £5000 per year would have a disallowable element of £1167 added back to profit.

(d) *Industrial buildings.* This is defined as a building in use for the purposes of a trade carried on in a mill or factory or a trade which consists in the manufacture of or subjection to any process of goods or materials. Buildings used for storage only qualify if associated with a manufacturer.

An initial allowance (25 per cent for 1985 and nil thereafter) is given and 4 per cent straight line thereafter. Special provisions apply to second-hand industrial buildings.

(e) *Hotels.* Hotels also attract a 4 per cent straight line allowance but the hotel must be open for at least four months from April to October, have ten letting bedrooms and supply services to guests.

(f) *Special enterprise zones.* Special enterprise zones have more attractive capital allowances but these zones are in depressed inner cities or areas of high unemployment. There are at least twenty-five such zones as of 1985.

(g) *Leasing.* Complex rules governing leased equipment were introduced in the Finance Acts 1980 and 1982. Generally, there are restrictions on equipment leased out by corporations. These are somewhat specialized but care should be taken by the lessor.

(h) *Capital gains.* Corporations have no relief for capital gains (unlike individuals) apart from inflationary elements which are based on indices supplied by the Treasury. The rules applying to pools of assets or shares are very complex and these should be left to specialist financial advisers to determine what rates apply. Capital gains are effectively only taxed at 30 per cent on a corporation although the mainstream corporation tax rate is higher for other profits in the business. No capital gain arises on the disposal of a tangible moveable asset of less than £3000.

Implementation of corporation tax

The rate is 29 per cent where taxable income is less than £100 000 and tapering relief is granted up to £500 000 profits when the full rate is charged. The full rate is 35 per cent for the year to 31 March 1987.

   If dividends are paid by the corporation then the Advance Corporation Tax (ACT) of three sevenths must be paid to the Revenue in the quarter when the dividend is paid. This ACT can, subject to certain conditions, be offset against the mainstream corporation tax due on the corporation's year-end assessment but not against capital gains taxations.

Example

Taxable income for year to 31 March 1984		£150 000
Dividends		119 000
ACT on 119 000 = 3/7	£51 000	

Corporation tax payable on £150 000 @ 50%   75 000
(assuming no reduction for small company rate)
ACT set-off
restricted to 30% × £150 000   45 000
Mainstream corporation tax   30 000
Surplus ACT (£51 000 − £45 000)   6 000

The Surplus ACT, subject to certain conditions, can be carried back and set off against corporation tax for the preceding six years. It may be carried forward without time limit so long as there is no change in ownership coupled with a major change in the nature of the business.

Shareholders receive a tax credit for the ACT suffered, that is, the dividend is treated as a gross receipt less tax already deducted. Higher rated tax payers may need to pay additional tax on their gross income but investment income surcharge is no longer in force.

Payment of tax

(a)   ACT is normally paid in the quarters ending March, June, September and December.
(b)   Mainstream corporation tax is due nine months after the end of the accounting period or 30 days after issue of notice of assessment, whichever is later. Companies formed before 31 March 1976 can pay after nine months and up to twenty months in some instances. There used to be some merit in having 6 April year end but this has largely disappeared and only affects companies formed before 31 March 1976.
(c)   Certain withholding taxes must be deducted at 30 per cent from annual payments and rents paid to non-residents. Double taxation agreements prevent double taxation on the recipient but the payer must deduct tax at source otherwise the payer could be held liable for the tax not withheld.

Miscellaneous corporation tax receipts

(a)   Stock relief was abolished in the Finance Act 1984 and is not applicable after 12 March 1984.
(b)   Losses can be carried forward against trading profits with no time limit. Losses can be offset against other profits in the period in which the loss was incurred, including capital gains, but

subject to restrictions on charges on income. Losses can be carried back for one year.

(c) Groups can be treated in essence as one corporation and losses can be used against profits of other group companies. A subsidiary is one where 51 per cent of its shares is owned by another corporation.

(d) Capital gains tax can be 'rolled over' when the gain is reinvested in another chargeable asset. The reinvestment can be twelve months before or three years after disposal of the first chargeable asset.

(e) Companies can now purchase their own shares – Companies Act 1981 – and this has major effects on capital gains as opposed to corporation tax planning, that is, the payment to the shareholders is no longer a distribution of profits but is regarded as a reduction of issued share capital. This is ideal for small family companies where a shareholder wishes to retire or an executor has to realise the value of shares.

VALUE ADDED TAX

VAT came into operation on 1 April 1973 and is administered by the Customs and Excise. It is collected at each stage of the production process, or supply of service. For VAT purposes, goods are classed either as inputs or outputs. Input tax will be suffered when a registered trader buys goods or services. Output tax is charged by a registered trader on goods or services supplied to customers. VAT returns are made up on a quarterly basis and if the input tax suffered exceeds the output tax, the taxable person is entitled to a refund. In the reverse case a payment must be made to the Customs and Excise office.

When VAT was first introduced the rate was 10 per cent on sales; subsequently, this was reduced to 8 per cent in July 1974. Since then there have been a number of changes, mainly affecting particular goods or categories of goods. For instance, the rate on petrol was increased to 25 per cent in November 1974 and this rate was also extended to a number of other goods in the 1975 Budget. In the 1976 Budget, the 25 per cent rate on petrol and on certain other goods was reduced to 12 ½ per cent, although in the case of petrol, there was a duty increase to compensate for the reduction in VAT. The Finance Act 1979 standardized VAT at 15 per cent.

Certain types of goods, though taxable, have a zero VAT rate. Obviously, this makes it easy for the government to increase the rate in the future. Food, water, books, newspapers, fuel and power are among the most important of the zero-rated goods.

Some goods and services are exempt from VAT; they include land, health, education, insurance and banking. Where a person supplies exempt goods or services he need not register for VAT, but if he does not, he cannot reclaim a refund on his input tax; if he does register he can reclaim the input tax.

Who is liable to VAT? Anyone who supplies taxable goods or services in excess of £21 500 per annum (the original limit was £5 000).

SUMMARY

Financial managers, directors, controllers and accountants need not know the detailed taxation provisions. These are very cumbersome and up to date knowledge is necessary. This chapter is meant to give an overview of the main taxes affecting corporations. A great deal of recent legislation is an attempt to harmonize the taxation rules with the European Economic Community (EEC) especially on VAT and other Customs and Excise related duties. The recent Finance Acts have also tried to simplify the application of quite complex rules and the stated aim of the Chancellor in his Budget speech in 1984 was to make the system easier to administer and understand. Perhaps he should consider the maxim of a 17th Century French Chancellor, Jean Baptiste Colbert

'The art of taxation consists of plucking the goose so as to obtain the largest amount of feathers with the least possible amount of hissing.'

Annotated bibliography

General

The following books provide a comprehensive discussion of corporate finance in a UK context:

Franks, J.R. and Broyles, J.E. *Modern Managerial Finance*, (Wiley, Chichester, 1979)

Samuels, J.A. and Wilkes, F.M. *Management of Company Finance*, (Nelson, Walton on Thames, 1982)

Weston, J.F. and Brigham, E.F. *Essentials of Managerial Finance*, (Holt, Reinhart and Winston, UK Edition, Eastbourne, 1979)

Useful textbooks which are more slanted to a US audience include:

Brealey, R.A. and Myres, S.C. *Principles of Corporate Finance*, (McGraw-Hill, New York, 1981)

Brigham, E.F. *Financial Management Theory and Practice*, (Dryden Press, Hinsdale, 1982, Third Edition)

Van Horne, J.C. *Financial Management and Policy*, (Prentice-Hall, Englewood Cliffs, NJ, 1983, Sixth Edition)

A very clear introduction to financial accounting is provided in:

Reid, W. and Myddelton, D.R. *The Meaning of Company Accounts*, (Gower, Aldershot, 1982)

Warren, R.A. *How to Understand and Use Company Accounts*, (Business Books Ltd, London, 1983)

Arnold, J., Hope, T. and Southworth, A. *Financial Accounting*, (Prentice-Hall, Englewood Cliffs, NJ, 1985)

Management accounting discussed in a UK and USA context respectively can be obtained from:

Sizer, J. *An Insight into Management Accounting*, (Pitman, London, 2nd Edition, 1979)

Horngren, C.T. *Introduction to Management Accounting*, (Prentice-Hall, Englewood Cliffs, NJ, 1984, Sixth Edition)

A useful collection of pertinent journal papers can be found in:

Lee, C.F. *Financial Analysis and Planning, Theory and Application: A Book of Readings*, (Addison-Wesley Publishing Company, New York, 1983)

A more detailed treatment of capital budgeting and capital project appraisal is given in:

Bierman, H. Jr. and Smidt, S. *The Capital Budgeting Decision: Economic Analysis of Investment Projects*, (Macmillan, London, 1980, Fifth Edition)

FINANCIAL CONTROL

Two books covering the general topic of planning and control are:

Dermer, J. *Management Planning and Control Systems,* (Irwin, Homewood, IL, 1977)

Anthony, R.V. and Dearden, J. *Management Control Systems*, (Irwin, Homewood, IL, 1976)

The first of these books is mainly concerned with the overall design of information systems for organizational planning and control, while the second deals with accounting aspects.

A comprehensive basic textbook on costing and internal pricing is:

Horngren, C.T. *Cost Accounting: A Managerial Emphasis*, (Prentice-Hall, Englewood Cliffs, NJ, 1981)

A useful treatment of techniques of preparation, production and analysis of accounts is given in the Reid/Myddelton book referred to in the general section above.

FINANCIAL STRUCTURE

Funding instruments and mechanisms for funding are dynamic and evolving. A résumé of many of these developments can be found in:

Shearlock, P. and Hutchinson A. (Eds), *Finance Director International,* UK Edition. (Sterling Publishing Group, Poole, 1986)

General discussions of the methods which investors use to appraise investment are given in:

Sharpe, W.F. *Investments*, (Prentice-Hall, Englewood Cliffs, NJ, 1978)

Richards, P. *United Kingdom and European Share Price Behaviour: The Evidence,* (Kogan Page, London, 1978)

A discussion of financial statement analysis from the investor's point of view can be found in:

Holmes, G. and Sugden, A. *Interpreting Company Reports and Accounts,* (Woodhead-Faulkner, Cambridge, 1979)

An elementary introduction to the UK stock market is contained in:

Investors Chronicle, Beginners Please, (Throgmorton Publications, 1973)

More detailed references on going public are provided at the end of Chapter 13.
    A general description of UK financial institutions is given in:

Revell, J. *The British Financial System*, (Macmillan, London, 1980)

THE EXTERNAL ENVIRONMENT

A good discussion of the issues in mergers and acquisitions is given in the books by Samuels and Wilkes and by Franks and Broyles referred to above. These books also review the general implications of taxation for corporate financial decisions.

Money and exchange risk management are comprehensively covered in:

Prindl, A. R. *Foreign Exchange Risk,* (Wiley, New York, 1976)

Index